Political Sociology

A New Grammar of Politics

Ali Ashraf
L.N. Sharma

Universities Press

POLITICAL SOCIOLOGY

UNIVERSITIES PRESS (INDIA) PRIVATE LIMITED

Registered Office
3-6-747/1/A & 3-6-754/1, Himayatnagar,
Hyderabad 500 029 (Telangana), INDIA
e-mail: info@universitiespress.com

Distributed by
Orient Blackswan Private Limited

Registered Office
3-6-752 Himayatnagar, Hyderabad 500 029 (Telangana,), INDIA

Other Offices
Bengaluru, Chennai, Guwahati, Hyderabad,
Kolkata, Mumbai, New Delhi, Noida, Patna

First published 1983
Reprinted 1988, 1190, 1992, 1995, 1999, 2004, 2006, 2007
2010, 2012, 2015, 2016, 2018, 2019, 2020, 2022, 2023, 2024

ISBN: 978-81-7371-016-2

Design Compilation & Cartography by
Sangam Books (India) Pvt. Ltd.

502132

Printed in India at
B.B. Press, Tronica City, Ghaziabad 201 102

Published by
Universities Press (India) Private Limited
3-6-747/1/A & 3-6-754/1, Himayatnagar,
Hyderabad 500 029 (Telangana), India

Contents

Preface *v*
1. Political Sociology : Nature, Scope and Emergence
2. Approaches in Political Analysis 18
3. Political Power and Social Stratification : Class and Caste 42
4. The Elite Theory of Political Power 53
5. The Group Theory of Politics 76
6. Political Parties and Political System 88
7. Bureaucracy, Society and Politics 106
8. Political Development, Modernization and Political Culture 120
9. Political Participation and Electoral Process 140
10. Public Opinion and Political Socialization 167

Notes and References 179

Glossary: Important Thinkers 201

Terms and Concepts 210

Index 221

Preface

During the past couple of decades the language of social sciences has changed perceptibly. The change had, of course, begun even earlier, but the study of government as the study of political processes has become more important in recent times. The integration of various disciplines such as political science, sociology and psychology and the growing preoccupation with the scientific method have contributed to the need for the indepth analysis of political phenomena beyond the formal constitutions of institutions of the government. The rise of the third world, with its myriad problems of socioeconomic change and political development, has further highlighted the need for an integrated and interdisciplinary approach to the study of political, socio-cultural and economic development. The cumulative effect has been a number of conceptual innovations and methodological experiments in the realm of social sciences.

The trouble with intellectual enterprise is that not all innovations stand the test of time, and some novelties are ephemeral. Students cannot, however, wait until the present day academic changes become classics, and it is essential that we constantly attempt to understand what is happening in the field. This is a difficult task, partly because good deal of innovation is interdisciplinary, and our present day education hardly equips us to acquire broad interdisciplinary understanding. Also, academic trends start in the western world, and the literature concerned not only takes time to cross the seas but also reflects the bias of the Western scholars. Their themes and orientations are, naturally, culture-bound and for the great part, reflect their own experiences and research efforts in the areas under consideration. Any attempt to apply the same model to developing societies is beset with certain limitations, notwithstanding the technical efficacy of the model and the perspective involved.

To keep pace with the West, by overcoming and modifying the ethnocentric bias of the Western writers and for a perceptive understanding of our own culture, society and politics, the pragmatic course of action is to observe developments and do our own thinking and writing. It is neither necessary nor desirable to be swept away by the intellectual snowballing of the West. We must, while keeping abreast of the developments in the West, make our own contribution to the mainstream of intellectual culture, on an international level.

Some works of insight have emerged in the field of Indian politics but they are yet to be fully absorbed into the syllabi of the universities and into the discipline of the social sciences. The essential equipment and training required to study the new idiom of social sciences is beset with limitations. Innovative writings are scattered in the form of articles, monographs and dissertations; they are not as yet available in the form of a text. This book, it is hoped, will fulfil the need for an integrated approach to various issues, concepts and approaches, germane to the field of political sociology. This text is, as it were, a new grammar of politics.

Many universities have recently thought it necessary to introduce a course in political sociology and the University Grants Commission has rightly encouraged it. University students grapple with the themes discussed in this book in papers such as modern political analysis, modern or behavioural political theory, and political sociology.

One of the problems facing students of political sociology is that no one textbook refers to exactly the same topics as the other. Each author defines his own outline of the discipline and as a result there is hardly any consensus about its boundaries. However, it is an accepted fact that this field is of profound significance for students of politics. It provides a perspective which should permeate the study of political science as well as that of sociology. Given these facts this book brings political sociology closer to students and other serious readers in related disciplines.

We appreciate the assistance rendered to us by Dr. N. Pant, Dr. A.K. Lal, Dr. Zafar Nizami, Mujtaba Khan, C.P. Sharma, Sangeeta Sharma, Jitendra Kishore Prasad Singh and Shahid Ashraf, in putting together the final version of the draft.

Ali Ashraf
L.N. Sharma

1. Political Sociology : Nature, Scope and Emergence

Nature

Political sociology seeks to understand the process of interaction between government and society, decision making authorities and conflicting social forces and interests. It is the study of interactions and linkages between politics and society; between a political system and its social, economic and cultural environment. It is concerned with problems regarding the management of conflict, the articulation of interests and issues, and political integration and organization. The focal point in all these concerns is the interdependence and the interplay of socio-cultural, economic and political elements.

The perspective of political sociology is distinguished from that of institutionalism and behaviouralism. The institutionalists have been concerned primarily with institutional types of political organization, and their study has been characterized by legality and formality. The behaviouralists have focused on the individual actor in the political arena; and their central concern has been the psychological traits, namely, motives, attitudes, perceptions and the role of individuals. The task of the political sociologist is to study the political process as a continuum of interactions between society and its decision makers, and between the decision making institutions and social forces.

Political sociology provides a new vista in political analysis. Yet it is closely linked with the issues which have been raised in political philosophy. Political philosophy as we know, has a rich and long tradition of political thought that began with the ancient Indian and Greek philosophers, and that has amply flowered since Machiavelli, who made a bold departure from Greek idealism and medieval scholasticism. It was Karl Marx however, who brought into sharp focus issues concerning the nature of political power and its relationship with social or economic organization. The Marxist theory of economic determinism of political power laid the foundation for the sociology of politics.[1] Marx was, however, neither the first nor the only thinker to conceive of government as an organ of the dominant economic class. The Arabian scholar Ibn Khaldun,[2] and several European predecessors of Marx, had argued that ideology and power were superstructures of economy. Plato and Aristotle had, much earlier, discussed government in terms of social and economic institutions. Aristotle, in particular, analyzed political stability in terms of social classes. It is nevertheless true that it was Karl Marx with his vigorous enunciation of the doctrine of historical materialism and class struggle who unreservedly revealed the economic reality lurking behind political power. His conclusion that political power is the handmaid of the economic elite, and that it serves the interests of those who own the means of production and exchange, reduced politics to the status of epiphenomenon of economic reality. The tenets of Marxism have been challenged by a rival tradition upholding the autonomy of politics. This tradition has precedence in the ideas of Kautilya and Machiavelli and is upheld by the neo-Machiavellians such as Pareto, Mosca and Michels. It is characteristic of the Machiavellian analysis of statecraft that it is rooted in the creative role of the ruling elite that relies on its personal talents and skills, uninhibited by social, economic and moral constraints. The Machiavellians have focused on the role of leadership in power dynamics and on a natural tendency towards the dominance of the 'political' minority.

The Marxist or the Machiavellian views, diametrically opposed to each other as they are, have one thing in common. Both inject, in their own different ways, a high sense of realism into the understanding of politics. They suggest that one must look behind the forms and facades of government to acquire a comprehensive view of political reality. The pertinent question then is who controls power. In providing an answer to this question, however, Marx and Machiavelli differ. For the Marxists, political process is determined by the class that owns the means of production and exchange; whereas for the Machiavellians, it is dominated by leaders endowed with exceptional personal and political qualities. In this dialectical controversy, the two different dimensions of political reality involve questions of interrelationship between society and politics, and the relative influence or control each has over the other. Both the Marxist and Machiavellian perspectives, representing the primacy of society and politics respectively, are the two major strands in the mainstream of the realistic study of politics.

There is another important sense in which Marx and Machiavelli differ. The concern of the realist is primarily with the world as it is, and his analysis aims at what is feasible. His pragmatic sense is concerned with the realities of the political process. Marx and Machiavelli, both champions of realism, differed in this vital respect; namely, in their conception of the value and the function of politics in society. Marx was forthright in perceiving class consciousness, class struggle and exploitation, but in his conception of communism and in prescribing ways to achieve classless society, he threw overboard his sense of realism and yielded to a messianic vision of an apolitical society that would be free from class conflict, exploitation and alienation. Machiavelli, on the other hand, was a hard-headed realist who considered politics a dynamic process, emphasized the role of leadership in the management of a society, and thus believed that political management is indispensable; and no society or polity, no matter how it is organized, can escape the impact of politics and the need for political leadership.

Given the inevitability of the political role in society, a body of thinkers from Aristotle to Tocqueville has rightly emphasized the point that instead of deploring the evils of human nature or social circumstances, it is more prudent and worthwhile to accept the 'given', and improve it for the good of man and society. If conflict, for example, is inherent in society, it is wiser to face it and to manage it so as to achieve reconciliation and accommodation. Conflict, though apparently an evil, is a condition of freedom, as it prevents the concentration of power. This kind of political realism recognizes the necessity and utility of the political management of conflict through compromise and adjustment among various social forces and interests. Political sociology aims at understanding the sources and the social bases of conflict, as well as the process of the management of conflict.

Men can live and fulfil themselves only in ordered societies. Order implies the organization and management of public affairs, that is, the affairs that concern the civic community or the state. This is the concern and the dominion of politics. The management of public affairs, however, is not a mechanical task. It involves and is preceded by clashes of ideas, values and interests. It is natural for people to project their own sectional ideas and interests as public interest. What begins and ends with the 'public' passes through a series of private, personal or group goals and interests. It is the function of politics to achieve public order out of myriad private interests, and to achieve consensus out of conflicts through compromise and accommodation. The transition from conflict to consensus is achieved by politics through the means of persuasion as well as coercion.

The fact of social conflict is ubiquitous, but the sources of conflict and the methods of their management differ. The sources of conflict reside either in what Hobbes called 'men's perpetual desire of power after power that ceaseth only in death' or in what Rousseau considered a departure from natural equality, or in what Madison called 'the diversities in the faculties of men', and 'social circumstances'.[3] On the other hand, the Marxist viewpoint looks upon conflict as entirely the result of economic inequality based on the possession or the want of property.

The further significant difference is with regard to the attitude toward conflict itself. The earliest evidence of such a difference in point of view is indicated by Plato and Aristotle. Plato perceived conflict as a disease of which the city must be cured, and he prescribed the subordination of power to reason in order to achieve justice on the basis of functional specialization and exclusive discharge of one's duties. Such societal justice alone was the guarantee of civic unity and harmony. Aristotle raised the pertinent question of limits to civic unity. Plato sought to unify a city to the extent that it would cease to be a city. He stressed the fact that the 'political' concerned the management of 'public' affairs, while Aristotle rightly drew the line between the 'public' and the 'totalitarian'.

Conflicts are rooted in human nature and social circumstances. As long as diversity of interests and insatiable demands in a world of scarcity persist, there is no escape from conflicts of interests. Politics is a continuous and dynamic process constantly in a state of flux, and there is no final solution to the problem of conflicts. Political process is a way of processing and controlling social conflicts so as to achieve the goal of order. But total elimination of conflicts, even if it were feasible, requires a degree of control that would destroy human liberty. An ordered society is not a totalitarian society that achieves unity and denies diversity, that imposes discipline and destroys dissent, that orders conformity and subverts spontaneity. Order can be achieved instead through the perception of mutual interests and the evolution of consensus, without compromising the canons of popular participation and due observance of the 'rules of the game'.

Scope

The broad aim of political sociology is to study and examine the interaction between social and political structures. The determination of the boundaries of what is social and political, however, raises some questions. The relevant question in delineating the scope of political sociology is that of the kinds of groups which form part of the study of the discipline of political sociology. Some scholars believe that politics depends on some settled order created by the state. Hence the state is political, and is the subject matter of political sociology, and not the groups. According to Bernard Crick, small groups are part of the order created by the state. They may help to create politics, but their internal behaviour is not political because their function is different from that of the state.[4] Crick's observations are limited to small groups and their internal mechanisms, but there are scholars who would exclude the study of even such large groups as trade unions, the church, the business firm, or other non-state organizations from political analysis because they are not political in the strict sense of the term. Drawing upon this viewpoint, Greer and Orleans explain political sociology as being mainly concerned with the description, analysis and sociological explanation of the peculiar social structure called the state.[5]

There is another school according to which politics is present in almost all social relations. Individuals and small groups try to enforce their preferences on their parent organizations, family, club, or college, and thus indulge in the exercise of 'power'.[6] Writers like Merriam and Lasswell see force and power, especially in the struggle and conflict among groups or classes, as an inherent aspect of political relationship. Lasswell explains that since the entire society is characterized by the interplay of influence, influential and influenced, politics pervades all of society.[7] Politics permeates every social group and association, class and profession. Each point at which power and influence manifest themselves is political. Elaborating this point further, Dahl treats 'any persistent pattern of human relationship' as political which involves 'to a significant extent, power, rule or authority'.[8] Ignoring the import of Dahl's words 'to a significant extent', this school argues that the politics of unorganized communities, associations and families is political and is an appropriate subject matter of study in political sociology.

The latter view may, however, be considered as carrying the point too far and there is an inherent weakness in stretching this argument to such an extreme. Bendix cogently points out that if we analyze without discrimination the political aspect of a family or a business corporation, the scope of our study would become too broad to exclude anything.[9] Such an extension of the scope of the 'political' would be too wide to be meaningful for any academic enterprise. On the other hand, it would be wrong to confine the scope of our study to the state alone, thus missing the central focus on forces with which the political system interacts.

Sheldon S. Wolin takes quite a reasonable view of the word 'political', which according to him, means three things:[10]

(*a*) a form of activity centering around the quest for competitive advantage between groups, individuals, or societies;
(*b*) a form of activity conditioned by the fact that it occurs within a situation of change and relative scarcity; and
(*c*) a form of activity in which the pursuit of advantage produces consequences of such a magnitude that they affect, in a significant way, the whole society or a substantial portion of it.

Wolin's definition rightly restricts the scope of politics to those activities only which 'affect in a significant way the whole society or a substantial portion of it'. The politics of the trade unions as a constituent of the British Labour Party, or of the FICCI as a pressure group in India, are relevant matters for study in political sociology. The politics of a club, a students' union or a teachers' association is 'political' when other groups in the society are affected vitally by their activities. On this point, Arthur F. Bentley's viewpoint is very clear. 'No group can be stated, or defined, or valued, except in terms of other groups. No group has meaning except in its relation to other groups.'[11] The rationale behind Bentley's statement is that it is not groups as such, but interactions and linkages of public significance among groups, that are relevant for political analysis. Social and political behaviour that has bearings on political decisions and policies, and which correlates significantly with the 'authoritative allocation of values in a society' make up the subject matter of political sociology.

Two groups of scholars have discussed the scope of political sociology in two different ways. According to Greer and Orleans, political sociology is concerned with the structure of the state; the nature and conditions of legitimacy; the nature of the monopoly of force and its use by the state; and the nature of the sub units and their relation with the state.[12] They treat political sociology in terms of consensus and legitimacy, participation and representation, and the relationship between economic development and political change. By implication, whatever is related to the state is alone held as the subject matter of political sociology. Andreu Effrat takes a broader view of the picture and suggests that political sociology is concerned with the causes, patterns, and consequences of the distribution and process of power and authority 'in all social systems'.[13] Among social systems he includes small groups and families, educational and religious groups, as well as governmental or political institutions.

Lipset and Bendix suggest a more representative catalogue of topics when they describe the main areas of interest to political sociologists, as voting behaviour; concentration of economic power and political decision making; ideologies of political movements and interest groups; political parties, voluntary associations, the problems of oligarchy and psychological correlates of political behaviour; and the problem of bureaucracy.[14] To Dowse and Hughes, one area of substantive concern for the political sociologist is the problem of social order and political obedience.[15]

Richard G. Braungart has pointed out that political sociologists are concerned with the dynamic association among and between (*a*) the social origins of politics, (*b*) the structure of politics or the political process, and (*c*) the effects of politics on the surrounding society and culture.[16] We would suggest that political sociology should include five areas: political structures (social class/caste, elite, interest groups, bureaucracy, political parties and factions); political life (electoral process, political communication, opinion formation and so on); political leadership (bases, types and operation of community power structure); and political development (concept and indices of its measurement, its social bases and prerequisites and its relationship to social change and modernization). To illustrate, we may point out that on the one hand, sociologists focus their attention on the sub areas of the social system, and political scientists concentrate on the study of law, local , state and national governments, comparative government, political systems, public administration, and international relations. On the other hand, political sociologists ought to be concerned with topics of social stratification and political power: socio-economic systems and political regimes, interest groups, political parties, bureaucracy, political socialization, electoral behaviour, social movements and political mobilization.

A significant concern for political sociology is the analysis of socio-political factors in economic development. The problems of administrative development, of bureaucracy steeped in a country's native culture and society, of the relationship between the bureaucratic officials and the political leaders, and of the role of citizens in development activities, are of such practical significance that governments as well as academicians have been forced to take notice of the sociology and politics of development. A kindred field that illustrates this is urban politics where one encounters problems of social change and mobilization, political institutions and popular participation, and organization and management of government functions on an increasing scale. Villages and towns are seen as microcosms of nations that are confronted with problems of social change, political participation and administrative management. There is a growing realization that the problems of development are not merely technical or bureaucratic in the narrow sense, but essentially socio-political in the wider sense, and that political forces must be organized in a way to ensure effective implementation of development plans. It is now appreciated that social and political insights are crucial requisites for achieving change and development in the Afro-Asian states.

Sociology and Politics

The bulk of discussion regarding the substance and scope of political sociology focuses on political phenomena as the epiphenomena of social and economic factors. Political sociology in its earlier incarnation came to be identified with the study of the social bases of political behaviour and institutions. Political variables (that is, political factors or conditions) were deemed to be dependent upon sociological variables. Whereas sociological variables such as society, class and status were held as independent factors, political variables such as the state, law, constitution and political parties were seen as dependent on them. This was Lipset's position in his *Political Man*, which became an essential text of political sociology.[17] Lipset's dominant thrust was towards identifying the social determinants or bases of political behaviour. Political institutions and phenomena were, according to him, to be studied and analyzed in terms of sociological variables such as class and group. Symptomatic of this approach are the psephological studies, which remained a favourite with social psychologists who sought to explain voting behaviour in terms of psychological factors or motives, and with sociologists who explained it in terms of sociological variables such as class, ethnicity, religion as well as attitudes and orientations towards participation. This viewpoint dominates the perspective of those scholars who treat political sociology as a branch of sociology. Typical of this attitude is the definition of political sociology given by Bendix and Lipset—that it 'starts with society and examines how it affects the state', whereas 'political science starts with the state and examines how it affects society'.[18] Coser is even clearer, when he says that 'political sociology is *that branch of sociology* which is concerned with the social causes and consequences of given power distribution within or between societies, and with the social and political conflicts that lead to changes in the allocation of power'[19] (emphasis added). It is to be admitted though, that Coser does not regard political sociology as a branch of political science at all.

This view regarding the nature and scope of political sociology has been effectively challenged by the Italian political scientist Sartori, who seeks to emphasize the autonomy of politics, and the impact of politics on the moulding of social and economic structure or behaviour.[20] He points out that it is one thing to study how class factors influence political behaviour, and quite another to examine how the system affects class in its political process. It is a common observation that political institutions and decision making agencies of government influence and mould social processes. It has even been pointed out that an electoral system adopted in a particular country influences group identification among diverse strata in the society, and determines the number and kind of parties that the country will have.[21] Nations that use a system of proportional representation are likely to develop a multi-party system. On the contrary, in countries such as the USA and Britain which use a majority system, groups are impelled to merge their identities in a major party, thus favouring the emergence of a bi-polar system. Governmental taxation policy has the effect of redistributing income or concentrating it, thereby changing the system of social stratification. Political leadership redirects attitudes and calls values into question. Even if one were to believe that social cleavages and conflicts translate themselves into party competition, the roles played by the managers of the translation process must be properly appreciated.[22]

The issue of autonomy of politics is indeed of profound significance, because if psychological and sociological variables are identified as determinants of political behaviour, the findings will throw light on the political actor's personality or social affiliations, but will not do justice to the process of politics. It is equally if not more important to know how, and with what consequences, political factors influence social and personal aspects of public life. To take a random example, the effect of elections and the electoral process on the parties and party system, as well as on the government and the political system, may be studied because they influence and reflect in combination, not in isolation, the general culture and spirit of political life.[23]

In any case, the earlier approach which is rightly identified as sociology of politics reduces political phenomena to non-political factors, and hence Sartori's argument that 'the sociology of politics' is 'sociological reduction of politics' has great force and value. Any view which ignores the independent and creative role of politics in bringing about social change is a distortion of the facts and the ideals of political life. Social and political explanatory variables must be treated as interdependent variables that interact closely with each other.

Since political sociology as it has been used in the past is a misnomer, Sartori seeks to distinguish sharply 'sociology of politics' from 'political sociology'. He argues that political sociology is only born when the sociological and "politological" approaches are combined at their point of intersection. Both political as well as non political causes of human behaviour have to be looked for. 'If the "sociology of politics" deals with the non political reasons why people act the way they do in political life, political sociology should include also the political reasons why people act the way they do', writes Sartori. The sociology of politics made headway because of the technical sophistication of research methods but there grew an increasing awareness of the inadequacy of its conceptual framework. Sartori therefore, rejects the suggestion to treat political sociology as a branch of sociology, and rightly demands that *political sociology should develop as an interdependent but primarily political study.*

It is strange that even after such valiant efforts, text books continue to refer to political sociology as 'a branch of sociology'.[24] The conflict goes on between political scientists and sociologists who reflect different orientations and approaches. While a sociologist generally emphasizes the primacy of social forces, a political scientist stresses the autonomy and creative role of politics. But the ideological commitment of the scholars in question also intrude into the controversy. The Marxist scholars treat economic or social variables as determinants of political phenomena. They find it difficult to accept politics as an autonomous and interdependent (or independent) function. They do not appreciate the autonomy of politics because they believe in the dogma that politics is the superstructure, the character of which is totally conditioned by the modes and relations of production, and it cannot but reflect the dominant class interests in a given society.

We want to emphasize that from the point of view of political sociology, political life should not be treated as the product of any one force, such as a class or some special social group, but as a result of multiple forces including political ones.[25] Multi-causal and multi-dimensional explanations are more realistic as public policy arises out of a complex network through the interaction of various social elements. Political decision making involves government and other political institutions and a number of social forces and groups. Raymond Aron aptly points out that the analysis of the economic structure should be combined with the analysis of the social structure, the structure of the groups within the elites and the structure of the constitutional system, to bring rich dividends.[26] A society cannot be characterized only by the class which owns the means of production or by the psychological and social nature of the elite. Hence, there is a sound case for the synthesis of the two perspectives. Political sociology must develop as a theoretical and methodological bridge between the two disciplines of political science and sociology. A political sociologist studies political behaviour within a sociological perspective. But while doing so, he must pay due attention to political questions and political parameters.

Emergence of Political Sociology

The social basis of government has been a concern of political scientists down the ages. Plato and Aristotle did not make a distinction between society and state, and they emphasized the social underpinnings of government. During the Middle Ages, the distinction between church and state was made, although the state was considered subservient to the city of God. The liberal, bourgeois conception of the state emphasized the value of the limited jurisdiction of governments to facilitate free enterprise so much so that even after Hegel's glorification of the concept, the state could not establish its complete supremacy. As against the absolutist conception of the state which dominated the writings of Hobbes and Hegel, the works of Locke, Adam Smith and Rousseau emphasized the distinction between society and state.

Major developments occurred however, in the social sciences, in the wake of the Industrial Revolution, which destroyed the feudal society based on an ascriptive hierarchy of landed nobility and peasantry, the pervasive authority of the church, and the cumulative character of political power.[27] The social forces and problems unleashed by the tremendous changes brought about by industrialization led to the study of concrete social phenomena. This endeavour paved the way for the development of sociology as a separate empirical discipline. Initially concerned primarily with the problems of industrial society, sociology continued to expand its scope, making its concerns comprehensive enough to include not only the sociology of politics, but also those of many other branches such as law, education, religion, family, art, science, medicine, leisure and knowledge.[28]

While Auguste Comte invented the term 'sociology', Von Stein was the first to discuss society as an independent concept. It was Karl Marx however, with his criticism of Hegel's philosophy of state, his materialistic interpretation of history and his conception of class as the basic variable for social or political explanation, who started the 'sociology of politics'. Taking this point into consideration, Runciman correctly identifies the 1840's as the period of the first empirical delineation of the discipline.[29]

After Karl Marx, the most significant contribution to political sociology was made by the German sociologist Max Weber, who made power the focal point of his social analysis.[30] He laid the foundations of political sociology by his original and exciting ideas regarding types of authority, the ideal type of bureaucracy, and the concepts of status and party as supplements to that of class. Weber provided brilliant insights into the forces and directions of social and political development, and also offered a liberal modification of the Marxist philosophy of historical materialism.

The trend towards 'realism' in political analysis was on the upsurge in America in the latter part of the nineteenth century. This was one of the causes of a move into research in the realm of 'political process' and 'political behaviour', the stuff of which political sociology is made. The focus on 'behavioural' rather than merely legal or formal aspects of institutions, the aim to make social sciences 'scientific' by integrating theory and empirical research, the use of sophisticated methods of analysis; and also, the development of an interdisciplinary approach calling attention to the effects of social, cultural and personal factors on politics, have significantly contributed to making the discipline of political sociology a major interdisciplinary concern in the social science field. But for many years, it continued to be an American phenomenon, with the successive appearance of the work of scholars such as Arthur Bentley, Charles Merriam, Franz Neumann, Sigmund Neumann, Paul Lazersfeld, Hans Speir, Hans Gerth, Reinhard Bendix, Seymour Lipset and others.

There were certain special reasons which motivated the American social scientists to undertake studies in political sociology. In the years following World War I, they grew conscious of the pathologies and shortcomings of the democratic framework of their country.[31] Inspired by the progressive movement and by its zeal for reform, they were drawn to themes such as the nature and degree of political participation, pressure groups and lobbies, 'boss' and 'machine', and the power and control over the mass media.[32] Some scholars were drawn into methodological experimentation and studied in depth the relations between social structure and process, personality formation and political behaviour. The psychoanalytic theories and the politico-sociological theories of Weber, Durkheim, Pareto, Toennies and others found great appreciation in America during this period.

But American studies by and large suffered from the fault of a limited vision, confined as they were to the framework of British and American versions of political democracy. They focused on the Anglo-Saxon political experience of a stable democracy and its institutions, and showed an inability to study or to appreciate political institutions or processes different from their own. They assumed the inevitability of Western democracy and looked upon communism and fascism as temporary disorders or deviations. This optimistic view of democracy and the tendency to view non liberal systems as aberrations did not suit the intellectual structure of the discipline in the period after World War II, especially in view of the emergence of a large number of free nations in Asia, Africa and South America. The bewildering variety of cultures, social institutions and political forms of these new states required a broad focus and new approaches and methods to study them.

Political sociology advanced after World War II, largely in response to this changing global situation, and in order to fill up a major gap in political studies. European and American cultures had provided most of its data and inspired most of its theory in the past. As the non Western states swamped the field, the study of political behaviour in these 'old societies' brought with it intrinsic attractions as well as extrinsic rewards for this discipline.[33] The scholars were now induced to move from the study of the 'first world' of the Western democracies and the 'second world' of the Soviet bloc to the 'third world' of the Afro-Asian variety, and to initiate the construction of this new perspective for looking at politics. The new states offered massive laboratories for research. Often these research interests were combined with interdisciplinary perspectives, and the studies were related to themes such as 'modernization' or 'nation building'.[34] The earlier efforts aiming at a 'nomothetic' analysis of a few states was in the course of time replaced by an 'ideographic' analysis of several nation states.[35] This precipitated the wave of area studies inspired by the view that governmental systems should be understood against their ecological background, and in the total context of their historical, geographical, and cultural settings.[36] The tenor of the studies was 'macrosociological'.[37] The new approach emphasized the study of societies, and even when focusing on parts of these societies, it studied their contribution to the functioning of the society as a 'whole'.

The sheer number of the emergent new states which were old societies, was one of the factors which accounted for the need to study not only their distinct characteristics independently, but also in comparison. This gave rise to a vast literature on comparative politics imbued with a politico-sociological perspective. Comparative politics studied the elements that were comparable in the political process, and sought to understand the interaction of politics with social and cultural dynamics. An early exponent of this view was Gabriel

Almond who attempted the taxonomy of systems on this basis. In an earlier formulation, he classified political systems under categories such as Anglo-American, European, totalitarian and 'pre-industrial'.[38] He subsequently revised this classification in favour of a broad division along the lines of 'traditional', 'transitional' and 'modern', and still later offered a general theoretical framework of functional analysis,[39] which has been pursued by several scholars engaged in studies of independent countries.[40]

The politico-sociological perspective was accepted in the study of politics also because of its broad concerns. The transplantation of political and administrative institutions in the newly freed states raised the question of the evolution and operation of these institutions in a social and cultural milieu vastly different from the countries of their origin. Concern with successful imitation of Western forms of governmental institutions and democratic norms forced attention on their social and functional prerequisites. The Western countries had debated these problems in their own context in the period following the Industrial Revolution. But the resurrection of these problems in the context of the third world countries has revived questions that are central to political sociology.

The Relevance of Political Sociology

The relevance of political sociology has been discussed on different wavelengths. To Duverger, the terms 'political sociology' and 'political science' are synonyms.[41] The term 'political science' reflects a certain tendency toward isolating the study of political phenomena, by limiting its contacts with other branches of the social sciences. The term 'political sociology' on the other hand, indicates a desire to restore political phenomena to their proper place within the broad spectrum of social phenomena, to remove barriers between disciplines, and to emphasize the essential unity of all the social sciences. It also implies a firm intention to use empirical and experimental methods of research instead of philosophical reasoning. And in this sense, argues Duverger, the term 'political sociology' is preferable to 'political science'. To some other commentators, political sociology is a hybrid and possibly upstart discipline, lacking a precise identity of its own. These viewpoints however, are not mutually exclusive.

Political sociology is relevant to political science in many ways. Political sociology has broadened the area of our enquiry by widening the scope of what is considered 'political' phenomena today. It has established that political variables influence social, cultural and economic variables as the latter influence the former. In grappling with the new demands of discipline, political sociology has opened new frontiers of research and has experimented with new methods of analysis. While behaviouralism which believes in action theory veered toward the behaviour of the individual in the political process, political sociology which believes in functional theory corrected the emphasis by focusing upon the function of groups in society.[42]

Political sociology involves an ongoing search for a more comprehensive scope, as well as more realistic, precise and theory conscious analysis. The non Western studies which have appeared recently break new ground in a theoretical as well as a methodological sense. They analyse comparative politics as a political theorist would, basing their analysis on the empirical data gathered from the specific area of their investigation. They formulate generalizations on aspects of politics which have significance for the general theory of political systems. The attainment of depth and realism in the study of political systems enables us to locate the dynamic forces of politics wherever they exist—in social class, in culture, in economic and social change, in the political elite, or in the international environment.

Comparative analysis on the basis of survey methods had led to cross-national, cross-cultural and cross-societal research of considerable value.[43] Concepts such as the state, the constitution, representation, and the rights and duties of citizens, can no longer contain and explain the activities of political parties, pressure groups and the media of mass communication, much less relate them to child rearing, educational practices and other civic norms. Political sociology fills up this serious gap by building theoretical formulations around single central concepts such as group, power, decision or conflict, and also by introducing comprehensive and highly abstract formulations such as system, process, development or communication. Role analysis, focusing on problems such as role conflict, role consensus and role structures, combined with theoretical notions such as system, decision making or power, has been useful in structural-functional approaches to the political process, and especially useful in closing the gap between the macro-analysis and micro-analysis of politics. New concepts of role and political socialization, together with functional categories including the conversion functions, capabilities of the system, and system maintenance and adaptation functions, have gained currency today because of their usefulness, and not merely as a matter of fashion. This has resulted in not only the re-establishment of the classical relationship between comparative government and political theory, but has also opened a new vista. The world community is viewed today as a political system, and the recognition of the intimate relationship between domestic politics and international relations has brought comparative and international politics closer together. In this sense, political sociology has made a seminal contribution, by making possible greater and more meaningful unity of the various sub-fields of political science.

2. Approaches in Political Analysis

The attempt to systematize political knowledge is reflected in various ways of looking at political phenomena. These ways or perspectives are the analytical systems, approaches or paradigms. An analytical system or approach underlies all scientific investigations. The kind of questions that are asked and the way one seeks to answer these questions depend however, upon certain assumptions or models of the world of inquiry. What are the questions to be asked? Which facts or observations should be collected? And how should these be collected and interpreted? There is no single method, but this does not mean that a scientific inquiry need be subjective. It only implies that there are no paradigms that are universally agreed upon. Researchers have different concerns and preferences; various interests and values influence their research enterprises. The variability of values however does not destroy the requirement of formal consistency and the empirical validity of political analysis. It is true though, that in the absence of a clear grasp of an analytical framework, much of political theory degenerates into idle speculation, and behavioural study becomes a collection of meaningless facts.

David Apter identifies six major traditions or themes that mark the emergence of political analysis.[1] These are (*a*) political philosophy, (*b*) institutionalism, (*c*) behaviouralism, (*d*) pluralism, (*e*) structuralism, and (*f*) developmentalism. We can say, as Apter did, that political philosophy is concerned with ends and purposes; institutionalism with political organization; behaviouralism with motivations and mechanism of human behaviour; pluralism with the interaction among groups and organizations; structuralism with the connection between the individual and the community, and especially the broad social relationships as determinants of power; and developmentalism with the process of growth, industrialization, and change, and their impact on governmental forms and policies. This classification of Apter is good in that it shows the main dimensions of political analysis. However, Apter's sixfold classification does not highlight the key issues in the controversy of modern political analysis. These issues centre around the following themes in the current discussions on the philosophy of social sciences: (*a*) behaviouralism and structuralism; (*b*) systems approach, structural-functional analysis and Marxism; and (*c*) science and history.

Behaviouralism and Structuralism

The main achievement of behaviouralism is that it has changed the emphasis of study from structures and institutions to the behaviour of individuals in political situations and roles.[2] It has posited that institutions do not work by themselves, or in a vacuum, and it is the attitudes, motives and perceptions of individual actors in the political arena which make up the mainspring of their political action. In the words of Heinz Eulau, an ardent champion of behaviouralism, 'the political behaviourist concentrates on the behaviour of individuals whose interactions and transactions make up collective behaviour, even if he is concerned with describing and explaining the actions of groups, organizations, or other large collectivities'.[3] The explanatory variables in behaviouralism are for the most part orientations, attitudes and personality traits, and their consequences, that is, their effect on political action.

Another important achievement of behaviouralism is that it has provided tools and techniques for the scientific study of politics. But as the unit of analysis in behaviouralism is the individual, its methods and techniques tend to be primarily psychological notwithstanding its emphasis on an interdisciplinary approach. The methods of psychological tests used in behavioural studies are usually sample surveys, structured schedules and questionnaires.[4] Equally rigorous methods of data analysis such as coding, statistical relationships of correlation and variance and factor analysis are used to measure the characteristics and relationships of variables. The behavioural approach seeks to achieve a precise measurement and quantification of an individual actor's characteristics and behaviour. It hopes to build empirical theories on the basis of data collected and analyzed.

We can make an incisive analysis of behaviouralism by taking up some of its authoritative texts for elucidation. Early in this century, Graham Wallas in *Human Nature in Politics* was particularly concerned about identifying psychological factors, as opposed to an exclusive concern with economic factors.[5] The later rise of fascism led to a much more intensive interest in the impact of psychopathology on the politics of extremism. Harold Lasswell's works spelt out the psychological basis of political leadership. His book *The Psychopathology of Politics* (1930), and his famous formulation that political activity arises from the displacement of personal frustrations on to public causes, gave valuable insight into the psychological basis of the radical political leadership and movement.[6] The psychology of individuals was later used to explain the behaviour of social groups or political institutions but it created the problem of faulty generalization.

Lucian Pye's study of Burma used psychological complexes of the Burmese bureaucracy to explain its administrative behaviour.[7] This case study is most typical in so far as it attempts generalizations about a macro-system on the basis of personality traits and needs of its individual members. Such generalizations raise two difficult questions. In the first place, individual traits and needs do not form an adequate basis of generalizations about a group. Secondly, the psychological needs of individual members may be fulfilled in different ways, and any generalization about individuals may be highly problematic. The socio-cultural and political factors that mediate between individual psychology and group behaviour are indeterminate variables of fundamental importance. Psychological explanations are reductionist explanations because they attempt to reduce group phenomena to individual psychology.

The trouble with the behavioural approach is that it seeks to explain a macro-system in terms of micro-characteristics. Several problems arise with regard to the validity of a generalization about a social group or political institution on the basis of individual psychology. A social group cannot be studied fully by analyzing the isolated individuals who constitute it because individual psychology is different from social psychology. The interpretation of social behaviour depends not only upon the interaction of individual with individual, but upon many other situations such as the interaction of individuals with a group (leader-follower situation), of a group with a group, and of a group with an individual. Antony F.C. Wallace has made very appropriate observations on this aspect of a socio-psychological explanation of a macro-system.[8]

1. The statistical fallacy offers an enumeration of the properties of individual persons as if it were a description of a social or cultural system without any demonstration of a non-random relationship among the dimensions considered.

2. It is sometimes said that personality is culture 'internalized' by the individual; that cultural change has an 'impact' on the individual; and that culture 'moulds' the individual. Such expressions and theoretical formulations are meaningless in any literal sense. To use transitive metaphors such as 'internalize', 'impact', 'mould' and so on to describe the relation between culture and personality is comparable to claiming that a circle has an 'impact on', or that it 'moulds' the points which constitute it. Thus behaviouralism that is based on the psychological approach suffers from either the statistical fallacy or the internalization fallacy, or both.

Insufficiency also characterizes those studies of voting behaviour which are based on survey methods alone. A leading behaviouralist, Eldersveld, admits that panel studies cannot answer basic questions of political theory such as : What is the nature of the electoral basis for the acquisition of power and the exercise of power? Which conditions and motivations induce power to change hands? How effective are the instruments for democratic action and discussion—elections, party, group and the media of communication?[9]

We must point out that the greatest failure of the behavioural approach stems precisely from its achievement. In its preoccupation with methodological precision, it tends to ignore the 'substantive issues' and 'brute realities' which are more difficult to quantify and measure.[10] Its methodological requirements confine its achievements to the quantifiable phenomena, which are often trivial in substance.[11] What is more serious is that 'methodism' itself turns into an ideology.[12] Because of its emphasis on stating what is (and not what 'ought to be') that is what actually happens (no matter, good or bad), behaviouralism is reduced to a barren defence of the status quo.

Some scholars seek the explanation of political action in structural factors. Politics, according to this school, is structured into social categories and their moral, cultural and ideological characteristics. In the political process, these structures or groups and even belief systems, develop their own identities and interests which bind their members into wholes. An individual is not always a free agent as he cannot behave completely independently of his group affiliations. Structuralism focuses on social categories and belief systems of ideologies, and discrete or joint factors in social action or change. In other words, it seeks a socio-economic and cultural explanation of social phenomena.

Durkheim, Weber and Marx may be considered well-known examples of structuralist thinking and a few illustrations of structural analysis from each will contribute to the clarification of the approach. Durkheim seeks to understand the phenomenon of suicide and finds its explanation not in psychological reasons, but in the common characteristics or structural features of certain groups more prone to suicidal tendencies.[13] These structural features represent an 'anomic' condition that is loss of social norms or moral meaning due to social mobility. Anomie is a problem afflicting a group that suffers downward mobility, deprivation and moral confusion. Max Weber also analyzes the rise of capitalism in terms of the puritan culture of the bourgeoisie.[14] The ethos of puritanism produced in the middle class a spirit of hard work and enterprise. Thus the cultural roots of capitalism lay in the 'protestant ethic' of individual enterprise and the motivation for individual achievement and success. Marx recognized the revolutionary role of the bourgeoisie in promoting technical capability for efficient production, but emphasized the development of inner contradictions that would render the capitalist system non-viable.[15] Marx also used the social category of class to indicate the phenomenon of class conflict, and the contradictions in society leading to the dialectical process of social and political change. All these statements, reflective of a structural approach, are holistic, and emphasize the role of a social, cultural or economic group characteristic as a factor in social action. Structural analysis therefore involves macro-analysis.

It may be stressed that in identifying the moral, cultural and ideological character of a social group, psychological insights are of great significance. But while behaviouralist explanation relies on experimental psychology and has built-in reductionism in psychological analysis, structuralism relies on the tangible and concrete expression of individual characteristics and the psychology of social phenomena, thus establishing patterns of human behaviour or social action, as manifest in a group phenomenon and the totality of a situation. As Apter points out, 'Despite major differences between the schools of thought, they share common concerns. They interpret events, episodes, and the activities of social life—including politics. They represent paradigmatic thinking; that is, thinking in terms of wholes. They use deductive methods.[16] Thus structuralism appears to be more suitable than behaviouralism as an approach to the understanding and analysis of the macro-phenomena of a social or political system. Structuralism sees an individual action or human behaviour in the context of a social, cultural or economic setting, and thus helps to indicate the context and the limits within which action can occur. Human behaviour is structured and not whimsical or completely individualistic. Anomie, bureaucracy or class refer to social categories, and are expressions of a group rather than that of isolated individuals. Like human behaviour, politics is also structured in terms of caste, class and elite, which together constitute different patterns of power structures. Political action is the result of certain political configurations, not fixed for all times, but certainly definite at a particular point of time when a political action takes place. A common error committed in structural analysis, however, is the assumption that structures are permanent or independent; whereas they are also subject to change by political action. While structures indicate the limits of action, the limits themselves are not immutable.

Systems Approach, Structural-Functional Analysis and Marxism

Systems analysis is the most explicit form of dealing with any system as a whole or in its wholeness. The concept of a system means that all the elements in the system are organically linked together and are mutually interdependent. Initially taken from biology, the concept of system as an organism has been replaced subsequently with the concept of a dynamic, self-sustaining system set against the background of a changing natural environment. Comprehensiveness, interdependence and boundary maintenance (with the environment) are the three main properties of a system. It is also conceived of as a coherent and endurable whole.[17]

Inspired by its previous use in biology, anthropology, sociology and psychology, systems analysis in its various forms has been used by Easton, Almond, Deutsch and Kaplan in the analysis of political systems.[18] Easton is credited with the introduction of the concepts of inputs and outputs of a political system. Deutsch concerns himself with how a political system 'steers' information and directs it into, or away from, particular channels of communication. Deutsch is influenced by cybernetics—the science of control and communication—and he conceives of society as a machine. Almond links systems analysis to structural functionalism and development, and makes it fit the needs of comparative analysis. All these attempts are part of a larger effort to unify natural and social sciences.

The aim of systems analysis is to understand systems belonging to various disciplines through a common conceptual framework, and furthermore to build a general theory of systems on the basis of this understanding. General systems theory (introduced in the 1930s and '40s), as conceived by its famous exponent Ludwig Von Bertalanffy, is an interdisciplinary doctrine 'elaborating principles and models that apply to systems in general, irrespective of their particular kind, elements, and "forces" involved'.[19] This is based on the assumption that there are parallelisms or isomorphisms in certain general aspects of different systems. Hence if independent disciplines deal with things pertaining to their specific area through a common conceptual framework, a general theory of systems would emerge. Needless to say, this was too ambitious and unrealistic a plan, and it was cause for little wonder therefore, that after a few years of initial euphoria, systems analysis has abandoned its pretensions of developing a general theory. It now devotes itself to the next best thing, the development of a systematic or coherent conceptual framework.

For political sociology, the relevance of systems analysis consists in being a way of ordering the study of politics by appreciating the interrelationship and interconnectedness of politics with other parameters. As a method, systems analysis marks a shift from analysis to synthesis.[20] Classical science in its various disciplines (be it chemistry, biology, psychology or the social sciences) tried to isolate the elements of the observed universe (the method of analysis) in an attempt to understand them separately. Systems analysis starts the other way around. It weaves together the previous pieces of specialized knowledge into a coherent picture (the method of synthesis) and places special emphasis on the interrelationship between one element and the other in the belief that a part can be understood only as a part of the whole, and not as a part in itself. The observed universe is an interconnected and interdependent system of nature and can be appropriately approached by understanding systemic order and interdependence of elements. The world we live in is too inter-related and interdependent for nations, groups or individuals to act with indifference to their action's consequences for others, at home or abroad. Hence, the universe can be understood only in relation to its inner elements as well as the environment.

In operational terms, systems analysis aims to describe, classify and explain the working of systems at various times and places. It is particularly interested in the work that a system does and how it does that work. According to David Easton, it looks for what goes into a system (inputs), how these inputs are converted into policies (outputs), how the latter react on succeeding rounds of inputs (feedback), and what their effects are on the system and systemic goals. The specific research undertaken in this connection is to identify the inputs and the forces that shape and change them, to trace the processes through which they are transformed into outputs, to describe the general conditions under which such processes can be maintained, and to establish the relationship between outputs and succeeding inputs of the system.[21] Inputs, outputs, conversion and feedback are the main activities of political systems (or any system) which systems analysis looks for.

Functionalists posit that certain functions must be performed by the political system (or any system) in order that it may maintain itself and survive. Functionalists also identify various parts or sub-systems within a system, and stress the study of interaction within a system which is essentially a functioning whole. The essence of a system's functioning lies in the fact that it brings about a state of equilibrium.

In a recent article, David Easton has argued that systems analysis does not include either functionalism or equilibrium.[22] Systems analysis does not postulate that the maintenance of a political system depends upon the fulfilment of specific functions. It is interested in identifying and describing the major kinds of activities which explain the operation of a political system. Deutsch, for example, stresses the steering of information by the political system through scanning, selecting and processing information. Out of the total load of information, the political system responds selectively in the form of what is known as its 'gain'. It operates in different societies and times by lagging (delaying) or leading (reacting) to predictions about the consequences of decisions and actions. Easton identifies the demands from the environment, and support to the community, regime or government generated from within the system.

Demand and support together modify and shape the operations of the political system. The authorities, through decisions, make an authoritative allocation of values, and through a process of feedback loop, cope with stresses coming from the intra-societal and extra-societal environment. Thus systems analysis looks at a political system in active or dynamic terms. It interprets a system as a complex organized form of behaviour through which something gets done. It views a system as an active set of relationships.

Functionalism is differentiated from systems analysis in the sense that it emphasizes the process of interaction. Functionalism views a system as a collection of parts that interact with each other. The components of the system adjust to and influence each other to bring about any resulting new state of the system. Systems analysis is basically interested in the process of transformation; functionalism in the process of interaction. However, this is more an instance of hair-splitting than a basic distinction.

We may point out that systems analysis avoids the shortcomings and pitfalls of the psychological approach of behaviouralism. As against the 'atomistic' model of behaviouralism, systems thinking is holistic. As against reductionism (which Frankl says is 'a mask for nihilism'), systems analysis takes a full view of the picture and takes due account of the interrelations within and beyond.[23] It has merits which recommend its use. Kaplan has particularly stressed the following merits of systems analysis.[24]

1. It accounts for a large number of descriptive concepts and categories which can be used for the interpretation of new facts, and for the study of new areas. Its categories are explicit and the framework of reference need not shift as new facts are brought in.

2. It makes possible the integration of variables that do not fall within a single discipline. It is possible to generate a hypothesis by indicating structural similarities with other subject matter. We imagine a homeostatic political system like a human body or an air conditioner. The concepts of 'closed' or 'open' systems or feedback process make us imagine systems in other disciplines. Such parallelisms, if based on sound reasoning, will result in greater clarity of understanding.

3. It makes explicit what is incomplete in analysis. Its insights are helpful in furthering research. It is particularly of value in sorting

out a large quantity of data and in recognizing the patterns and uniformities that tie the elements of a system together.

4. It has suggestive value as it is a heuristic method of gaining knowledge and interpreting the real world.

David Easton argues that the chief merit of systems analysis lies in the fact that by identifying the major classes of variables that require investigation, and by explaining the operation of political systems, it provides the criteria of relevance for the collection of data and presents a coherent perspective or conceptual framework for the analysis of political systems. Easton's notion of support for political objects (the authorities, the regime and the political community) has become more relevant today since various societies are experiencing different stages of decline in the input of support. Similarly, Easton's output of policies has assumed great significance as policy analysis has become the crucial concern of political scientists in the seventies.

Attention ought to be drawn also to certain disadvantages of systems analysis among which are the following:

1. Spiro doubts the usefulness of systems analysis in analyzing politics because the concepts drawn from biology, physics and so on, are sometimes irrelevant and the analyst falls into the trap of misplaced analogies.[25]

2. Systems analysis is useful in macro-analysis, but not very useful in a micro-analysis of forces which constitute a large part of social interaction. Systems analysis does not take note of the complete psychological aspects of the interaction function. Young rightly says that it does not offer very much for studies dealing with the political aspects of such matters as 'perception, expectation, cognition'.[26]

3. Systems analysis may not be able to answer questions such as those on the scope and depth of power as it was being used. Nor does it help us to understand the strategies and tactics involved in the exercise of power.

4. Systems analysis provides for a large number of concepts, some of which may not be relevant in a particular study, and some of the notions of which are not of practical utility.

5. A proper application of theory would require a very high level of theoretical consciousness which is generally difficult to acquire, and its application is possible only in a programme of research requiring abstract analysis of a high order. This leads to difficulties in empirical operationalization.

6. Kaplan argues that the use of systems analysis in social sciences

can be made only with certain reservations and awareness of its limitations.[27] As social objects lack the fixed and definite character of natural objects, particularization in social and political forms is just not possible. We cannot construct models that copy faithfully the particularities of the real world. Our mathematical and computer tools are inadequate in representing the complex inter-relationship between social and political structures. The highly complex models 'run the risk of being artifacts' because the more complex a model, the more sensitive it is to slight variations. Highly particularized models lack both generality and relevance to any specific problem of social science. On the other hand, a completely general theory may lack explanatory power. It might enunciate the most elementary truisms about social and political structures, or alternatively, mislead by attempting to do something which it cannot accomplish. Hence, it is better to make use of the comparative method and theory, or confine oneself to saying different things about distinguishable systems rather than the same thing about every system.

The ideas of structural-functional analysis are spelt out by Gabriel Almond in his famous introduction to *The Politics of the Developing Areas*. It would, however, be worthwhile to trace functionalism to earlier contributors. The concept of functionalism refers to the social system as an organic body in which certain vital functions must be performed by different organs and structures in order that the social system may maintain itself and survive. A social system, for instance, must perform recruitment and socialization functions so that a society is able to have its members in constant supply and that these members are socialized into common norms and values to maintain social cohesion. From this basic 'organismic' notion of a social system, there followed a number of ideas: (*a*) that the functions are necessary for the survival of a social system, and that therefore, (*b*) the functions are universal. The earlier version of functionalism, as associated with Radcliffe-Brown and Malinowski in particular, emphasized three main principles: functional unity, functional universalism and functional indispensability.[28] According to Radcliffe-Brown, the function of a social activity or institution is the contribution it makes to the total social life. Malinowski further maintained that every social institution or tradition fulfils some vital function, and every custom or belief therefore, is indispensable.

Robert Merton has subjected this version of functionalism to scathing criticism and provided necessary correctives.[29] He first points out that the same social institution or item may have multiple functions, and that the same function can be diversely fulfilled by alternative items. The concept of a functional alternative, equivalent or substitute therefore, removes the commitment to, or the value of, particular social items as universal categories serving the entire society. Merton also introduces the concept of dysfunctions, and points out that some structures or institutions may indeed produce consequences harmful to the society. As he points out, functions are 'those observed consequences which make for the adaptation or adjustment of a given system', and dysfunctions, 'those observed consequences which lessen the adaptation or adjustment'. He further adds that there is also the possibility of non-functional consequences, which are simply irrelevant to the system.

Another important contribution to structural-functionalism comes from Talcott Parsons.[30] His theory of action is determined by a structural relationship between culture, personality and the social system. There are five pattern-variables in each set of contrasting modes. They are: (*a*) affectivity or affective neutrality, that is, emotional gratification or detachment; (*b*) self-orientation or collective orientation; (*c*) universalism or particularism; (*d*) achievement or ascription; and (*e*) specificity or diffuseness. These pattern-variables are alternative and contrasting modes of behaviour or organization. However, all social systems are based on the fulfilment of four basic functions: adaptability, goal achievement, integration and pattern maintenance. These functions, it was initially believed, are characteristic of a 'social system', and it was deemed desirable to search for 'appropriate' functional categories for the analysis of 'political systems' which though part of the social system, at times attempt to engulf the whole, or at least to affect it substantially.

Almond introduced a structural-functional approach to political science, and though his scheme followed Easton and Lasswell, he was the first to apply this approach to the analysis of politics. In Almond's formulation, the modern political system is distinguished from the traditional one on two major dimensions: (*a*) structural differentiation-structural non-differentiation and (*b*) secular-theocratic. In addition, there are several secondary dimensions which point out certain aspects of style. By structural differentiation, Almond means that there are structures in the political system that have a 'functional distinctiveness, and which tend to perform a regulatory role in relation to that function within the political system as a whole'.[31] In order to operationalize the concept of structural differentiation, he identifies the functions that all political systems are supposed to have in common. Almond classifies these functions into four input functions, namely, (*a*) political socialization and recruitment, (*b*) interest articulation, (*c*) interest aggregation, and (*d*) political communication; and three output functions, namely, (*a*) rule-making, (*b*) rule-application, and (c) rule-adjudication. They are called conversion functions because inputs are converted into outputs by the political process. A modern system, according to Almond, is a differentiated political system because in each of these functional areas, there exist specialized and distinct structures which regulate that function. The modern style or mode is distinguished from, or contrasted against, the traditional style of regulating such functions on the dimensions suggested by Parsons.

Almond's conceptual analysis of the modern political system provides a useful framework for the analysis of some highly significant problems in cross-cultural research. His framework, however, appears to have certain limitations which prevent it from being completely effective as a basis for developing more general theories of political modernization. It is difficult to apply his scheme on a broad basis to include both historical and contemporary cases. The formulation tends in effect to equate the modern political system with the modern Anglo-American democratic system, and it cannot be applied to the societies which have adopted a totalitarian form of government or which are as yet underdeveloped. Holt and Turner point out that its definitions employ too many dimensions, and that it neglects the study of societal functions.[32] Holt and Turner suggest the following guidelines for use.

(*a*) A useful approach to the study of political modernization must be able to accommodate both the democratic, and the autocratic or totalitarian states.

(*b*) Different types of systems should be defined by a very limited number of characteristics.

(*c*) Particular attention must be devoted to the societal functions of government.

(*d*) Instead of psychological explanation (reductive explanations of macro-social phenomena), efforts should be focused upon sociological (emergent) explanation, with an explicit attempt to achieve maximum closure and autonomy.[33]

Holt and Turner in their studies of France (1600-1789), China

(1644-1911), Japan (1603-1868) and England (1558-1780), present another version of structural-functionalism for the analysis of political factors in economic growth, and also develop hypotheses on the role of these factors in economic development. In their framework, they are mainly concerned with 'the social system at the societal level', and have adopted the four basic functional requisites postulated by Parsons. They are: (*a*) adaptation, which is concerned with the relationship of the social system with the non-human part of environment; (*b*) goal attainment, which is concerned with the achievement of a system's goals in relationship to the material, cultural, and other aspects of societies; (*c*) pattern maintenance, which is concerned with maintaining conformity with the belief-value (cultural system); and (*d*) integration, which is concerned with achieving necessary coordination among differentiated but interdependent roles.

The overview of systems and structural-functional analysis attempted above leads us to the following critical observations.

(*a*) There is no universal acceptance of what exactly constitutes the political functions. Different authors put forward different versions or inventories of functions. (*b*) Functionalism is based on the notion of equilibrium, and provides little understanding of conflict which is the heart of the political process. The organismic implications of functionalism, even after Merton's correctives, does not fully account for the growth and development of the political system. (*c*) Functionalism does not reckon with history, and the historicity of political phenomena. The implication of universal functional requisites assumes the full development of political systems, and disregards the developmental problems and perspectives of new nations. (*d*) An uncritical application of functionalism is likely to result in the neglect of factors and events unique to a political society. It is in the context of each country's historical compulsions and political choices that the politics and political development of a country can be understood.[34] To proceed with functional analysis on a universal basis is to distort the proper focus and to rob political analysis of its significance.

The inability of systems analysis and structural-functional analysis to deal with developing countries in particular are ably summed up by D.L. Sheth.[35] According to him,

1. The systems theory proceeds with the assumption that territorial entities called nation-states have acquired the formal

characteristics of an ongoing system.

2. The relationship of variables and their conceptualization presupposes a uniform pattern in all countries, which is not warranted by facts.

3. The approach wishes away the inconvenient aspects of political change which are difficult to quantify; and the will and ability of human individuals to intervene in the causal process of development. In developing countries faced with the task of nation and state building, conflicts and crises of growth and development involve factors and situations that cannot be meaningfully explained in terms of a given version of political functions.

There is however, one aspect of functionalism that holds great promise in political analysis. Political functions may be understood as the consequences of political actions, and as such, may focus on the conditions and consequences of political events in a particular country. This would also deal with the problem of historicity by taking account of an individual or a discrete institution or event.

The Marxian approach, on the other hand, distinguishes itself not only as a revolutionary doctrine but as the one which seeks to revolutionize political analysis by its way of thinking about social, economic and political phenomena. Marxian analysis is rooted in dialectical and historical materialism according to which history progresses through a conflict between two classes in which society is perpetually divided. 'All past history', according to Marx and Engels, 'with the exception of its primitive stages, was the history of class struggles'.[36] These warring classes are the products of the modes of production and of exchange. History is the record of class conflict between those who own the means of production and others who do not, and this class conflict is the central theme and motive power in politics.

The modes of production in all times determine production relations, resulting in the existence of classes and a new kind of social relations. These social or economic relations, that is class situations, determine men's ideas and mental behaviour. 'It is not the consciousness of men that determines their existence but, on the contrary, their social existence determines their consciousness.'[37] Social existence or social relations are the determinants of the character of society, politics and religion. With the passage of time, men develop new and advanced methods of production; so correspondingly new relations of production and further new ideas, laws, customs, morals and social and political relations develop.[38] With the change of the economic foundation, the entire superstructure is transformed.

Marx identified four broad stages through which society has evolved.[39] These are the Asiatic, ancient, feudal and bourgeois stages. At each stage of development, the new material forces of production come into conflict with the existing and established relations of production, and related laws, ideas and morals, inducing change and progress. Each stage was characterized by antagonism resulting from a situation when forces of production outstripped the firmly established relations of production of an earlier stage of development. This created disharmony between the modes of production and the existing social relations. Struggle follows conflict, and is resolved by the victory of the new and advanced forces over the old. Marx analyzed the contemporary situation as most disharmonious, because the Industrial Revolution had exposed the contradictions between modern technology and feudal social and political organization. The rise of the bourgeoisie provided a balance between free enterprise and modern technology. This balance was however faced with inner contradictions between increasing technological efficiency and the concentration of wealth in the hands of the leaders of monopoly capitalism on the one hand, and growing pauperization of the working classes on the other. These trends, Marx predicted, would make the capitalist system collapse under the weight of its own inner contradictions which could be resolved only by eliminating private control of the productive forces.[40]

Marxian analysis illustrates the progress of history according to a definite course. History follows regular laws. These laws of history or principles of social change are based on certain basic postulates which are as follows:[41]

1. Society is always in motion. It is never stagnant or unchanging; it is never in a fixed or solid state. All phenomena of nature are in a state of continuous change and development. The change is not visible to us at any one moment; but we can notice the change over long periods because it is constantly occurring. In the words of Stalin, 'nature is not a state of rest, but a state of continuous movement and change where something is always arising and developing and something always extinguishing and dying away'.

2. Social change is from quantity to quality—from the lower to the higher order. Over a period of time, this change becomes perceptible, for example, in the evolution of human beings and civilizations,

in the nature of state and family, or in our ways of looking at things. The change from primitive society (Asiatic) to slavery (ancient), from slavery to feudalism, and from feudalism to capitalism, is a qualitative change or development. Following this logic, it will qualitatively develop further, from capitalism to socialism, (through the phase of the dictatorship of the proletariat) and finally lead to communism through the withering away of the state.

3. Progress is a dialectical process. It takes place through the process of a clash of opposites or contradictions which bring in synthesis. In any existing state, every phenomenon contains elements of contradictions which make for motion and change. Contradictions are inherent in all things, for they have their positive and negative sides, a past and a future. At each stage, something is dying away and something new is developing; so within every phenomenon, there is a struggle between the being and the becoming. This struggle is the internal content of the transformation of quantitative changes into qualitative changes.

Marx placed undue emphasis on the progress of history through class antagonism, and conceived of no moral or political values independent of the class interest. Interests or ideas not conforming to his logic of dialectical materialism became matters of false consciousness. Religion or nationalism, for example, became aberrations marring the main motive power of history, class conflict. Marx showed that conflict actually existed, and that it has always existed in the past. One can argue that these conflicts may not always appear as class struggles and that they may follow other lines. Similarly, one may not agree with Marx's prescription that this process will cease with the establishment of communism where the source of conflict—private ownership of productive forces—is eliminated and where the government of people is replaced by the administration of things. The emergence of a classless or stateless society is a romantic utopia and not part of Marx's otherwise brilliant scientific analysis.

The Marxist approach is based on a logical view of economic determinism, but it ignores non-economic and cultural movements in the development of history. Orthodox Marxism also ignored the forces of nationalism and of national polity as the dominant factor in modern politics. Marxism not only reduces politics to the dependent status of epiphenomenon, but by ignoring religion, language, ethnicity and above all, nationalism, it fails to provide an understanding of political developments, whether in the first, second or the third world. Moreover, the massive range of Marxist ideas has lent itself to different interpretations in the twentieth century which have been extremely polemical as a result of the East-West cold war and international rivalry. Thus there is not one version of Marxism-Leninism, but many, and still more have cropped up recently.

There is one common point however, in systems analysis and Marxism. Both believe in the unity and the interconnection, the interdependence and totality of the process. Both find it necessary to take into account the surrounding environment for the understanding of a particular system. Systems analysis has in its later incarnations, shown concern for the historical development of things, but it does not share the concern of the Marxists with the material development of things. Above all, they differ in their assumptions about the world of inquiry. While a systems analyst would consider a political system capable of transforming social inputs into outputs, a Marxist would consider it necessary for social and economic inputs to change the political system itself. Also, while a systems analyst introduces the notions of stability and equilibrium, and postulates the existence of such a system, a Marxist assumes that things are transient and that nature is in a constant flux; so that the notion of rest or stability is notionally repugnant to the Marxian thesis. So inspite of the persuasion of the systems analysts that they can account for change and transformation, it has to be admitted that stability is the central idea in systems analysis, while change is the principal focus of Marxism.

It is true that systems analysts are making strenuous efforts to give a lie to the charge that their approach describes the elements which create equilibirum, and that systems analysis is hence not suited to the study of societies which are undergoing transformation and social change. Kaplan has argued that its model can be useful for the study of systems in disequilibrium and for diagnosing 'disintegration, decay or breakdown'.[42] The absence of factors which create equilibrium will produce instability or disequilibrium. *International Political Science Review* has devoted its full length in Vol. I, No. 1, 1980, to articles dealing with the transformation of systems. Yet the stigma of being pro-status quo remains, their basic parameter being system maintenance or endurance. Even the revised formulations of Almond refer to the capabilities of a political system and to the ways in which political systems maintain or adapt themselves to pressures for change in the long run. Gouldner cogently argues that 'what makes a theory conservative (or radical) is its posture toward the institutions of its own surrounding society. A theory is conservative to the extent that it treats these institutions as given and unchangeable in essentials; proposes remedies for them so that they may work better, rather than devising alternatives to them; foresees no future that can be essentially better than the present, the conditions that already exist, and explicitly or implicitly, counsels acceptance of or resignation to what exists, rather than struggling against it.'[43] Systems analysis is conservative in this sense; and Marxism radical, because it regards the present as transitory, views development from lower to higher and is committed to change.

It is a measure of the success of systems analysis that it has not only proved useful for handling problems in industry, commerce, and politics, but has impressed progressive thinkers in the world. From the Soviet side, Blauberg, Sadovsky and Yudin have suggested a 'philosophy of systems' to 'explicate the characteristics of the systems world view' and tackle its methodological and epistemological problems.[44] General systems theory, pioneered by Kenneth Boulding, Anatol Rapoport and others, promise the blending of scientific information with sophisticated methodologies and conceptual analysis—thus bringing science and philosophy together.[45]

Neither functionalism nor Marxism however, pays attention to the peculiar problems of statecraft and nation building, and to the creative role of politics in tackling these problems. This perspective is important in the context of world politics of the late twentieth century and it provides a major agenda of research and theory building. These inadequacies however do not negate the value of these approaches, as political science must continue to live with competing paradigms. Also, different situations may demand different approaches of study and understanding.

Science and History

The recent trend in political science is dominated above all by attempts to make it empirical, that is, to focus on rigorous methods of collection and analysis of data. The application of scientific methods in empirical political studies has received increasing attention. The trend reflects developments in all social sciences, but especially in psychology, sociology and economics. Behaviouralism, that insists on the study of what men do, calls for empiricism and the scientific study of political phenomena. *Political sociology incorporates the empirical dimension of behavioural analysis but broadens it in the context of political system; political sociology, methodologically speaking, is concerned with 'systemic' analysis in which structural factors hold the focus.* Behavioural factors in terms of motives and attitudes have found a place in areas of psephology and political culture, but they are still part of a larger concern with political structures.

The trend toward a more scientific character of social sciences, including political science, is reflected in the attempt to produce theory not in terms of speculative philosophy, but in terms of generalized statements showing the relationship among variables.[46] The body of modern political theory has not yet yielded any ground breaking theory from which propositions regarding political behaviour may be drawn. Yet many attempts have been made in the recent past to offer conceptual frameworks or paradigms according to which systematic empirical studies may be undertaken. These frameworks, paradigms or models are designed to lay down basic concepts and views of political phenomena and of the way the political process takes place.

The models provide the approach towards the understanding of politics, and lay down the criteria for the choice of facts that are relevant to political analysis. It is not enough to know facts; it is necessary to know which facts are relevant, and in order to know the relevant facts, one must know the criteria of relevance. It is the function of a framework or paradigm to define the criteria of relevance for a particular enquiry. To proceed with an enquiry, one must have a problem, not merely in the sense of a social problem, but in terms of a scientific problem, which originates in but is distinguished from, a social problem in being an intellectual puzzle. The solution of this scientific problem depends upon its analysis with regard to finding an explanation or seeking an understanding but not necessarily a cure. A theory thus explains a phenomenon and contributes to the understanding of its how's and why's.[47] This is feasible in the context of a model of how or why things happen the way they happen. It is this model that determines the significance of facts required, or relevant for explanation.

Debate continues on whether a scientific study of political phenomena is feasible, and if feasible, desirable. There are, on the one hand, those who demand that political science should aim at being mathematical. They advocate that political science should acquire technical proficiency, pursue basic understanding divorced from practical interests, and exclude moral valuations or value specifications. Only facts, publicly verifiable, testable and sensually perceived, should be admitted as basic data for research. As Holt and Turner point out, 'our suggestion is that political scientists must turn to mathematics for rules of logic and until this is done, the grand schemata will remain essentially heuristic'.[48] Likewise, the session of the International Political Science Association on mathematical political science, at its conference in the summer of 1964, put forward proposals to elucidate the application of mathematics to political study.[49] It is, however, interesting to note that opinions were sharply divided and there were at least as many critics, as defenders of mathematical politics.

The main thrust for mathematical political science can be seen in the *Social Science Yearbook for Politics* published in 1976.[50] The book has two underlying currents: one relates to the substantive and specific subject of various papers read, and the other to basic questions about the scientific character of political science. The latter includes the more substantive aspect of the discussion in the book and is a useful contribution to the philosophy of social science in general. The conceptual and methodological developments in the field of political science have raised basic questions relating to the nature of the social sciences in general, and political science in particular. The central question relates to how 'scientific' social sciences can be and should be. What is the status of measurement and prediction in social theory? The dissatisfaction with normative speculations, and the need to quantify in order to establish a relationship between variables and to predict, has led to efforts at model building and searching for universal paradigms. The debate on these issues has already made us familiar with claims and counter-claims for and against the use of statistical methods in the study of politics. Indeed, the present preoccupation with such newfangled methods has been criticized on the ground that this results in disorientation with the substantive concerns of the discipline, and ends up with an obsession with the techniques of measurement.

The main trouble with mathematical political scientists is that being believers in scientism, they are prepared to sacrifice questions of relevance and significance for the sake of scientific precision and prediction. Holt and Richardson Jr. for example, maintain that

> A science that is heavily committed to dealing with socially and morally relevant problems finds little use for this kind of paradigm or for the commitment to mathematics that it requires. For political science to advance, it must shed this professional commitment to solving social and moral problems.[51]

This, indeed, is the crux of the problem. It is unacceptable to a vast number of social scientists who cannot accept the dictum that social science can, or should be, divorced from the social context and the moral goals of man.[52]

It is further argued that social and political phenomena and social facts, being highly complex and variable; less, if at all, repeatable; less directly observable; and less uniform than natural phenomena and objects, cannot be studied through the methods and process of the natural sciences.[53] We cannot isolate one factor from a host of factors to establish the fact of causation or correlation. Even in natural sciences, following Einstein's theory of relativity, scientists establish only probabilistic relationships and not absolute relationships. Heinsenberg has argued that a physicist cannot specify accurately both the position and the velocity of a particle.[54] The more accurately the position is stipulated, the less accurate the measurement of velocity becomes.

It is important to appreciate the fact that there are differences between the cognitive intention and aims of the natural sciences and social sciences.[55] Social sciences aim at interpretation and explanation; they do not deal only with facts, but with subjective feelings and emotions of human beings. If social scientists choose to remain aloof from contemporary crises, they are bound to become conservatives, and defenders of the status quo. Even visionary or speculative philosophy then, would have greater orientation towards change than 'scientific' social science.

The necessity of amenability to quantification and measurement has one more limitation. It limits not only aims and concerns, but also areas of research. Quantification has two aspects—statistical and mathematical. The use of statistics as quantitative data affected by a multiplicity of causes, fits in with the study of political participation, voting or political culture. The framework of analysis in such areas is empirical, and data give a more precise idea of the number of voters voting and breakdowns of different forms of participation or political attitudes. Quantification is useful in such areas where it can provide an accurate picture of what is going on. It is also possible to manipulate the quantifiable data to demonstrate correlations or variance of relevant factors in the behaviour of various groups of political actors.

In the contemporary debate however, this meaning and use of statistics is hardly controversial except when used merely as plain tables or figures without offering plausible interpretation and explanation of these figures. Tables in themselves are meaningless, and such statistical work in political analysis is a collection of data lacking in coherent meaning or significance. The charge against such statistical use or abuse however, is of triviality rather than major philosophical or scientific distortions. Contemporary political science is confronted with a challenging choice as to its epistemology as well as methodology. All the evidence however, shows that mathematical politics is often concerned with the trivial, or what is ancillary to politics, and has hardly produced works of great understanding and insight.

The historical method, insofar as it illuminates the past and provides a common denominator for comparison between the origins and development of social and political phenomena, is fruitful. Good historical works can provide a better understanding of political development than mathematical manipulations can.[56] However, by historical works we do not refer to those which merely narrate events and uncorrelated facts. As Lester Salmon rightly points out: 'Perhaps it is the social scientist with a firm understanding of history who can be most useful in the research for fruitful modes of modernization. Comparative history can generate readily testable hypotheses firmly grounded in empirical reality'.[57] Salmon refers to three studies as examples—C.E. Black, *The Dynamics of Modernization* (1966); Barrington Moore, *Social Origins of Dictatorship and Democracy* (1966); and S. Huntington, *Political Order in Changing Societies* (1968). Indeed, it may be said that works such as these relying on historical insight and explanation make for a better understanding than those employing mathematical models.

To argue for history against mathematics in the study of politics is not to dismiss all the concerns of sociological and behavioural approaches, perspectives or frameworks. Certainly even history cannot escape the impact of behavioural sciences, and there is a definite trend towards developing the social, economic and cultural history of groups and forces. Much of new history tends to be sociological, and some sociology also tends to be historical. History as a method is increasingly applied to the analysis of social categories, and social categories are more and more employed in the study of history. Thus the blending of the historical method and sociological concepts and theories, may be an answer to the current perplexities surrounding the discipline of political science. In the field of political sociology, there is great potential for such blending which can ensure a systematic and significant treatment of political life and its problems.

3. Political Power and Social Stratification : Class and Caste

Class

The stratification or division of a society into several ranks is a characteristic of most social systems. Social class is the most popular and powerful concept of stratification which social scientists have used as an explanation of social organization, social movements and power structure. Plato conceived of three classes based on natural faculties. He thought that an ideal republic could be achieved if each class performed the function that naturally belonged to it, that is, for the discharge of which it was most capable and equipped. The ancient *varna* classification of Hindu society was based on a similar functional division of fourfold classes which eventually evolved into the caste system.

Aristotle analyzed the state in terms of three classes which were distinguished from one another by the amount of wealth each possessed, and the virtues or vices that each acquired as a result of its economic condition. His conclusions that the best political community is formed by citizens of the middle class, and that those states in which the middle class component is large are likely to be well administered, were the earliest significant pronouncements in the field of political sociology.

In modern times Marx made the concept of class conflict central to his theory of dialectical materialism. According to him, all those who occupy an identical position in the process of production and in relation to the means of production and exchange, belong to a class. The basic distinction is between the class which owns and the one which does not own the means of production, and these two groups constitute two separate and antagonistic classes. The concept of conflict is essential to Marx's philosophy of dialectical materialism. Classes are pitted against each other with the owning class exploiting the dispossessed class. The social and political mechanisms of control are designed to support and reinforce such exploitation. The class system is characterized by consciousness of identity and solidarity within each class, and mutual hostility between them. To cite Marx and Engels,

> The separate individuals form a class only insofar as they have to carry on a common battle against another class; otherwise they are on hostile terms with each other as competitors. On the other hand, the class in its turn achieves an independent existence over against the individuals, so that the latter find their conditions of existence predestined, and hence have their position in life and their personal development assigned to them by their class, become subsumed under it. This is the same phenomenon as the subjection of the separate individuals to the division of labour and can only be removed by the abolition of private property and of labour itself.[1]

Bendix and Lipset rightly emphasize that the important aspect of the Marxist concept of class is the individual's position in relation to the control over the organization of production.

> It is the position which the individual occupies in the social organization of production that indicates to which social class he belongs. The fundamental determinant of class is the way in which the individual cooperates with others in the satisfaction of his basic needs of food, clothing, and shelter. Other indices such as income, consumption patterns, educational attainment, or occupation are so many clues to the distribution of material goods and prestige symbols. The income or occupation of an individual is *not*, according to Marx, an indication of his class position. For example, if two men are carpenters, they belong to the same occupation, but one may run a small shop of his own, while another works in a plant manufacturing pre-fabricated housing. The two men belong to the same occupation, but to different social classes.[2]

The concept of alienation is also an important element of the Marxist theory of class conflict. According to Marx, capitalist society is divided between the bourgeoisie and the proletariat and the latter are alienated from their labour, and the fruits of their labour. As Fritz Pattenheim points out,

> The social framework of modern industrialized nations described by Marx is in many ways the archetype of Tonnies' *Gesellschaft.* The concept of "capitalist society" is used by Marx in a polemical sense, to express his condemnation of a social system with inherent exploitation and injustices. But he also uses it to describe the structure of a social order in which the strong communal organization of previous societies no longer exists. In such societies individuals have become so separated and isolated that they establish contact only when they can use each other as means to particular ends; bonds between human beings are supplanted by useful associations, not of whole persons, but of particularized individuals.[3]

The harsh, inexorable logic of class conflict described by Marx, was modified by Max Weber, who while acknowledging the fact of social differences and even of economic class, repudiated the Marxist idea of revolutionary class conflict, and diffused the concept of class by introducing the concepts of status and power. While a man's class is determined by his individual place in the market situation, his status is derived from a different set of criteria such as occupation, lifestyle and social prestige. Weber further pointed out that classes are not communities. A community is characterized by a feeling among its members that they belong together. This implies a sense of identity and cohesion. A community may indeed provide a sharing of lifestyle in its totality, which, says Weber, is not true of economic classes that are determined by the individual's place in the market or economic situation. There could therefore be no direct relation between classes and the social behaviour of members constituting a class. Weber defines class as follows:

> We may speak of "class" when (1) a number of people have in common a specific causal component of their life chances, insofar as (2) this component is represented exclusively by economic interests in the possession of goods and opportunities for income, and (3) is represented under the conditions of the commodity or labour market.[4]

Max Weber goes on to point out that 'in our terminology "classes" are not "communities"; they merely represent possible and frequent bases for communal action.[5] Thus class is a basis of human action, but not the conditioning factor. Men tend to be more closely identified with social groups that are communities rather than classes. A community represents the closest possible identification between an individual and a group, and cuts across classes. Class is one dimension of the totality of life that is defined at a time by the community. As Gordon Leff says:

> All evidence of history points away from class as the basis of action and consciousness. The group, whether nation, tribe, class, and the myths which it engenders, has been incomparably the most potent factor in mobilizing men's allegiance. The actual community to which men belong is that with which they identify themselves, often to the point of dying for it. For it, unlike class, is where life is lived in association with others.[6]

Thus Max Weber modifies the concept of class as a comprehensive social category, by employing the concept of status based on social honour or prestige, to make a distinction between class and community, denying that class is a community. Indeed the social structure of India provides ample illustration of Weber's concept of status. Even the poor brahmin in India enjoys some measure of prestige and influence. The decisive role of lifestyle in determining status regardless of income or occupation, reduces the significance of the economic factor.

While discussing Pareto's ideas in this connection, Robert Michels points out that

> Pareto does not want to contest the value of faith, opinions, and feelings to the development of politics and even individual human life. Rather, he thinks that faith and the struggle between the various faiths is an indispensable element to a sane and active life, alone able to prevent sloth and laziness. Non-logical actions have their own profound reason for existence, which consists precisely in this: the ingenuous supposition that "man could do away entirely with religion and substitute for it simple scientific notions" is an infantile error.[7]

Thus economic interests, however powerful or fundamental, do not exhaust the totality of individual and community life. Another idea that Max Weber uses to modify the concept of class is that of party.

> Whereas the genuine place of "classes" is within the economic order, the place of "status groups" is within social order, that is, within the distribution of "honour". But parties live in a house of power. Their action is oriented toward the acquisition of social "power", that is to say toward influencing a communal action no matter what its content may be. In any individual case, parties may represent interests determined through "class situation" or "status situation" and they may recruit their following respectively from one or the other. But they need be neither purely "class" nor purely "status" parties. In most cases they are partly class parties and partly status parties, but sometimes they are neither.[8]

Marx treats the concept of class as if it were the only rational and empirical reality. Concepts are artifacts or constructs and not empirical facts. Marxist theory with its commitment to class conflict is more an arsenal of revolution than a tool for understanding, and therefore lacks the flexibility characteristic of Weber's analysis of class, community and party. The Marxist view endows the concept of class with the characteristics of a categorical imperative, rigid in its composition and absolute in its character as the determinant of human consciousness and social and political action. Thus the idea of class as invariable or fixed in composition and absolute in its role is untenable.

Discussing the implications of the Marxian analysis of class for social action, Gordon Leff says that

> This allows no place for developments within a class or an ideology so far as class is concerned, to maintain it as the universal and basic category is to make all human activity dependent upon it; and since class is in turn dependent upon changes in the forces of production, there is a double dependence in social action. This is in fact a doctrine of social statics rather then dynamics.[9]

This would indeed eliminate the creative and autonomous role of political action and leadership. The contingent and variable character of historical events rule out the universal determination of social action on the basis of class. Leff further argues that

> Social categories do not have the status of those of nature. To begin with, they are abstractions from qualities which are themselves abstracted. Secondly, social phenomena lack the universality and invariability of natural phenomena. A class is

not a species just because it is not common or necessary to all men at all times and in the same way as an inseparable accompaniment of social organization.[10]

A similar view is expressed by Ralf Dahrendorf,[11] who has extended further Weber's sociology and politics concerning class. Dahrendorf proceeds with the inevitability of conflict in society but rejects the Marxist thesis that property alone is the cause of power and dominance. He defines class in relation to authority. Classes arise because some groups participate in the exercise of authority while others are excluded from it. This may give an impression of class conflict akin to Marxist dichotomy between the owners of property and those without it. Dahrendorf however, maintains that an industrial society tends to be pluralist in which patterns of domination and subjection are spread over the entire society in a number of associations. There is no monopoly of power in a single class in all the spheres of life and therefore there is no simple polarization of class conflict.

Criticism of the Marxist view of 'class' does not however eliminate the phenomenon of status cleavage or social differences. Class and status differences have characterized the older societies, and even in modern society, social cleavages based on economic interests are easily observed. As the authors of *The American Voter* have noted, 'competition between upper and lower status groups appears to have been an element of some importance in political matters since the birth of the American Republic'.[12]

Number ten of *The Federalist Papers* recognized the importance of the economic causes of social inequality and cleavage. To quote its author,

The most common and durable source of factions has been the various and unequal distribution of property. Those who hold and those who are without property have even formed distinct interests in society. Those who are creditors, and those who are debtors, fall under a like discrimination. A landed interest, a manufacturing interest, a mercantile interest, a moneyed interest, with many lesser interests grow up of necessity in civilized nations and divide them into different classes, actuated by different sentiments and views. The regulation of these various and interfering interests forms the principal task of modern legislation and involves the

> spirit of party and faction in the necessary and ordinary operations of the government.[13]

The Federalist approach to class is fundamentally different from the Marxist. Although both recognize the importance of economic interests, the Federalist approach stresses plurality of interests. The Federalist view of class is characterized by pluralism and political reconciliation among group interests. Social class is conceived of as a group, and the group reality of the class is amenable to manipulation and adjustment by the political process.

The group reality is a variable because it is a function more of subjective identification and shared interests, rather than affiliation with an economic category alone based on income or property. Such a subjectivist view as against the Marxist view of class is presented by Richard Centers in his book entitled *The Psychology of Social Classes*.[14] Social class as a group is real only in the minds of its members. This is independent of the economic condition. The objective class distinction is described by the term 'stratification' and it is the consciousness arising from the objective condition that makes the group a social class. A social class is, therefore, a group of people who feel a sense of identification and shared interest as a result of membership in a common stratum of the society. It is, therefore, a question of empirical investigation whether class and stratum correspond or differ.

On the question of conceptualizing social class, V.O. Key sums up the alternative approaches in the following words:

> The problem of social class in politics becomes a bit slippery when one attempts to define social classes. One method is to define them by some plausible objective criteria, such as occupation, income, level of education, property ownership or another similar standard. Political theorists characteristically hold this conception of class. The trouble with it is that the persons so grouped are not necessarily aware of their class position. A person obviously proletarian by the objective criteria may neither regard himself as a proletarian nor act politically as such. An alternative mode of demarcation of classes is to discover with what class, if any, people identify. Do they regard themselves as upper, middle or lower class? How strong is their sense of class identification? If they have a sense of class consciousness, a sense of belonging to one group rather than to another, class takes on political significance.[15]

Sociologists use class as a concept in social stratification and seek to explore the conditions of and the means for, stratification, and the consequences thereof. Stratification, of course, implies inequality and it is the business of sociologists to seek an analysis of the phenomenon of social inequality. The primary concern of the sociologist is with the why and how of stratification, and the category of social class. The political sociologist, on the other hand, is interested in understanding the relationship between social class and political process. Political analysis is aimed at exploring the impact of class, status and parties on the authoritative allocation of values, and also the impact of such allocation on class and other groups. It is this mutual interaction between social class, status groups and political action, that forms a major field of inquiry for political sociology.

There has been a good deal of controversy about the relation between class or status and politics. As we have seen earlier, Marx projected class struggle as the key factor in the march of history. The theory of class conflict and the tenet of dialectical materialism implies that technology and economy are basic, and that society, polity and culture are reflections of the economy. We have also observed that the Marxist dialectical process aims at a classless society.

In opposition to the Marxist view, the neo-Machiavellians,[16] headed by Mosca and Pareto, put forward the theory that in all societies, two classes of people exist: a class that rules and a class that is ruled. There is always a minority of influential persons to which the majority defer. Mosca was rather confused about the basis of a political class and talked about a tendency for power to be perpetuated in some distinguished families. Pareto concentrated on the psychological and personal qualities of superior people who excel and dominate in their respective fields. Pareto emphasized that in view of class circulation, the governing elite is in a state of slow but continuous transformation.

The question then is, what is the relation between social differentiation and political hierarchy in modern societies? Discussing this question with reference to France, Raymond Aron maintains that the Marxists refuse to take into account political hierarchy; and that the Paretoans ignore social differentiation.[17] Marx equated economic resources with political power. For him, the political elite remains firmly grounded in social and economic relationships. Since economic power was the basis of political power, and society was divided into two classes, the inescapable conclusion was that the class that owned the means of production and exchange controlled the government. It was inconceivable that political power should belong to a class other than the bourgeoisie which controlled the economy. Pareto's elite, on the other hand, stand outside the social structure altogether. The basis of his elite formation lies in bio-psychological factors. The struggle between groups for power or an elite position is a struggle between personality types—the lions and the foxes.

Lasswell adds another dimension to the understanding of class formation and political structure.[18] His analysis of recruitment and movement of the elite follows closely Pareto's approach, but in addition to personality traits, he adds the dimension of managerial skills required by all modern governments. The rise of the managerial class as a dominant elite of modern states is an almost universal trend. Modern industrial society everywhere has emerged as a society of organizations, increasingly controlled and directed by an expanding class of managers, bureaucrats and technocrats.

Along with these theories concerning social class and political power, the authors of *The American Voter* put forward the view 'that the group reality of social class is variable'.[19] The social class as such rarely becomes formalized as an organization. There is no formal class leadership and there is no official class policy. Furthermore, it is very difficult to decide who belongs to which class. The debate regarding the precise relationship between social differentiation and political power goes on. Economic control, personal qualities, managerial skills and leadership acumen are significant parameters, but it is an empirical question as to which one determines what, and to what extent. There is no doubt that economic interests are important but it is problematic that these interests are polarized into two clearcut, homogeneous and monolithic classes; that these interests are necessarily and irreconcilably antagonistic, and that public ownership of means of production will eliminate class conflicts. The diversity of economic interests and the variation of social prestige make the determination of social classes and their relative influence, an issue of continuous articulation and adjustment.

In modern societies, a significant fact with a bearing on this problem is that of organization. Social groups are often divided into organized and unorganized sectors. The organized sector wields influence; the unorganized are powerless. The organized trade unions can command great leverage and hold industry, and even society, to ransom until their demands are met. The complexity of modern society and the interdependence of all its parts means that those engaged in essential services can succeed in paralyzing the entire economy. Organization has therefore helped to bring to the members of an association the means of collective strength to protect and promote their interests. The transformation of an entrepreneurial society into a managerial one, and the formation of professional and trade associations, have made both Marxist analysis and classical liberalism rather obsolete.

The transformation of a bourgeois society based on free enterprise into what Robert Presthus[20] calls an organizational society, is a trend evident not only in the United States or Western Europe alone but also in all developing as well as modern industrial societies. Technological, economic and administrative needs account for this slow but pervasive trend towards the emergence of an organized, bureaucratic society in modern times. There is no doubt that organizations are the new centres of power, be they government, business or labour unions. They demand more management skills and there is an increasing displacement of the entrepreneur or even the professional by the manager and the administrator in many walks of life. The managerial class represents the new class, combining both managerial and political skills. The polarization between the bourgeoisie and the proletariat that Marx emphasized has thus been yielding place to the new gulf between the organized and the unorganized sectors, between the managers and the masses.

Caste

Caste is a distinctive category in the Indian social system. Though it had its beginnings in the Hindu philosophy of four *varnas* corresponding to four functional divisions, it has resulted in the perpetuation of several caste groups by birth among the Hindus, leaving about one third of them outcastes (called harijans by Mahatma Gandhi). By impact or otherwise, caste also extends to other religious communities in India, such as the Muslims and the Christians.[21]

In terms of a social group, caste is an occupationally specialized group which is close-knit on account of the fact that social custom sanctions marriage within the same caste.[22] The caste system is characterized by the fact of ascriptive inequality among the component groups in matters of social status and privileges, dominance and subordination. Traditionally it is the hierarchical arrangement of castes according to different degrees of dominance and privilege, which makes Indian society a highly stratified one.

Caste is a 'community' as it is based on kinship and primordial affinity, whereas class is an occupational and economic category and hence limited in social interaction.[23] A caste contains classes within itself and tends to neutralize the phenomenon of class conflict. The poor in one caste entertain a feeling of proximity to, or identity with, the rich in the same caste rather than the poor in another. But instances of an opposite nature may also be found. Hence both 'classes' and 'castes' are social realities of Indian culture and society.

A pertinent question to examine is the impact of the modernization and democratization processes on caste. The answers to this question are as varied as they were when Marx and Weber debated them in their writings. Marx believed that the growth of industrialization would lead to the dissolution of the caste system, and its gradual replacement by a class system.[24] Weber argued that the caste system was inimical to the emergence of 'capitalism', and would always stand in the way of the growth of legal-rational norms inherent in the development of a modern polity.[25] A glance at the literature produced in India on this topic will show that the social scientists in India are still fighting the battle of Marx and Weber. Whereas M.N. Srinivas insists that caste structures persist and even expand under the impact of adult franchise and political parties, Andre Beteille holds that social stratification is undergoing a transformation under the influence of modern secular and political institutions, and is being replaced.

It cannot be claimed that Indian caste society is a static social order. In reality, the people of India have kept adjusting their social systems, and at times have made fundamental changes in them. It is also noted that lower groups tend to move up and occasionally even gain so much strength as to challenge their superiors. The caste system has introduced even systemic changes. Whereas the Vedas reflect a system of relatively open classes, the trend towards a comprehensive caste structure began after about 600 B.C. In the next phase, a number of features of 'classic' caste society developed, to be followed by the modern caste system around the tenth or eleventh century. The fact is that the difference between the Indian caste and the western class is a function of time span. Changes have taken place in the caste system, though these have necessarily taken a longer time to be felt. Western society also has a stratification that shows persistence of classes. The aristocracy or the upper classes continue to enjoy their privileges and a higher social status. Thus it is not possible to say either that the Indian caste system is an entirely closed society, nor is it possible to say that the western class system is an entirely open one. It is more important to appreciate the fact that caste has assumed new functions and roles under new circumstances and under the impact of modern forces and demands.

Representative Politics Strengthens Caste: In the process of arguing that representative politics has strengthened rather than weakened castes, some important concepts have come to be developed which deserve our attention. One such concept is 'Sanskritization', which denotes that a status group aspiring to upward mobility in the system of social stratification, tends to emulate the lifestyle of higher castes, and seeks its acceptance within the great tradition of Sanskritic norms and the *varna* system.[26] This tendency among the backward castes, says Srinivas, is responsible for the continuity of the traditional structure of caste. Another concept that Srinivas uses is that of 'dominant caste'. He calls a caste dominant if it preponderates numerically over other castes, and also when it wields preponderant economic and political power.[27] Adult franchise has made the numerical strength of a caste an important criterion of dominance. The expansion of economic opportunities and the introduction of the Panchayati Raj make it possible for lower status groups to move towards dominance. But Srinivas makes an important point when he says that even a large and powerful caste group can be 'dominant' only if its position in the local caste hierarchy is not too low. The 'intermediate castes' such as the Jats in Uttar Pradesh, Punjab and Haryana, and the Kurmies, Koeries and Yadavas in Bihar (who once formed a Triveni Sangh), aspire for a dominant position not only in the villages, but also in recruitment to various elective and bureaucratic posts. These intermediate castes, in the process of their upward mobility, have emerged as rivals of the upper castes.

The scheduled castes, untouchables or Harijans still find it difficult to become a 'dominant caste'. Some outcastes in Bihar, such as Dusadhs and Domes, endowed with physical strength and traditionally in the service of landlords as musclemen, often clash with members of intermediate and upper castes. The reservation of jobs for 'backward classes' (in Bihar and Uttar Pradesh, practically identified with backward castes) is likely to aid and formalize the entry, particularly of the intermediate castes, to the services, thus facilitating their upward mobility. But we may join Srinivas in expressing the doubt that these shifts in the dominant status of caste groups may not entirely disrupt the traditional structure of social stratification. It is true that the caste system has been strengthened rather than weakened by the introduction of adult franchise and representative politics in India. There may be changes in the dominant status of particular castes, and dominance may change hands because of mobility of castes, but the caste system as such has not been disrupted. M. N. Srinivas has cogently argued that such shifts have occurred throughout the history of the caste system in India without disrupting the traditional structure.

Representative Politics Transforms and Replaces Caste : There is another point of view which holds that social stratification is undergoing a change as other elements of status such as power and class are coming to the fore. Under the influence of modernization, secularization and democratization, caste is being replaced by social circles, social networks, political factions or factional alignments, pressure groups and even socio-economic classes. Andre Beteille argues that with the changes in the criteria of status in Indian society, there has occurred 'transformation from closed status groups based on caste to more open ones which accommodate other components as well'.[28]

An important factor in this transformation is the change in the pattern of ownership of land, an important source of rural power. The class of ex-landlords is shifting to urban areas and the rural scene is subject to domination by an emerging class of landowners. Instances may be cited of Jats in Haryana and western Uttar Pradesh, Kammas and Reddis in Andhra Pradesh, Marathas in Maharashtra and Yadavas in Bihar. Changes in the pattern of land ownership and occupations lead to changes in the rigid hierarchy of the traditional caste system.

Education tends to diversify the social base of the intellectual and professional elite, and education is no longer the monopoly of any one caste. It is true that those castes which received English education first, such as the Kayasthas in UP and Bihar, still tend to dominate the bureaucracy both at the higher and lower levels. But there is growing competition, not only among the upper castes, but also in the form of increasing challenge from intermediate castes. The Harijans are still far less educated numerically but the educated among them can enter services with the help of job reservation. Legally, occupations and professions are open to all, and there is a growing tendency among various castes to utilize these new opportunities.

It is argued that the phenomenon of 'white collar townsmen' or urban middle classes cannot be explained in the 'caste frame of reference'. It may, however, be noted that 'an urban middle class' emancipated from caste hierarchy is still a newspaper myth except perhaps in a few metropolitan cities. In towns, universities, the professions and the bureaucracy, caste groups continue to survive and operate.

Social reforms have led to the emergence of new social sets or circles such as the Brahmos in Bengal who cannot be described as either a caste or a class. But a very important factor of change is political power itself. If political power comes into the hands of a particular caste at a particular place, that caste tends to improve its status. Politics tends to divide castes rather than unite them at all times. Political parties, in their bid to secure support of different castes, promote dissent among them and enter into alliances across castes. It has been argued that these processes of generation and distribution of power, tend to loosen the traditional structure.

Some village studies point out that the older system of inter-caste competition has been replaced by cooperation among castes in the villages. Conflicts in villages are not always caste conflicts. Members of the same caste may be grouped against each other in league with the members of other castes, and the issues of conflict may be control over economic resources, social domination, self assertion, or the desire for autonomy. Indeed, it is often pointed out that political factions have replaced castes in villages, and that there is no one dominant caste there.

The entire argument hinges on the point that the factors of economic and political change, such as universal education, social legislation, land reform, urbanization, industrialization, emergence of 'caste free' occupations, the penetration of impersonal bureaucratic norms; the new institutions of planning, Panchayati Raj and community development; elections based on adult franchise, a competitive party system and decentralization of political power at state, district and local levels, have transformed castes and replaced them by other status groups. Andre Beteille builds up the argument that the behaviour of castes in India is like that of a status group in any other society.

Caste Assumes New Functions and Roles: According to a third perspective, caste has assumed new functions, such as the provision of educational, welfare and employment facilities, and other economic benefits for its members. Caste associations and caste federations have been formed which contribute to the social mobility and economic well-being of its members. But it is to be emphasized that caste functions today more as a political group than as a social or economic group. Hence, the phenomenon of 'politicization of castes' must assume a special significance in any discussion of caste-politics interaction.

Foreign scholars who have studied caste have tended to grant a positive role to it. Rudolph and Rudolph, for instance, point out that caste is a medium of political mobilization, and an instrument of political education.[29] Caste is also seen as an infrastructure of a modern democratic society and it is held by some that tradition is not antithetical to the functioning of modern political institutions. India's success in managing important crises of political development, especially those of political participation and mobilization is attributed, among other things, to the ability of a traditional society to contain the disruptive effects of rapid political mobilization. On the other hand, there are volumes of literature referring to the baneful effects of caste and its harmful influence on politics and administration; and such descriptions generally end with a plea not only for reforming the system of caste but eradicating it altogether. Both these positions are extreme, though both are partially true.

We must concentrate on assessing the role of caste at various levels of politics, to develop a proper perspective of caste-politics interaction. The caste orientation of local politics has been the aspect most often emphasized. Panchayats and cooperatives are said to have come under the increasing control of dominant caste groups and their leaders. Political factions are also said to be based on caste. A number of case studies describe how competition for political power in elections and political parties has brought about basic changes in leadership processes and power structures of local communities.[30] Iqbal Narain refers to the emergence of a new leadership in the Panchayati Raj which represents interests other than economic ones.[31] Others have referred to the increasing political autonomy of local leaders, and the growth of political factions which operate more as interest groups than as caste groups. Basing their observations on the data indicating changes in the social composition of caste leaders from election to election, it is emphasized that the political skills of a leader are more important than his caste.

Politics in Indian states has also been viewed in terms of competition among major caste groups for political power. Iqbal Narain, for instance, stresses the interaction between political parties and social groups.[32] It may be said that as chief contenders for power, caste groups work through political parties. However, it has also been argued that the necessity of a heterogeneous support base for a political party undermines the exclusive importance of caste as a factor in state politics.[33]

Caste is also said to fractionalize national politics. The preponderance of a certain caste (of Brahmins) in the central cabinet has been cited as an instance to prove the impact of caste.[34] A scholar has argued at length that politics has bred caste parties.[35] For example, he points out that the Congress in the Travancore-Cochin region of Kerala is predominantly Catholic, and in the Malabar area, it is a party of the locally influential Nairs. At the close of the thirties, it was pro-Brahmin in Madras and now it is anti-Brahmin. It tends increasingly to be a Marathan party in Maharashtra and a Reddi party in Andhra, and so on. Similarly, the PSP (Praja Socialist Party) or SP (Socialist Party) sought its strength mostly from the Nairs in Kerala and the Brahmins in Maharashtra; and in UP, it was favoured more by the non-Brahmins. The CPI has been as much caste-ridden as the Congress and the SP. It is a party of the Nairs in Kerala, the Kammas and their supporters in Andhra and the Sikh leftists in the Punjab, whereas its top leadership is substantially Brahmin. In Bengal, like other parties, it is a Brahmin-Vaidya-Kayastha alliance. However, we may point out that though political parties do want to maintain their bases among caste-clientele, it is not appropriate to call any of these 'caste-parties'. It is also a sweeping generalization to say that 'behind every defection, every faction, every splinter group and every new formation of party is invariably a caste or a combination of castes'.[36] Caste operates more as a faction than as the determinant of party formation.

One area in which the role of caste has been most emphasized is that of voting behaviour. Rajni Kothari and Ghanshyam Shah, in their study of Modasa constituency in the 1962 general election, pointed out that caste loyalties proved more important than party affiliation both to voters and to political activists.[37] V.M. Sirsikar confirmed the influence of caste in Poona, though he also referred to the impact of other 'irrational factors'.[38] Sirsikar found the same trend again in his studies of the 1967 elections.[39] Many other studies show how caste sentiments and loyalties are used during elections. It has been shown, for instance, that castes play significant roles in committing and extending support to political parties or candidates during elections. This is said to have resulted in the creation of the institution of 'caste-leaders' at various levels of society. We may point out that there exist 'official' caste-leaders as well as 'unofficial' ones—both being distinguished by their recognition among the members of their caste. It is possible to identify the leader of a particular caste who is recognized by the men of his caste as their leader and who will, as a consequence, muster greater electoral support than the rival but unofficial leaders of the same caste. Through political brokers or subleaders, the message from the caste-leader at the state level percolates down to the lower echelons of caste groups and at times this results in overnight electoral swings cutting across party lines.

Politicians find caste a handy and convenient instrument for use during elections. It is convenient because it has permanent membership which can be mobilized with little canvassing. It also means less expense in terms of time and money, while yielding rich dividends in terms of consequences. This fact is responsible for the recruitment of candidates of dominant castes in particular constituencies by political parties during elections. There are 32 constituencies in Bihar which have returned candidates of a particular caste to the legislature in each election since independence. No matter to which party the candidate has belonged, caste has been the permanent variable dictating selection of candidates and electoral consequences. On the basis of these facts, it is argued that inter-party competition in fact reflects caste-based cleavages, rather than differences in the political identification and party loyalties of the electorate.

A good number of voting studies on the other hand emphasize the role of non-caste factors in determining voting behaviour. Rajni Kothari and Tarun Sheth in their studies of Baroda East in the 1962 general elections, found that elite groups were riven by leadership and factional conflicts, and that few communities voted as a block.[40] The defeat of the Congress in all the three by-elections in 1963 is also attributed to the state of Congress organization in those areas and the consolidation of the opposition forces.[41] Rajni Kothari stresses the sequential relationship between electoral behaviour, party system and political development.[42] Many other studies have shown how caste loyalties and caste identities are often undermined by political factors such as the party loyalties of the electorate, ideological appeals of political parties, and issue orientation of voters. Instances of split voting in the same castes and factional alignments between and across castes are cited in support of the argument.[43] Thus empirical studies show that while at some places and in some elections, caste plays an important role in influencing voting behaviour, at other places and at other times, it has not been so important an element.

Our discussion on the interaction between caste and politics shows that under the impact of democratization and modernization, caste as a traditional social structure has changed its functions and roles, maintaining itself in the process. It would be wrong however, to interpret the political process solely in terms of caste interests and struggles.[44] Caste has been influencing and changing politics while politics has also been influencing and changing the caste system and its stratification of society. We may conclude with D.L. Sheth, that

> By drawing castes into its competitive structure politics finds its bases in society, and by subjecting itself to the rules of competitive politics, caste acquires political characteristics. The controversy whether caste serves functions of politics or politics serves functions of caste is, therefore, misplaced. Indeed, the interaction between caste and politics should be conceived as a two-way process of politicization of castes and institutionalization of politics.[45]

It has to be stressed however, that even though caste politics has helped the process of political mobilization, participation and even development, it has aggravated caste antagonism and social tensions. Also, fierce caste competition has favoured the already rich entrenched groups and handicapped the weaker caste groups, especially those indigent as well as unorganized, or dependent on the support and patronage of dominant castes. It is common knowledge that development programmes have helped the haves and rural kulaks more than they have poor peasants or landless farmers. Thus the imbalance and inequality aggravated by development activities and the competition of castes favouring the strong among them, have led to the neglect of the public interest of 'equal development of all' and especially for the economically backward and the depressed. This is however, a matter of incomplete and imbalanced political mobilization; and an unfinished task, as yet to be performed by political parties, intellectuals, leaders, public interest groups and parliamentary institutions.

4. The Elite Theory of Political Power

There are three distinct perspectives on the distribution of power in society. The first is the notion of classical democracy that postulates the rule of the majority. Freudian psychology and the exposure of human infirmities and irrationality in public as well as private affairs, and the increasing complexity of the business of government, have combined to destroy the myth that democracy is based on the will of the majority or on the will of the people. The second view is that even a democracy depends on leadership, and the conception of democracy therefore must come to terms with the realities of unequal distribution of resources and skills of leadership and power in society. Among those who have attempted to reconcile the value of democracy with the fact of power, Schumpeter stands out as a prominent thinker. According to him, it is not the people but the few who rule with the consent of the majority.[1]

The third view is elitist and proclaims that it is not only a fact but also a desirable phenomenon that a dominant minority rules regardless of the forms of government. This is the view of Wilfredo Pareto, Gaetano Mosca and Robert Michels — the Italian neo-Machiavellians who were opposed to both democracy and socialism. They were sceptical about democracy because it is the few who possess the necessary power and skill to rule; and as they are specially endowed to rule, it is as well that they should rule. Their hostility to Marxian socialism was based on the argument that since it is the few who have always ruled, it is that few who will continue to rule even in a socialist society.

These neo-Machiavellians, anti-democratic and anti-socialist as they were, did not reject liberalism. Indeed, they were individualists, and Mosca even defended social and constitutional pluralism. In the heated controversy about the place of the elite in a democracy, elitism versus pluralism has become a prominent debating theme of political theory and political sociology. This theme has dominated Western thought, particularly since the turn of the last century, even though pluralism, in recent times, is making a bid to suggest revisions in the elitist doctrine. Political scientists and sociologists interested in the distribution of power, influence, and decision making authority in society, have made significant beginnings in both directions.

The core of the elitist thesis is that in any society, there is, and must be, a minority of the population which makes the major decisions in the society and rules over the majority. This minority, the 'political class' or the 'governing elite', includes the wider circle of those who influence governmental decisions as well as those who formally 'decide' policies. The minority gains its dominant position by means beyond ordinary elections. Its influence may be due to its embodying certain social or religious values, heredity or certain personal qualities. James Miesel has pointed out that elitism thrives because of its three characteristics: group cohesion, consciousness and conspiracy.[2] Elite rule can exist only when an elite is united, and when it self-consciously and covertly seeks to maintain its power and privileges in society. An important reason for all this, of course, is that power by its very nature is cumulative. Power gives access to more power as it becomes a means to obtain other social goods—economic influence, social status, wealth, educational advantages for children, and so on. The latter two are in themselves powers and tend to maintain the elite's domination in subsequent generations. The elitists have described in various ways the qualities and social opportunities a group needs to possess in order to gain an elite position.

While Mosca and Michels emphasize organizational abilities, Pareto examines the psychological make-up of both elite and non elite. Whereas Burnham concentrates on control of economic resources, Mills explores the positions they hold in a number of key institutions within society. The elitist doctrine further believes that the dominant minority cannot be controlled by the majority regardless of the democratic mechanism used. Both Pareto and Mosca describe the phenomenon of the circulation of elites. There is circulation among different categories of the governing elite itself and there is circulation between the elite and the rest of the population. Thus the elite is not necessarily made up of a group of permanent members or members of the one and the same class that rules; rather, the membership of the group changes over a period of time. This is the humane climax of the elitist doctrine like Marx's classless society. We may comment, however, that the fact of personal and social circulation, and the competition among elite groups, may be significant enough to preclude the elitist monopoly of leadership and power.

Pareto uses the word 'elite' in its etymological sense, referring to the strongest, the most energetic and the most capable for good as well as evil.[3] For him, elite is a value free term inclusive of all those who score high on scales measuring any social value or commodity, such as power, wealth or knowledge. Though he is for the most part dealing with the economic and political elite, he is ready to extend the use of the term to religion (the most holy), to art (the most artistic), and even to ethics (the most virtuous)—in short to all those who constitute the higher stratum in society. The higher stratum, according to him, comprises two classes: a governing elite, consisting of individuals who directly or indirectly play a considerable role in government; and a non-governing elite, including the rest. Pareto is convinced that the study of historical change revolves to a great extent round the study of the elite, and that events and decisions among the elite have more consequences for the history of a society than those which occur among its masses.

In the opening chapter of *The Rise and Fall of Elites*, Pareto enunciates several propositions, of which the first two deserve special mention. He says: 'The greater part of human actions have their origin not in logical reasoning but in sentiment.' Further: 'Man, although impelled to act by non-logical motives, likes to tie his actions logically to certain principles; he therefore invents these *a posteriori* in order to justify his actions'. On this psychological basis, he says that human actions are the combination of 'residues' and 'derivations', the former being the major motivations and the latter the external elaboration of human actions. Pareto locates six residues: combination or a tendency to invent and embark on adventures; persistence or preservation; expressiveness or a tendency to make feelings manifest through symbolization; sociability; integrity; and sex.[4] In his analysis of elites, Pareto makes use primarily of the first two residues which he calls the 'instinct for combination' or innovation, and the 'persistence of aggregates' or consolidation. Persons possessing those aptitudes are correspondingly called 'innovators' and 'consolidators'. Thus Schumpeter's 'entrepreneurs' and Weber's 'modern capitalists' are innovators in Pareto's phraseology.

Derivations are the ways in which actions assume the appearance of logical actions. They are for the most part expressed through speeches. Derivations are classified by Pareto in four categories—assertion, appeals to authority, appeals to sentiments or principles and verbal proof.[5] Pareto used this categorization in a content analysis of ideologies. But it does not play a significant part in his analysis of elites. The more important discussion centers around the residues. For example, he considers the dominant residues in an elite:[6]

Dominant Residue	Economic Elite	Political Elite
Combination	Speculator(S)	Fox
Preservation	Rentier(R)	Lion

The focal point of the whole discussion is that by means of the two residues, that is combination (foxlike quality of cunning) and preservation (lionlike persistence or use of force), the elite keeps itself in power. But in order to rationalize or justify its actions (or in order to use power), it takes recourse to derivations or myths which help it to dupe the masses.

Pareto's concept of the circulation of elites implies more than the idea that new men of money or power replace old ones. It means that the dominant residue in the elite changes: consolidators become innovators in the course of time, and conservatism gives way to radicalism. The circulation of elites by this means is irregular but incessant. Pareto expresses this idea in a phrase that both resembles and modifies Marx's dictum of history:

'The history of man is the history of the continuous replacement of elites: as one ascends, another declines.'[7] In *Les System Socialistes*, Pareto lists war and differential fertility among the causes of this historical change.[8] War tends to kill a higher proportion of the elite than of the general population. Elite families also tend to die out, since they have fewer children than the masses. But a more serious cause is discussed in Chapters 12 and 13 of *A Treatise on General Sociology*. Both the residues of combination and preservation are called for in the elite. When the elite consists of innovators only, or consolidators only, it is not able to meet effectively the normal exigencies of life. Elites must embark sometimes on innovative actions, and sometimes on consolidating actions. When they fail to do so, they are replaced. However, an imbalance between innovation and consolidation can be avoided by open recruitment into the elite.

It is noteworthy that usually an elite predominantly composed of consolidators admit intelligent innovators in its stratum. Failure to pursue this policy leads to difficulties, even to revolutions. In the words of Pareto:

> Revolutions come about through accumulations in the higher strata of society—either because of a slowing down in class-circulation, or from other causes of decadent elements no longer possessing the residues suitable for keeping them in power, and shrinking from the use of force; while meantime in the lower strata of society elements of superior quality are coming to the fore, possessing residues suitable for exercising the functions of government and willing enough to use force.[9]

The circulation of elites is aided and accompanied by rising religious-humanitarian sentiments. In such a climate, the existing elite becomes softer, milder, more humane and less apt to defend its own power.[10] If the innovators already dominate at such a stage, it spells doom for the elites. But the rising elite is also subject to speech habits justifying its drive to power (derivations), and these are also moulded by the same rising religious-humanitarian sentiments.[11] But after victory, the elite becomes more rigid and more exclusive.[12] The new elite is now established and the process can start all over again.

Mosca, the other celebrated writer on the elite, uses the term 'elite' in the sense of a political or ruling class. In a famous passage, he writes:

> In all societies—two classes of people appear—a class that rules and a class that is ruled. The first class, always the less numerous, performs all political functions, monopolizes power and enjoys the advantages that power brings, whereas the second, the more numerous class, is directed and controlled by the first, in a manner

> that is now more or less legal, now more or less arbitrary and violent, and supplies the first, in apperance at least, with material means of subsistence and with the instrumentalities that are essential to the vitality of the political organism.[13]

Mosca emphatically says that in all countries 'the management of public affairs is in the hands of a minority of influential persons, to whom, willingly or unwillingly, the majority defer.[14] He refers to two political facts.[15] In every political organism, there is one individual who is the chief among the leaders of the ruling class. Under special circumstances, two or three may discharge the functions of supreme control. Nevertheless, they may not always be the persons who hold power according to law. Secondly, in every political organism, pressures arising from the discontent of the masses who are governed, exert a certain amount of influence on the policies of the ruling or the political class.

Mosca proceeds to account for these political facts.[16] He says that in reality, it is always the few who rule. The minority is cohesive and organized (also because it is a minority), and its domination over the unorganized majority is therefore inevitable. The larger the political community, the more difficult it is for the majority to organize itself for reaction against the minority. Also, the ruling minorities are distinguished from the masses by certain personal and social qualities. Either they have themselves some material, intellectual or even moral superiority, or they are the heirs of individuals who possessed such qualities. Consequently they are esteemed and influential in their society. In primitive societies, military valour, and in advanced societies wealth, opens access to the political class.[17] Wealth produces political power just as political power has been producing wealth. 'To be rich is to become powerful.' Other agencies for exerting social influence—personal publicity, a good education, specialized training, a high rank in religious orders, public administration and the army—are more readily accessible to the rich than to the poor.

Mosca makes some interesting observations on the point of heredity. He says that all political classes tend to become hereditary in fact if not in law.[18] Political forces seem to possess a quality that is known in physics as the force of inertia. They have a tendency to stabilize themselves. Certain families develop the qualities for holding important offices and continue to be dominating for a long time. Even in democratic elections, successful candidates show certain hereditary characteristics. This is why we frequently see in the English, French and Italian Parliaments the sons, grandsons, brothers, nephews and sons-in-law of members and deputies, ex-members and ex-deputies. A hereditary caste, after gaining a dominating *de facto* status, turns itself into a *de jure* power holder. In this connection, Mosca refers to the hereditary castes in India too.

Like Pareto, Mosca says that the governing class justifies its actual exercise of power by resting it on some universal moral principle. He also talks of the 'circulation of elites' and forcefully makes the point that the whole history of civilized mankind comes down to a conflict between the tendency of dominant elements to monopolize political power and transmit it by inheritance, and the tendency toward a dislocation of old forces and an emergence of new forces; and 'this conflict produces an unending ferment of endosmosis and exosmosis between the upper classes and certain portions of the lower'.[19] Mosca says that as soon as there is a shift in the balance of political forces, when a need is felt for new capacities different from the old in the management of the state, the old capacities lose their importance and the constitution of the elite undergoes a change.[20] If a new source of wealth develops, knowledge grows, an old religion declines or a new one is born; a new current of ideas spreads, the ruling class faces serious chances of dislocation. Commerce with foreign peoples, forced emigrations, discoveries and war are the causes which create new poverty and new wealth, disseminate knowledge and bring in new moral, intellectual and religious currents. The political class undergoes changes in its membership, ordinarily by the recruitment of new individual members from the lower strata of society, sometimes by the incorporation of new social groups, and occasionally by the complete replacement of the established elite by a 'counter elite'.

Mosca however takes a modest view of the use of force and prefers change through persuasion. He advises the governing elite to bring about gradual alterations in the political system in order to make it conform to changes in public opinion. Mosca is in favour of multiplicity of social forces. He also introduces the concept of the 'sub-elite', consisting of civil servants, managers of industries, scientists and scholars, and treats this force as a vital element of society.

Robert Michels reveals another dimension of the elite phenomenon. He proposes a law governing all social organizations and calls it 'the iron law of oligarchy'.[21] He does not merely say, like Mosca, that organizational ability grants power, but stresses that the very structure of an organized society gives rise to an elite. In Michels' formulation, 'who says organization, says oligarchy'.[22] He proceeds to test the hypothesis by examining the organizations which would be expected to offer an outstanding counter example to the law. He analyzes the structure of decision making in the socialist parties of Europe, and in particular, the German Socialist Party in the years before the war. He found that these political parties, though committed to democracy and socialism, allowed power and privilege to a small group of leaders who controlled the party organization. Two sets of factors, namely the organizational and the psychological, are responsible for the phenomenon of concentration of power in the hands of a ruling minority.

Michels insists that mass members cannot control the large-scale organizations of the modern age. Leadership is 'technically indispensable'.[23]

> At the outset leaders arise *spontaneously*; their functions are *accessory* and *gratuitous*. Soon, however, they become *professional* leaders, and in this second stage of development they are *stable and irremovable*.[24]

A political party campaigning to gain power needs to organize its vote, canvass supporters, supply information for speakers, raise contributions, attend to the party's financial structure and its legal standing. It needs to establish a coordinated policy line for the sake of consistency and solidarity. All these activities require expertise which the mass of members may not have the aptitude to develop and for which they certainly lack the leisure. Mass control conflicts with efficiency and is, therefore, replaced by professional direction both in policy making and technical administration.

The leadership controls the party funds and the channels of communication. It selects parliamentary candidates and dispenses other kinds of patronage. Its activities are news, publicized even by the opposition press. The leadership works to gain the support of non-party members or those who are on the 'margin' of the party to ensure electoral success. To gain their allegiance, the party moderates its dogma and provides continuity of leadership to give an assurance of stability. These factors strengthen the hands of two groups—party bureaucrats (more interested in power than in principle) and the party's parliamentary representatives (who owe their electoral success to their electoral appeal). Even the attempts to maintain a proletarian leadership for the proletarian parties and to prevent the estrangement between leader and led is foredoomed to failure. Instead, a 'proletarian elite' emerges which ceases to be proletarian in anything but origin, as it exchanges manual for desk work and wages for salary.[25] The leaders are 'bourgeoisiefied', transformed into strangers to their class, and the party hierarchy becomes an established career, offering a rise in social status as well as income.

In his analysis of psychological causes, Michels says that the majority is apathetic towards public matters. Interest and influence in the party are represented by a pyramid—voluntary party officials, a large stratum of enrolled and active members, and down below, a large number of non-members who merely vote for the party.[26] The majority is only too glad to have others take on political responsibilities. Even revolutionary agitation has to be undertaken by a small minority on behalf of the majority. Such apathy, submissiveness, and deference on the part of the masses, provide ideal conditions for the few with the interest and the organizational ability to lead.

Burnham agrees with Marx that control of production gives rise to political power, social prestige as well as wealth, and also that capitalism is in decline.[27] But his explanation for the cause of its decline as well as his perception of the future set up are different. The capitalists were originally both managers and owners of their own enterprises which grew into large and complex organizations, which had to be left to professional managers. The bourgeoisie is thus gradually displaced by the technically indispensable managerial elite. Making similar projections about trends in government and public administration, Burnham predicts that government will increasingly be a matter of executive action rather than legislation, and will be run by the bureaucrats. Even before Burnham, Veblen had drawn the picture of the capitalists being replaced by the 'engineers' or the technical specialists.[28]

Djilas describes how after the Bolshevik Revolution in Russia, a new class, previously unknown to history, has been formed.[29] This new class, according to him, consists of the leaders of the party, who control the party organization and enjoy complete power and special privileges. The party leaders make up the elite, and use the party as an instrument of their own power and privilege. Djilas holds that the communist party creates this new class, but that this class grows and uses the party as a basis. 'The class grows stronger, while the party grows weaker; this is the inescapable fate of every Communist Party in power.'[30]

The new class Djilas speaks of springs from the proletariat but emerges as the newly formed elite. The new class obtains its power, privileges, ideology and its customs from one specific form of ownership—collective ownership—which the class administers and distributes in the name of nation and society.[31] Thus its chief weapons are industrialization and development of production. All changes initiated by the communist chiefs are dictated primarily by the interests and aspirations of the new class, which like every social group lives and reacts, defends itself and advances, with the aim of increasing its power. Having achieved industrialization, the new class can do nothing more than strengthen its political as well as administrative hegemony. Djilas bitterly predicts that 'when the new class leaves the historical scene—and this must happen—there will be less sorrow over its passing than there was for any other class before it'.[32]

Wright Mills makes an elitist analysis of American society and its power structure. He sees power in society as attached to institutions, and defines the power elite 'as those who occupy the command posts'.[33] He distinguishes three major elites in America—the corporation heads, the political leaders and the military chiefs. Mills refutes the comment that the elites in a functioning democracy are neither close-knit nor united. He insists that elites, even in a democracy, are a cohesive group, united by the ties of homogeneity and the identity of their social origins. Mills notes the close personal and family relationship and the frequency of interchange of personnel among the three spheres in the United States. He describes American society as a mass society in which the power elite decides all important issues and keeps the masses quiet by flattery, deception and entertainment. He refers to the corruption of the power elite which flourishes in the absence of an organized public to which the power elite would be responsible for its decisions.

Harold Lasswell is another distinguished writer on the subject of the elite phenomenon. For him, 'the study of politics is the study of influence and the influential'; and 'the influential are those who get the most of what there is to get'.[34] What people want to get is described by Lasswell as 'values', and he lists the basic values of deference, income and safety. Those who get the most of these values are elites; the rest are the masses. Elites differ as they command different values. For example, an elite of deference is not necessarily an elite of safety. Lasswell discusses the method by which the elites are protected or superseded. According to him, the fate of the elite is profoundly affected by the ways in which it manipulates the environment, whether by the use of violence, goods, symbols or practices.

> An elite defends and asserts itself in the name of symbols of the common destiny. Such symbols are the "ideology" of the established order and the "utopia" of counter-elites. By the use of sanctioned words and gestures, the elite elicits blood, work, taxes and applause from the masses.[35]

Lasswell finds the various forms of violence among the major means of elite attack and defence. He also refers to the personality and attitude of groups, and discusses the meaning of social change for the relative ascendancy of such formations. An elite is subject to domestic attack when it fails to bring in prosperity. The security of elites is tied up with shifts in goods and prices. Hence the elites resort to the rationing of pricing to direct the flow of goods and services. Lasswell, however, feels that the insecurities of the contemporary world, sharpened by the vicissitudes of a rapidly expanding and rapidly contracting economy, foster the conditions of perpetual crisis which favour the seizure of power by the agitator, and the retention of power by the man of ruthless violence.[36]

According to Lasswell, a revolution is a shift in the class composition of elites. The French Revolution marked the rise of the bourgeoisie; the Russian Revolution marked the rise of the lesser bourgeoisie, the skill groups. The next major revolutionary impulse may come in the name of the manual workers against the bureaucratic state fostered by socialism. Meanwhile, the scope of the elite which seized authority in Russia is being circumscribed by the same processes which restricted the scope of the elite in revolutionary France.[37]

Elite and Democracy

The idea of elitism is denied by those who uphold classical democratic or socialist ideas.[38] But Schumpeter has tried to show the compatibility of elitism and democracy. He defines democracy as 'an institutional arrangement for arriving at political decisions in which individuals acquire the power to decide by means of a competitive struggle for the people's vote'.[39] Others also point out that political democracy envisages that the choice of personnel should be 'open and subject to negotiation and bargaining,'[40] among the various elements of the population. Democracy provides an opportunity for the people to choose among competing elites. Dahl's concept of polyarchy stresses 'the continuing responsiveness of the government to the preferences of its citizens'.[41] In a recent book, Plamenatz suggests that as the 'will of the people' or 'the will of the majority' is a myth, so too is 'the will of the minority imposed on the majority'.[42]

Dahl, who advocates that citizens should be considered as political equals in a polyarchy, is painfully aware of the fact that the power resources in society are unequally distributed. Nevertheless, he points towards a general tendency or trend from cumulative concentration, to dispersal of these resources among various sections of society. He holds as untrue the assertion that an individual or group controlling one resource of power can automatically control other resources of power. But he does not deny that a small stratum of individuals is much more involved in political thought, discussion and action than the rest of the population.[43] Such leaders have direct influence on decisions in the sense that they can initiate proposals for policies, or successfully veto the proposals of others.[44] But behind these leaders, there is a corps of subleaders, followers and constituents, whose support the leader needs and maintains through a flow of rewards. It is this phenomenon that transforms elite rule into 'polyarchy'. Robert Dahl, along with Talcott Parsons and Morris Janowitz, identifies a 'bargaining model' in America in which political elite perform the mediating and adjusting role among the various institutional sectors of society. The basic issue according to them, is not the arbitrary exercise of power by a small, integrated elite, but the necessity of creating conditions under which a differentiated elite can make effective decisions.

Polsby also challenges the thesis that a socio-economic elite dominates political life or that there is a single all-purposive elite.[45] According to him, a general elite places great emphasis upon the maintenance of, and the sociability and contact with, a wide range of citizens in the community. Elites are free to commit the resources of the community when decisions are relatively routine and innocuous, but decisions of a non routine, unbureaucratized, or innovative variety require special consent by the non elites.

The foregoing discussion has tried to throw light on the fact that we can find a new conception of elitist democracy,[46] as against the classical concept of democracy. On the one hand, it is not realistic to deny the existence of the elite in all societies; on the other, it is not legitimate to consider elitism as a complete negation of democracy. Indeed, as democracy has come to be seen as a competitive, open and pluralistic polity, elitism is seen as a safeguard against the concentration of power that is a greater danger in a totalitarian society. The need for multiplicity of political forces and the importance of men of independent means and character, was rightly emphasized by Mosca. He was against socialism on this account. He wrote,

> Collectivism and Communism, like all doctrines that are based on the passions and the blind faith of the masses, tend to destroy multiplicity of political forces. They would abolish private wealth which in all mature societies has supplied many individuals with a means for acquiring independence and prestige apart from the assent and consent of the rulers of the state.[47]

Mosca further observed that the strength of socialism lies more in its negative aspects, its 'minute, pointed, merciless criticisms of our present organization of society'.[48] Other elitists try to refute Marx's theory of social elites on three points. First, the Marxist conception of a 'ruling class' is erroneous because there is, in fact, circulation of elites, and there is no stable and closed ruling class. Second, a classless society is impossible because in every society, there is and must be a minority which actually rules. Third, a class does not rule only by virtue of economic or military power, but because of the superior qualities of its members. These elitist theories are, therefore, obviously of an anti-Marxian tilt.

Elite theories are criticized on the ground that they do not fully explain the reality of the situation as it exists in different societies. Carl J. Friedrich points out that elitist doctrines are the 'offspring of a society containing feudal remnants'. G. Lukacs suggests that the elitist problem has been raised precisely in those countries where liberal traditions are weak.[49] The point of view that reinforces their argument is that the perceptions of the elitists are culture and time-bound. But whereas this may be true to some extent with regard to the classical elitists, this argument cannot be advanced against elitists who have successfully and empirically tested these theories in the contemporary scene in different societies. Empirical studies confirm elitism as an observable social phenomenon through which they seek to explain social life and political change. We may point out that elitism is relevant for the understanding of the politics of developing countries where economic, political and other changes are bringing about changes in social structure, prestige and power of different social groups and consequently, the rise and fall of elites. The new social forces are creating new elites in developing countries, and the activities of the elite are significant in the modernization process of developing societies. There exists a significant relationship between economic structure, social structure, the structure of the groups within the elite and the structure of the constitutional system.[50]

Elitism as a feature of a total society in the classical sense is not feasible in an industrial age. The question of organizational oligarchy however, assumes greater significance in an industrial society that becomes more and more bureaucratic. As a result, elitism as a phenomenon of organizational or bureaucratic oligarchy is a problem to be reckoned with. The loss of individual discretion and erosion of freedom in a society dominated by large organizations, pose threats to individual freedom and democratic rights. The safeguard against complete totalitarianism however, lies in organizational factionalism and the right to dissent on the one hand; and in the multiplicity of organizations that serve as veto groups and a check on each other's power. Internal conflict and external competition among organizations, whether business cooperatives or political parties, interest groups or bureaucracies, have their value in maintaining a democratic society by preventing the complete supremacy of a few centres of power. The elite does not exist in the classical sense of a single self-conscious, united and ruling group. Elites compete among themselves, checking each other, creating balance of power in society. This is far from the classical conception of elitism as a phenomenon of a ruling or political class. The question of who controls power has to be analyzed in this new perspective, especially as a society progresses from one stage of growth to another.

In developing countries like India, elitism has acquired different dimensions. In the rural setting, the convergence of caste, class and status as well as political power, help to sustain an elitist oligarchy of sorts. But the cities, which offer greater mobility and freedom, and increasing opportunities of migration not only to neighbouring towns or metropolitan cities but even beyond national borders, are contributing to social mobilization and political change. Notwithstanding enormous inequality, there are unmistakable signs that democratic politics and party competition are helping to accelerate social and political mobilization and restructuring.

5. The Group Theory of Politics

The concept of the group has been germane in all the social sciences, and especially in sociology.[1] However, in the form of social pluralism, the group idea also made its appearance in political theory.[2] Pluralists from Locke to G.D.H. Cole recognized the reality of groups against the classical liberal notion of a state of individuals held together by the sovereign power of the state. The group was conceived of as a mediator between individuals and the state. Thus pluralism was both a statement of political and social reality, and an ideology that sought to divide the monolithic power of the state. With the publication of Arthur F. Bentley's *The Process of Government* (1908), Earl Latham's *The Group Basis of Politics* (1952), and David B. Truman's *The Governmental Process* (1953), the group approach to politics has become one of the dominating themes in modern political science.

Briefly, the group theorists subscribe to the idea that political process can best be understood by examining the political structures called groups which play a significant role in political and governmental decision making. Particular sets of individuals seek specific policy goals suited to their social or economic interests, and engage in various kinds of activities to generate pressure which will influence decisions in their favour. Graham Wooton expresses this idea through the formulation PA=T:G, which means that private actors (other than political parties) seek to influence governmental targets to secure certain goals.[3] It is assumed that there is a close connection between socio-cultural, ethnic as well as economic interests, and political behaviour. Interests manifesting themselves through group activities create issues for political conflicts and deliberation, and one group tends to bring pressure upon other groups and the decision making apparatus, to score an advantage over its rivals. The main business of government is to effect reconciliation among a set of interest groups. Fundamentally, the study of politics, according to group theorists, means the study of groups of active men bound together by common interests; and political process is mainly the interaction between governmental institutions and pressure groups. With a characteristically sharp thrust, Bentley says,

> The great task in the study of any form of social life is the analysis of these groups. When the groups are adequately stated, everything is stated. When I say everything I mean everything.[4]

He suggests that political institutions, legislatures, courts and executive officers should be analyzed as groups and in terms of other groups. The American presidency for example includes a large number of people in and out of office and should hence be analyzed in terms of the president's involvements and interactions with various groupings.[5]

Bentley forcefully argues that the psychological explanations of politics are not satisfactory. They give 'an animistic semblance' of explaining society, but actually they block explanation.[6] Metaphysical terms such as 'civic virtue' or 'civilization' are also inadequate tools for explanation. Sometimes, an attempt at realism is made by referring to the 'boss', the 'machine' and the 'conduct of politicians', but this too cannot take us far because the boss is as formal an element as the president or the governor.[7] By referring to him, we do not describe the living society. Bentley suggests that we should 'go behind to find what are the real interests that are playing on each other' through formal agencies such as a presidency or governorship.[8]

Bentley's attempt to go beyond the formal agencies of power gave rise to his view of politics based on the equation: group=activity=interest=pressure=process. He starts with the premise that the raw material for a student of politics is not one man but many men taken together, acting with or upon each other, that is, participating in some activity. His chief interest consists of the 'actually performed' legislating-administering-adjudicating activities of the nation, and he recommends for study the streams and currents of activity that gather among the people and rush into these spheres. He depicts the situation like this: some men always try to shunt other men's conduct along changed lines; forces gather to overcome resistance to such alterations, and finally, one witnesses the dispersal of one grouping of forces by another grouping.[9]

Besides political groups Bentley attaches importance to 'underlying groups', though he appreciates the point that political groups are highly differentiated groups reflecting or representing other groups.[10] He generalizes that a corporation is nothing but the specialized activities of those constituting it.[11] If a corporation has to decide which of two kinds of plans it should pursue, it is the active groups of men which are important. For them, the plans are but symbols or tables. Further, he wants social scientists to be able to quantify and measure those activities because 'measure conquers chaos'.[12] He elucidates this by saying that the quantities are present in every bit of political life; and political process is nothing but a balancing of quantity against quantity.

Bentley emphasizes the inter-group conflict situation which he sees as the hallmark of politics. He points out that when we have a group that participates in the political process, we always have another group facing it on the same plane. It is not possible to get hold of one group interest except in relation to other group interests, and a group therefore can be understood only in terms of other groups. The size of a group or the number of its members is essential in determining the importance of a group. But even more important is its intensity. This refers to the concentration of interest by virtue of which a group is effective in its activity in the face of the opposition of other groups, and because of which it is in a position to use a variety of means to maintain the dominant position.

Bentley is against the notion of a 'social whole' or 'national interest', and he maintains that there are always some parts of the nation which are posed against other parts.[13] On testing the notion of a 'social whole', we find that it is merely the group tendency or demand represented by an individual or individuals, erected into the pretence of a universal demand of the society in question. In fact, if it were a comprehensive all-embracing interest of the society as a whole, it would have been an established condition and not a subject of discussion. The political interests and activities of any given group are directed against the activities of other men in other groups. Society consists of the complex of these various groups; and leadership and public opinion represent group activities.

The group phenomenon always involves force or what may appropriately be called pressure. It indicates the push and resistance between groups, whereas society balances these group pressures. Pressure includes all forms of group influence upon group, from battle, riot and other expressions of power, to abstract reasoning, call of conscience and sensitive morality.[14] Both the tendencies to activity, and the more visible activities, are examples of pressure.

All phenomena of government are those of groups pressing one another, forming one another, and pushing out new groups and group representatives to mediate the adjustments. It is only as we isolate these groups activities, determine other representative values, and get the whole process stated in terms of them, that we approach a satisfactory knowledge of government.[15] We have to study the interests that work through government, the laws representing the pressures having worked themselves through to a conclusion or balance. Government, finally, is to be viewed as a producer of balance, equilibrium or order among interacting groups.[16]

Group theory as it emerged from David Truman, pointed to the group as the only actor in the political process able to account for the patterns of uniformity and disparity in political behaviour and attitudes. As if to cover up the allegation that Bentley had failed to define group convincingly, his admirer and in a sense disciple, Truman, sought to concretize the group concept by clarifying its classification.

According to Truman, the term 'group' is applied in too broad a sense. It is used to describe any collection of individuals who have some characteristics in common. For example, the term 'group' may be used to denote persons of a given age level, those of similar income or social status, those living in a particular area, and assortments of individuals according to a variety of similarities such as farmers, alcoholics, insurance men, blondes, illiterates, neurotics, mothers, and so on. These are known as 'categoric groups'. But they are not basic social units for political analysis as they do not produce uniformities of behaviour. They can be called groups only when they interact with some frequency on the basis of their shared characteristics. As Truman says, 'it is the interaction that is crucial, not the shared characteristics for being designated a group' [17]

The most important groups from the standpoint of moulding the individual's personality and helping him to adjust to his surroundings are those that operate during infancy and childhood, such as the family, the neighbourhood, schools and friendship groups. They are characterized by face-to-face contact and physical proximity, and are known as primary groups. Secondary groups, such as the media of mass communication, are large formal groups in which indirect contacts are generally possible. Institutionalized groups are characterized by a relatively high degree of stability, uniformity, formality, and generality. Their accepted examples are executives, legislatures, courts and other political institutions, families, organized religious institutions, producers' establishments and so forth. Such groups show a tendency towards maintaining equilibrium, that is, they tend to stabilize themselves through the expected patterns of interaction of their participants.[18] They seek to achieve equilibrium along standardized lines so that the pattern is not altered or disrupted. It is characteristic of balanced groups that if the equilibrium is disturbed by some events outside the group, it is restored when the disturbance is over. But if the disturbance is of great intensity, and if it persists over a long period of time, a very different pattern of interaction might be established in place of the previous one.

'Interest group' refers to any group that, on the basis of one or more shared attitudes, makes certain claims or demands upon other groups in the society, for the establishment, maintenance or enhancement of forms of behaviour that are implied by the shared attitudes.[19] Truman identifies 'potential' as well as existing interest groups. 'Potential interest groups' are those which have widely held attitudes that are not expressed in interaction. Thus, like Bentley, Truman is also conscious of potential activities or 'tendencies of activity'. Only when a group makes its claims through or upon any of the institutions of government, it becomes a 'political interest group'. The term 'pressure group' suggests a method or a category of methods that may be used by an interest group to achieve its objectives. This term then denotes an advanced stage or phase of group activity. But the term 'interest group' is more inclusive and neutral than the term 'pressure group'.

The association is a type of group that grows out of 'tangent relations'.[20] There are individuals who participate in, or are common to, more than one group or subdivision. A family and school are tangent to one another through a child who interacts in both. If out of the family-school tangency, a number of mothers and teachers interact fairly regularly with one another, an association is born;

for example, the Parent-Teacher Association. An association is said to emerge when a considerable number of people have established tangent relations of the same sort and when they interact with one another regularly on that basis. It is a group, a continuing pattern of interaction, that functions as a 'bridge' between persons in two or more institutionalized groups or subdivisions. The function of an association is to stabilize the relationship of individuals in tangent groups. The association operates to relate and establish the interaction among persons in basic institutionalized groups. It influences the attitude, function and behaviour of its members. Associations operate both as interest groups and as political interest groups

A group of thinkers have held that the primary function of government is to establish and maintain a measure of order in the relationships among groups for various purposes.[21] The forms and methods of government depend upon the character of the groups and the purposes it serves. Hence groups determine the forms and methods of government, and not vice versa. Truman's theory that at any given moment in time, society consists of a number of groups which are always in a state of equilibrium is crucial. The equilibrium is maintained by internal and external checks that are inherent in the nature of the groups. Overlapping membership of groups prevents any one group from making demands that would result in serious conflicts with the other interests of its members. This equilibrium can be disrupted only as a result of some disturbing process of social change induced by factors such as increased division of labour, major changes in transportation, communications, economic organization, new technology, market fluctuations, war, depression and population shifts. But even after such disruptions, new groups are mobilized from the 'potential groups' that exist in the society at all times, leading to a restoration of the equilibrium.

Latham starts with the premise that organized groups are structures of power.[22] Like the philosophical pluralists, he holds that state and non-state associations belong to the same genus (although a different species), and the common factor between them is possession of power. Both are associations of people for the achievement of ends common to the members. Members try to achieve their goals through the application of the power of the association to the obstacles which block the goal. For Latham, the individual is the centre-piece of all group forms. Groups exist for the individuals; by his membership in them, the individual fulfils personal values and felt needs. Groups organize for the self-expression and security of the members which comprise them. Satisfaction in the fulfilment of the received purposes of the group is an important element in keeping groups intact. If these purposes are not fulfilled, the group would suffer a loss of morale, energy and dedication.

Unlike Bentley and Truman, Latham grants a positive, even superior role, to the state, which according to him represents the consensus by which the various groups exist in harmony. The state establishes the norms of permissible behaviour in group relations, and it enforces these norms. The fact that men have other group loyalties than the one they bear to the state does not in itself prescribe limits to the activity of the state. The role of the state is not limited to that of referee in group conflict. Established as the custodian of the consensus, the state helps to formulate and promote normative goals, as well as to police the rules agreed upon. In the exercise of its normative functions, it may even require the abolition of groups, or a radical revision of their internal structure. Latham also grants a role to the groups themselves in the process. He says that groups do not hold still; they are in a state of constant motion, and through this motion and its interaction, groups themselves generate the rules by which public policy is formulated and the community is governed.

If groups are allowed to struggle for survival in their environments, and to carry forward the aims and interests of their members in an entirely uninhibited manner, the ensuing struggle is likely to lead to violence and war. Social disapproval of most of the forms of direct action, however, reduces this struggle to an effort to write the rules, that is to agree upon the rules of the game by which groups live with each other, and according to which they would compete for existence and advantage. Statutes, administrative orders, decrees, rules, interpretations, and court judgements are examples of the written rules.

Returning to the topic of the relationship between groups and the state, Latham introduces the important concept of public and private government. According to him, organized groups are called systems of 'private government', whereas the organs of the state are said to represent a system of 'public government'. 'Public government' is associated with kings, presidents, governors, mayors, ministers, judges and other public office holders, and 'private government' with corporation managers, leaders of trade unions, bishops and so on. Both kinds of governments maintain bureaucracies of an almost similar nature. The phenomenon of power is present in both official and unofficial groups.

From the point of view of political sociology, it is indeed important to appreciate Latham's concept of 'officiality'. He argues that the state apparatus, through its manifold offices—legislatures, councils, agencies, departments, courts, and other fora—maintains a system of instrumentalities for the writing and enforcement of the formal rules by which the society is governed. All these instrumentalities however, are themselves groups, and they possess a strong sense of group belonging and identification. But they are 'official' in the sense that they are authorized by social understanding to exercise certain powers against all groups and individuals. This 'official' characteristic distinguishes public government from private government. The principal function of official groups is to provide various levels of compromise in the writing of the rules, all within the body of principles that form the consensus upon which the political community rests.

Each of the three principal branches of government has a special role in performing this function. The legislature referees the group struggle, ratifies the victories of the successful coalitions, and records the terms of the surrenders, compromises, and conquests in the form of statutes. Every statute tends to represent compromise because the very process of accommodating conflicts of group interest is one of deliberation and consent. The legislative vote on any issue thus tends to represent the composition of strength, that is, the balance of power among the contending groups at the moment of voting. Like the legislature, the judiciary also has a sense of identity and plays its own role in the process. Justices serve one more level of official compromise in the never-ending march and countermarch, thrust and parry, among economic groups, enforcement agencies, legislators, and executive functionaries. Finally, public policy announced by the executive is actually the equilibrium reached in the group struggle at any given moment, and it represents a balance which the contending factions of groups constantly strive to tilt in their favour.

Interest Groups in India

All sorts of institutional, associational, non-associational and anomic interest groups exist in India. Legislative blocs or lobbies and officer cliques or ideological cliques in bureaucracies, are instances of institutionalized interest groups. Among the associational interest groups, we find the existence of two specialized structures—business interest groups and labour interest groups. Most of these groups developed Truman-fashion, in response to the acceleration of social change brought about by British rule. *Kisan* associations are not structures as formally organized and specialized as business and labour structures, though *kisan* lobbies dominate politics in various states. Because of the concentration of land ownership in a few hands in the remote and widely dispersed rural areas throughout the country, over thousands of years, it has not been easy to bring about 'land reforms' by breaking the system of landlordism. A '*kisan* lobby' demanding ownership of land for the tiller, and actively helping in the enforcement of the *bataidari* and other progressive land legislations, is yet to emerge. We need therefore to focus on the two interest groups, business and labour.

The business groups are by far the best organized, with a sound financial base. The earliest association of business formed to promote business interests was the Federation of Indian Chambers of Commerce and Industry (FICCI) started in 1926 under the leadership of Purshotamdas Thakurdas and G.D. Birla. It later received the blessings of Mahatma Gandhi who was a personal friend of Birla. With its 137 member bodies (the Regional Chambers of Commerce etc.) and 286 associate members (Tata Iron and Steel, Hindustan Motors, etc.), the FICCI has a well-organized central office at Delhi. Its activities both in the pre-independence and post-independence eras have been significant. In 1957, the House of Tatas set the trend of contributing to the funds of political parties, by changing their memorandum which enabled business houses to come to terms specifically with the ruling party. But when the Swatantra Party emerged in 1959, Tatas began to contribute to the funds of both the Congress and the Swatantra. The fashion has caught on since then.

If the FICCI has in general spoken for big business and industry, the All India Manufacturers Organization (AIMO) founded in 1941 by Sir Visvesveriya and other industrialists, speaks for small scale industries. The two other less important groups are the Associated Chambers of Commerce (a foreign interest) and the All India Organization of Industrial Employers (almost a branch of FICCI). It would indeed be interesting to examine the influence these business houses exercise on the government and its policies.

India has a fairly large number of trade unions, but on the whole, they have not been able to exercise much influence. Both in terms of organization and finances, they compare very poorly with the American Federation of Labour. In the UK, trade unions have been able to influence the policy of labour governments considerably because parties allow trade union affiliation. Eighty six unions and five cooperatives are affiliated to the Labour Party. The conservative and liberal parties disallow affiliation of corporate bodies. In the UK, the labour unions promote and support candidates. Unions such as the Miners' Union, the National Union of General and Municipal Workers, the Transport and Salaried Staff Associations, set up, on an average, a hundred and thirty candidates every general election. Such a practice is unknown in India. In India, although the Congress Party has its own sponsored and supported trade union, the Indian National Trade Union Congress (INTUC), it is not as dependent for its political support on the union members as the British Labour Party is, and this accounts for the relatively insignificant influence of the union over the party. In fact, the objective in setting up the INTUC appears to have been to educate the workers, acquaint them with the Congress ideology and enlist their support for the party. This seems to be clear from the words of the resolution of the working committee of the Indian National Congress adopted in 1946, a year before the INTUC was born. The INTUC leaders however, insist that theirs is a completely independent organization. The truth is that all the labour unions are tied to their respective parties, acting more as party agents explaining the party's policies to workers and enlisting their support, than as independent interest groups seeking to influence government policy. But while the existence of unions has helped parties to develop a channel of influence downwards, it has, nevertheless, enabled a few union leaders to have access to politicians. According to Morris Jones, the top leaders of unions are not as independent of parties as the few 'local bosses' are.[23]

There are non-associational interest groups such as kinship and lineage groups, ethnic and religious groups in America as in India. In the USA the various ethnic minorities such as the Jews, the Blacks and the Italians, have their own fraternal organizations. It is estimated that there are 175 such groups in the USA.[24] The National Association for the Advancement of Coloured People and the Urban League have taken up the cause of equality among the blacks. American ethnic groups have strived for good relations between the USA and the country of their origin. The German-American Bund and the Irish Organizations prevented American entry into World War II. The various religious communities also have their groups. In India too, groups based on race, religion and language play an important part in the articulation and organization of the interests of their members. Thus religious communities, castes and sects, and regional and linguistic groups influence politics and administration.

Almost every Hindu caste operates in a sense as an interest group. C.H. Philips pertinently observes that caste is capable of functioning as an effective pressure group, and that its members cannot leave it and join another at will, places it into a position of a political power which cannot be ignored by the political parties depending for their mandate on the goodwill of their voters.[25] Several castes have associations such as the Kshatriya Samaj in Gujarat. Castes also tend to exert pressure by aligning with one group or another.

Anomic interest groups are more or less spontaneous breakthroughs into the political system from the society, in forms such as riots and demonstrations.[26] Even when organized and controlled, they have the potential to exceed limits and norms, and disturb or disrupt the political system. We must guard against considering every overt manifestation of rowdyism, riots, satyagrahas and fasts as representative reflections of the latent interests of the general population. Often it is a small group which resorts to street demonstrations and intimidation tactics of various types. Sometimes however, a movement anomic in origin may become such a force that it threatens the political system itself. The students' movement which started in Gujarat in 1974, spread to Bihar and under the leadership of Jayaprakash Narayan, engulfed the entire polity, is one such case.

We may conclude by saying that the actual ability of interest groups to influence Parliament or Government depends on the power base of individual interest groups, and on the general political culture of the country in which they operate. The power base usually consists of the organizational strength, quality of leadership and finances at the disposal of the interest group; its command over votes; its specialized knowledge; and above all, confined capacity to render benefits or services to its members. With respect to all these, interest groups in our country are very weak compared to interest groups in the developed countries. Whereas in industrialized and urbanized polities, political parties are largely directed and sustained by associational interest groups, in India, the reverse is the case. Non-political associations, interest groups and even voluntary organizations are in most cases sustained and directed by political parties in India. These groupings have largely functioned as wings of political parties which have more often than not created, staffed and dominated them. Perhaps as the size of the interest groups grows, political dictation by parties will decrease, thus changing the status of these groups from satellites of political parties to their controllers. Bargaining and self-assertion may become the new style and this may lead to political participation of a more relevant and autonomous nature. Industrialization and faster agricultural growth may lead to the creation of more pressure groups directed at the bureaucracy, administrative departments of government. These pressure groups may have an enhanced intensity, and a demanding style of functioning.

All the same, the political culture of the country is not conducive to the intense articulation of interests through associations or trade unions.[27] Collective action on the basis of secondary relationships is not the general case. As the repository of centralized governmental power, political and bureaucratic elites run the show, and pressures exerted by organized vested interests are generally held as 'dangerous' for the system. Commitment to planned economic development and the creation of a socialist pattern of society grant power to the government to control and regulate the internal affairs as well as external conduct of interest groups. Interest groups themselves play a defensive role and want to appease the government and the bureaucracy, rather than antagonize them. So far from being merely an outcome of interest group activity, as group theory would have it, public policy in India plays an important role in interest group mobilization and behaviour.

The interaction between interest groups and the political process is, in fact, far different from the early elaborations of group theory by Bentley or Truman, who because of the experiences of the United States tended to treat the political system as the dependent variable, and the groups as independent variables. The Indian political system sets the parameters for group activity, and groups can be understood only as part of the larger and more complex set of relationships. The Indian political system interacts with traditional and ascriptive groups which are based on birth or primary relationships such as kinship, castes, and religious, regional and linguistic groupings.

6. Political Parties and Political System

Political parties are the main intermediate and intermediary structures between society and government. They are central to both in the sense that they connect bridges to create a two-way communication process between them. Being the 'primary lubricants' and 'moving forces' of the govermental process, they are central also to modern political systems. In one way or the other, all forms of governments in all societies have turned to the political parties, and have maintained them as an essential institution of the political system. But precisely for this reason, there is conceptual ambiguity with regard to the meaning, functions, structural properties and classifications of parties or party systems. There have been various approaches to understanding parties, and we recapitulate the most important of these here.

Party : *Ideology and Power*: Edmund Burke, Benjamin Constant and others conceived of party as an ideological group. According to this school, the members of a party entertain a set of common basic convictions about public interest, and are ready to act in concert in pursuit of these ideals. According to Burke's definition, 'a party is a body of men for promoting by their joint endeavours the national interest, upon some particular principle in which they are all agreed'. Burke's definition represents a certain phase in the evolution of parties in the eighteenth century. Parties were regarded with some suspicion because of their long association with factions, which were considered an evil. Parties gradually acquired legitimacy as an instrument of government in the nineteenth century. Credit, therefore, goes to Burke for having distinguished parties from factions. But in the process he cast parties in an ideological mould by attributing to them a highly ideological orientation.

Most present day writers regard Burke's definition normative because of its insistence on 'principle', and unrealistic because it shuts its eyes to the power conflicts and machinations of parties. Duverger argues that often geographical proximity or the desire to defend one's profession or personal interest leads to the formation of parties; doctrine comes afterwards.[1] He cites the rise of parties in the French Constituent Assembly of 1789 as an instance. It is also argued that the 'doctrinal unity' of a party is often fictitious and accidental. Two socialist parties react in very different ways and find it difficult to collaborate. The fate of socialist and communist parties which are more ideologically based than others may be cited here.

As against the conception of party as a doctrinaire or ideological group, the more acceptable view is that the party is a power-seeking instrument. Schumpeter contradicts Burke by saying that 'a party is a group whose members propose to act in concert in the competitive struggle for political power.[2] The most distinguishing element of party is its bid to capture power or to assume governmental functions rather than its ideology. Max Weber's definition also supports this contention. According to him, a political party is 'an associative type of social relationship devoted to secure power within a co-operative group for its leaders in order to attain ideal or material advantages for its active members "which" may consist in the realization of certain objective policies or the attainment of personal advantages or both'.[3] Operationally speaking, we perceive political party as a political group that contests at elections, and is capable of placing through elections (free or nonfree), candidates for public office.[4] Indeed, it would be naive to suggest that either at the time of its inception or at the time of election, the members of a party are bound together solely by the force and rationality of an ideological stance. The desire to capture power is indeed the basic and primary motive and the animating force. It needs to be conceded, however, that political parties tend to rationalize the existing interests of groups or classes supporting them and articulate issues in ideological terms. While trying to control governmental power, they formulate issues in terms of ideological compulsions. They play the game of power in the name of an ideology.

We may therefore quote Bernard Hennessy who combines the

elements of both power and ideology in his definition of political parties. He writes:

> Political parties are social organizations that attempt to influence (1) the selection and tenure of the personnel of government by putting forward candidates for elective office; (2) the policies of government according to some general principles or proclivities upon which most of their members agree.[5]

Sociology of Political Parties

The communist view of a party as the representation of a class has inspired studies into the sociology of political parties. Behavioural enquiries have also been made concerning the relationship of the individual's standard of living, his profession and his education with his political affiliation. This school attributes the essence of the political party to the social composition of the rank-and-file membership, that is to their affiliation with identifiable social or economic classes in the population. Thus the Whig Party in England in the 17th and 18th centuries was connected with the great financial and mercantile interests, while the Tory Party stood for the landed nobility, the country squires, and the established church. In the United States, the Federalist Party was largely composed of bankers, businessmen, large capitalistic planters, and members of the professions, while the Democratic Republican Party of Jefferson represented the small farmers, inhabitants of black-country areas, city workers and skilled artisans.[6]

The tendency to treat parties as reflections of a particular class has been widespread in modern times. The approach has also been extended to tracing the influence of factors such as caste, ethnicity, nationality, race or religion, on political affiliation. This approach is based on the consideration that ideological and doctrinal beliefs are 'determined' by material factors or group affiliations. However, Avery Leiserson, among others, rightly argues that in many situations, the converse can be true. Many party leaders and personalities profess doctrinal beliefs and act in policy controversies squarely in contradiction with their class or caste situation and thus deliberately attempt to declass or decaste themselves. How do we explain such individuals' behaviour if we are to regard all behaviour as group behaviour ? Moreover, this approach neglects or minimizes the structural aspects, internal organization and external governmental relationships of the party and influences of leadership behaviour. It cannot explain deviations of party policy from the professed norms of group belief except on grounds of moral deficiency or political expediency. We must also appreciate that parties and party systems not only reflect society, but also seek to change and mould it.

Party as an Organizational Structure: Duverger said 'a party is a community with a particular structure'.[7] He also stated that 'a party is not a community but a collection of communities, a union of small groups dispersed throughout the country (branches, caucuses, local associations, etc.) and linked by coordinating institutions'.[8] In other words, he wanted to emphasize the study of the anatomy of parties. He was not the first do so.[9] In fact, earlier students of political parties were interested in the formal agencies for action within the party, its internal conflicts, and the structural relationship between the party leaders, the members, the active workers, and the bureaucracy. In 1888, James Bryce provided an extensive description of how the party machines operated in the United States.[10] However, the first major study of this kind was attempted by M.Y. Ostrogorski and published in 1902.[11] A little later, Robert Michels came out with his famous book enunciating 'the iron law of oligarchy'.[12] Some of his statements have been challenged by Neumann,[13] and more recently, by Eldersveld and others. All these studies raise and develop certain significant issues worthy of our consideration.

Parliamentary vs. Extra-Parliamentary Group: The question of who controls a political party is often raised. Ostrogorski held that the two major British parties, the Labour and the Conservative, were gradually being dominated by the extra-parliamentary section of the party. This view was challenged after fifty two years by Mackenzie, who argued that despite protestations to the contrary, both the Labour and the Conservative Parties were effectively dominated by their parliamentary wings.[14] The issue has been well-clinched by Duverger, by relating the issue to the origin of parties.

Duverger begins with the thesis that just as men bear the mark of their childhood all their lives, so parties are profoundly influenced by their origins. He refers to the two processes by which parties come into being. Some of them, like the British Conservative Party, are 'internally' created. They are born in response to the need to bring the 'new electors' to the party. The extension of popular suffrage (granted by the Reforms Act of 1832) and parliamentary prerogatives, led to the rise of parliamentary groups and electoral committees, and finally, to such parties in Britain first and subsequently in other countries. But some parties are externally created, which means that they come into being to realize revolutionary objectives.

Duverger finds important lines of distinction drawn between internally and externally created political parties. The externally created political parties are more centralized, more coherent and more disciplined than the internally created political parties. The top and the central bodies of an externally created party generates local committees and groups with limited liberty of action. On the other hand, the development of internally created parties starts at the base. Since local committees create a central body to coordinate their activities, they naturally see to it that they maintain their autonomy and grant limited powers to the central body. Because of this fact of origin, the attitudes of the two kinds of parties towards their parliamentary organizations and works differ. For the interior parties, the winning of seats in the legislature is the prime activity; while for the exterior parties, the electoral and parliamentary struggle is only one of the elements in its general activity to realize its political ends. This will be clear by looking at the functioning of communist parties which are more interested in organizing mass struggle than in fighting elections. As a result of this attitude, the parliamentary wing is less influential in externally created parties than in internally created ones. In fact, in the externally created political parties, there is a certain mistrust of the parliamentary wing and a desire to subject it to control. Duverger concludes that the leadership of the conservative and liberal parties in Britain is in the hands of parliamentary representatives; and that of the Labour Party in the hands of the party outside the parliament, that is the mass organization. However, after the Attlee-Laski controversy of 1945, the primacy of the parliamentary wing was established for the Labour Party as well.[15]

The Congress party of India and most of the parties in India are externally created, and hence the problem of adjustment between the two wings has been vexing. This problem was evident in the Congress party in the Nehru-Tandon conflict in 1951, and in the Mrs. Gandhi-Syndicate rift which led to the party's split in 1969. Even then, it can be said that for most of the years, the parliamentary wing held its sway over the mass organization. In the Janata Party also the same trend was discernible. Despite the heterogeneity and the persistent factional behaviour of its constituents, the pre-eminent position of the party leadership in the parliament had been asserted. But in the

CPI, the mass organization appears to have sway over the parliamentary wing. Thus both origin and continuing activities of the party decide which wing will dominate the other. But apparently the dominance of the parliamentary wing is more pronounced in the case of parties in power.

Direct vs. Indirect Structure: Duverger argues that some parties have direct structure, whereas others have indirect sturcture. The French socialist party, he says, has direct structure because its members sign a membership form, pay a monthly subscription and attend local branch meetings more or less regularly.[16] As an example of a party which has indirect structure, he cites the instance of the British Labour Party of 1900. In 1900, there were no party members in the Labour Party; persons who were members of trade uinons were supposed to be the members of the party. An indirect party supposes that there is no party community really distinct from the component social groups. However, Duverger admits that generally, we have direct parties; indirect parties are exceptional. If they are formed, it is usually in the initial period of struggle to get into parliament.

Cadre vs. Mass Parties: Duverger offered two contrasting models of party organization. One he calls the cadre party, the other the mass party.[17] He considers American political parties, cadre parties, and the European socialist parties mass parties. In the cadre party, voters have no formal ties with the organization, nor are they heavily involved in the internal decision making processes of the party. Control of the machinery of the party rests largely in the hands of an elite—influential persons of high repute, experts and financiers. It is also this cadre's performance which defines what the party stands for. The pre-eminent function of the cadre party is electoral. The mass party, on the other hand, is designed to involve the rank-and-file members in the decision making processes of the party. Typically, the organizational structure of the party is both articulated and detailed. The details of intra-party relationships are often specified in a party constitution and bye laws. Members do feel closely identified with the party of their choice, a feeling that is maintained in part by for mal membership in the party and the payment of annual dues. Presumably these organizational characteristics account for the existence of a large pool of talents from which party leaders are recruited. But the most important point is that for the mass party, the members are the very substance of the party, the stuff of its activity. The members are recruited, politically educated and trained. They contribute funds for electioneering and other party activities, this function being of paramount significance in as much as it substitutes the party's dependence upon big business for funds with 'democratic financing'. It is difficult to describe all existing parties as either 'purely' mass or cadre organizations, but most tend to lean one way or the other.

Oligarchy or Stratarchy: Robert Michels argued that all political parties—indeed all organizations and even the most democratic ones—are oligarchical in the sense that they are controlled by a minority of leaders.[18] On the basis of his studies of the socialist parties in Italy and Germany, Michels argued that decision making power lay centred in the top echelon of leadership. This thesis has generated a great deal of debate in the literature on parties.

Neumann holds that Michels' 'glittering generalization' is an 'overstatement' of the undeniable existence of oligarchical, hierarchical and centrapetal trends in every society. There are data to confirm the equally omnipresent democratic, leveling, and centrifugal forces encountered even within totalitarian regimes.[19] Neumann thinks that if instead of studying the Italian and German socialist parties, he had studied the British Labour Party, he would have reached different conclusions. Michels, like many social scientists, was biased towards the values of his time and society. Neumann mentioned several determinants which can account for different kinds of relationships within the party.[20] Among the factors he mentioned were variations in the character of the masses who are led and the existence of checks and balances exercised by an alert citizenry.

Samuel J. Eldersveld in his behavioural study of political parties explodes Michel's thesis and suggests a framework of the structure of political parties that is quite contrary.[21] As against the thesis of 'oligarchical' control over the party, Eldersveld advances the concept of 'stratarchy' (having borrowed the phrase from Lasswell and Kaplan's *Power and Society*), discusses the structural styles of parties, and suggests four theoretical constructs or dimensions about political parties.

1. The party is a clientele-oriented structure and is always 'potential clientele'-conscious. It is open at its base to new recruits for party work as well as to nonactivist supporters. It is often open at the higher level also, and indeed, at the elite apex, if such a strategy will profit the party's power aspirations. 2. The party is adaptive and its character is coalitional. The party is a structural system seeking to translate

means partnership, participation or sharing. The party in this sense emerged only as a part of a 'pluralistic society' and as the organ of not only a 'responsible' but 'responsive' government. 'A party system', says Sartori, 'is a pluralistic' system of 'parts' that forcibly 'express' the opinion of the government.[26] A pluralistic policy is a whole of parts and results from the interplay of its parts. The whole cannot be identified with just one party.[27] If the party is not a part, it is a pseudo-party; and if the whole is identified with just one party, it is a pseudo-whole. Even the assertion that the single party identifies with the whole needs to be qualified.[28] Sartori flatly rejects the idea of a whole resulting from a competitive interplay of parts.[29] Even within the single party, any kind of formalised intra-party division is banned. Thus communism, nazism and fascism testify to the existence of a monochromatic belief system based on the principle of unanimity and the horror of dissent.[30] According to this logic, single party systems bear no comparison with competitive party systems.

The next relevant question is, why one party instead of no parties? Sartori explains that the no-party notion comprises two different cases : (*a*) the partyless and the pre-party states such as Saudi Arabia, Yemen, Jordan, Afghanistan, Nepal and (*b*) the anti-party states, that is the regimes that have suppressed pre-existing parties, taken an anti-party stand or anti-party doctrine, such as military regimes in Bolivia, Brazil, Chile and Peru in South America and countries in Africa.

As Huntington says, 'the party state is the natural state for a traditional society. As a society modernizes, however, the no-party state becomes increasingly the anti-party state'.[31] Sartori adds that the more modernized and/or developed the society, the more anti-partism yields to unipartism, as the latter solution proves to be far less tangible and far more effective than the former.[32] If the society is politically developed but party pluralism fails, then the one party state becomes the end solution. Parties, in a state of politicization, become channeling agencies. The single party serves that purpose only too well. 'The modernized society has to be mobilized, persuaded, and asked for a trustful, if not an unconditional decision. The society is to be "chained". These are the uses to which the single party is put'.[33]

The Dual or Multi-party System: The party in a dual or multi-party system has functions quite different from what it has or can have in a single party system. The party in a single party system has only the function of channeling, but the party in a competitive party system is characterized by its 'expressive' function, that is, it performs more than a merely 'representative' function. As Sartori says

> Parties are more than upgoing transmission belts of claims and grievances. They transmit demands backed by pressure. The party throws its own weight into the demands it feels compelled to respond to.[34]

Sartori also emphasizes that more than expressing and reflecting public opinion, parties shape, and indeed manipulate, opinion.

> A party system lends itself to expression from below far more than to manipulation from above; if for no other reason than this that the people have no opinions of their own, or that their opinions are largely formed by opinion makers.

Both the channeling and expressive functions are fulfilled through communication. In fact, communication is common to both competitive and non-competitive systems; what distinguishes one from the other is control or freedom of communication media. V.O. Key stresses 'the interest-aggregation functions of parties'.[35] He writes,

> To the political parties falls the task of keeping the peace among group interests. Political parties both comprehend and transcend the special interests of society. They must take into account the demands of interest groups; they must also consider aspirations not represented by organized groups; they must seek to speak for the nation as a whole—or at least for a substantial majority—and not merely for a small part of it. Their energies activate the machinery of government, which is a powerful engine for the allocation of this world's goods among classes and groups. Yet parties must do more than combine interests for the satisfaction of mutually compatible greed; they must, at least in their American incarnation, implant a widespread belief that their policies promote the common weal.[36]

Key also writes that political parties perform an essential function in the management of succession to power, as well as in the process of obtaining popular consent to the course of public policy. They amass sufficient support to buttress the authority of governments; or, on the other hand, they attract or organize discontent and dissatisfaction sufficient to oust the government.

However, comments Theodore Lowi, some of the regular activities of parties, including nominating candidates and running candidates, are not to be confused with functions of parties. 'The activities are not functions'.[37] The functions of a party can be determined only by assessments of the consequences of party activities. And for a party to function as a channel of innovation for the political system at least, the following consequences of the activities would be required: the absorption of representation of prevailing values and conflicts, their organization into distinctive and simple alternatives, the shaping of electorates around these alternatives, and the translation of at least some of these into objectives once the party is in power. Quite obviously, the 'functions of party' are not actually functions but standards for the proper functioning of a party.

Lowi hypothesizes that in a party system, innovation is a function of the minority party. Innovation does not necessarily require the passage of new laws. It is also intended to include *inter alia*, new definitions of old problems, entirely new items for the policy agenda, the representation of new interests and new minorities, structural changes in government (reform), and new ways of organizing and mobilizing voters. It is in itself a condition that gives continuing reality to such specific activities as organizing elections, simplifying alternatives and running campaigns. Through the various forms of innovation, the parties remain in the 'vital centre' of the political process; for unless the parties somehow attach themselves to a fair proportion of the prevailing conflicts of the day, they lose their legitimacy, and are shunted aside from direct 'pressure group' action.

Besides functions of parties in competitive party systems, we have also to look into the question as to why any two parties function most of the time in Britain and the USA, whereas multi-partism exists in many other countries. This question assumes significance because it is related to the question of political stability.

V.O. Key explains that several variables such as the persistence of initial form, the popular election of the chief executive, certain patterns of popular political beliefs and attitudes, and a popular consensus on fundamentals, are some of the reasons for dualism in the USA.[38] Factors such as the homogeneity of populations, the stabilization of class order by the end of the nineteenth century, the national character and above all, the tradition and the particular nature of the evolution of parties, have been put forward to explain dualism in Britain. But some commentators hold that political stability or party dualism is related to the single member constituencies and the simple majority single ballot; whereas multi-partism is related to proportional representation and plural member constituencies. In a single member district where only two parties can contend for electoral victory with any hope of success, a third party is doomed to defeat. Minor parties are obstructed and encouraged to coalesce with a major party, for the system almost invariably reduces their share of the parliamentary seats below their proportion of the population vote. Thus a particular type of electoral system, according to the school of 'electocentrists', is responsible for a particular type of party system.

The validity of the single member district theory, however, has not been adequately tested. Maurice Klain has pointed out that almost half of the American state legislators are chosen from multi-membered districts, a practice of long standing in many states.[39] It appears that the single member district has a significant effect, principally when it exists in conjunction with other factors that predispose the mass of the electorate to a dual division.

Stability is not the creation of any electoral system. In fact, the electoral system is an offspring of the social system, and political stability is essentially governed by a number of active social factors or circumstances often variable and independent of the ballot mechanism. Identical social factors, regardless of the electoral system, are capable of producing stability or instability, in bipartism or in multipartism. It is the social groups, either specified or clearly identifiable, that are at the base of political parties, and they shape the electoral system as required for a given society. If circumstances are positive, the multi-party system can ensure ministries as stable as those offered by the biparty system, which in unfavourable social situations will yield as much to recurring instability as the former.

The contention of the electocentric school is based solely on the experience of France in the Third Republic. But in France, for the 24 elections between 1831 to 1935, single member constituencies were in existence; but this did not change the French political pattern. Hence, instability should be ascribed to political reasons or to lack of political consensus, and not to electoral form. In Belgium, multi-member constituencies and proportional representation were in use till 1899, but Belgium did not have more than three parties. Even the assumption that multi-partism foments political instability, and bipartism facilitates stable ministries is not borne out by facts. Australia with its tripartism, Canada with its quardripartism, Sweden with its pentapartism, Denmark with its hectapartism, Finland with its septapartism and Switzerland with its octapartism ensure governments as stable as those in the bipartisan countries.

Sadasivan is right therefore, in concluding that the party system in all democracies is a projection of the social system. Where society is divided into assertive groups, irrespective of the prevailing ballot system, parties are bound to multiply, and unless effective means are evolved to reconcile group differences, political stability cannot be realized.[40] In Britain and the USA, the main divisions are two; hence bipartism has developed. In India, where society has numerous ramifications, multiplicity of parties is but a social reflection. In certain states like Tamil Nadu where society has developed such cohesion as to make two broad political divisions possible, there is an emerging trend towards bipartism. Similarly, through social agreement, a coalition government can be formed as it has been in the past, in Kerala for example. In fact, political stability in India is to be sought in the ability of the various parties to achieve enduring social agreement to forge a national coalition.

In multi-partism again, we find large variations. India, for instance, has a multi-party system but the Congress has been a 'dominant party', and the 'Congress system' has been responsible for a particular orientation of the party system. This has had significant implications for the functioning of the Indian political system. We shall examine this point in some detail.

One Dominant Party System : India

The Indian political system has been analyzed by quite a few scholars and commentators as a 'one dominant party system'.[41] The concept was popularized in the sixties by W.H. Morris-Jones and Rajni Kothari.[42] For a basic elucidation of the term, however, one has to go to Maurice Durverger who used the expression as early as 1951.[43] Even earlier, V.O. Key used the concept in his study of the politics of the Southern states in the USA, where he dealt with the nature and consequences of one-party factionalism.[44] But it was Duverger who gave a workable definition of the concept. According to him, a party is dominant if it displays the two following characteristics in a two-party or a multi-party system.[45] (*a*) It clearly outdistances its rivals over an extended period of time (even if occasionally sustaining an electoral defeat); and (*b*) it identifies itself with the nation as a whole. Its doctrines, ideas and even its style coincide with those of the times.

The radical party in France during a certain phase of the Third Republic, and the social-democratic parties in Scandinavia, were the prototypes on which Duverger based his definition. Later, this was applied to the prevailing models in India, and certain republics of Africa.

Notwithstanding the comment that 'one party dominance' is a subjective and relativistic concept rather than one possessing an objective definitional standard,[46] it appears that this concept provides a useful tool for the analysis of the Indian political system. In operational terms, the concept characterizes a system in which the party in power cannot be seriously challenged by the opposition party or parties as the latter are too weak to replace the former. But there are certain considerations in an evalution of the degree of dominance of a certain party in a particular system. First, there is the time factor; how long has a party been pre-eminent? The Indian political system has been dominated by the Congress Party ever since Independence, as it has been in a position to rule the centre[17] and most of the states. There has been a communist government in Kerala (1957-59), and there were non-Congress governments in many states after the fourth general election. Even at the centre, the overwhelming majority of the Congress was reduced in 1967, and there was a minority government between November 1969 and December 1970;[48] and in 1977, the dominance of the Congress was effectively challenged with the election to power of the Janata Party. But these exceptions are already implicit in Duverger's elucidation of the concept.

Second, perceived dominance is affected by the margin of victory of the major party over the minor party or parties. A party that attracts 60 or 70 per cent of the votes may be perceived as more dominant than a party that is winning regularly but by less substantial margins. The Congress Party has not won an absolute majority of the popular votes in any national election.[49] Thus the dominance of the party is a result of the multi-party character of the system, and the division of votes among the opposition parties. However, the Congress Party is still the single largest party in India in terms of popular votes. The third important factor is the 'identification' role of the party mentioned by Duverger. Many opposition parties in India reflected facts of Indian political life which were not always present in the Congress.[50] It is characteristic of the 'dominant party' to try to identify itself with the nation as a whole, or at least to a greater part of the whole. The fourth factor relates to how the 'dominance' operates in the governing of the country, and what its impact is.

It is true that one-party dominance in India is different not only from the non-party states,[51] but also from the one dominant party systems of Ghana, Mexico, Algeria and Egypt. The Indian system is 'democratic', 'representative' and 'constitutional'.[52] The reason for this is the perpetuation of the 'Congress system' in India.[53] We may add that the Janata Party, though different in name and historical origin, share some of the characteristics of the Congress system. Let us first analyze the Congress system and then examine the Janata rule to find out if it conforms to the definition of the 'Congress system'.

The Congress Party faced organized political and pressure groups and had to maintain a political dialogue with them. The Congress and the opposition groups had emerged from the same class and they did not project diverse socio-economic interests.[54] There were no clear lines between government and opposition and the boundaries were also at times unclear between 'government' and 'party'.[55] The Congress Party maintained an 'umbrella' character in its role as dominant party. It tried to build 'consensus', and in the process, accommodated various shades of political opinions and interests. Intra-party 'factional' competition (mostly at the state and local levels) kept the party 'open and democratic'. The party, by widening its base, contained the emerging or incoming groups. Parties of pressure (opposition groups) enjoyed influence because of the nebulous and loose structure of the party. Thus some sort of linkage between the opposition groups and the Congress factions that think along the same lines has been in evidence.[56] The role of 'personalities' in mediating political relationships in the country has also been apparent.[57]

The Congress system provided political stability to the country through the mechanisms of strong leadership at the centre and the consensus-building approach. India was able to hold elections and make changes in leadership through democratic processes. Even power conflict at the top (1969-70 and 1974-77) was resolved through parliamentary devices. All these have been the plus points of the 'system', but there were minus points too. The Congress maintained ideological ambiguity in socio-economic matters, and resorted to non-committal general declarations in favour of a 'socialistic pattern of society' or a 'socialist state'. It attempted to be at the centre, and the description of its nature made by Nehru in 1936-37, continued to be valid even after Independence with slight variations. Nehru said, 'Politically, the Congress is overwhelmingly left, socially it has leftist leanings but is predominantly centre. In matters affecting the peasantry it is pro-peasant'.[58] As a leader, Nehru wanted to carry the masses with him and with that end in view, was willing to proceed with caution in bringing about socio-economic reforms.[59] The net result was the lack of programmatic commitment or a production-oriented, target-achieving performance which created a lag between promises and fulfilment. This has been one of the most important causes of the ferment and mounting frustrations in India, particularly since 1967.

In order to arrest the erosion of confidence exposed so blatantly by the outcome of the fourth general election, a section of the Congress Party felt convinced that the key to the survival of Congress dominance was a radical ideological posture, and matching action which would close the gap between policy and implementation.[60] The activist ideology, it was felt, would enable Congressmen to transcend factionalism, and this in turn could enable the party to bring social and economic change. After passing through a phase of intense intra-factional competition at the top level, the Congress received substantial majorities in 1971-72, with promise in favour of performance-orientation. But even then the Congress system could not bring about radical changes. The new feature was the politics of populism, opportunism and of naked power.

While the Congress under Mahatma Gandhi and Nehru was attuned to thinking in terms of 'unity', 'purity' and 'sacrifice', it came to be identified with gratification politics in the latter part of the sixties. The paradox of issue orientation and a quest for power going hand in hand became more prominent. The dominant party ruled through the mechanism of centralization of command. Even the tendency to impose leadership on the states seemed to grow,[61] and in the process, intra-party democracy weakened to the extent that it could not prevent its leader from imposing internal 'emergency' without the prior approval or consent of the cabinet. However, it has to be admitted that power politics enhanced the cleavage between the communal-secular and the radical-status quo divisions in Indian society, and that the ruling party had the advantageous position of identifying itself with the secular and radical slogans.

All these features—ideological ambiguity, a consensus-building approach, nebulous and loose structure and factionalism—were very much in existence in the Janata Party also. Some sections of the Janata Party engaged in dialogue with the opposition parties, particularly the Congress (I) and the Congress (S). Factionalism effectively kept checks on the growth of a dominant majority in the Lok Sabha. It continued to speak both in terms of agriculture vs. industry, private vs. public sector, and maintained enough ambiguity to disappoint neither of the two sections connected with them. Thus the Janata system represented, to a great extent, the elements of the Congress system. It is possible to state therefore that one-party dominance' appears to be a feature of our political life. It seems to be correlated with our cultural and religious system. Hinduism, the religion of the dominant majority in India, is also loose, nebulous and consensus-building in approach. But we must concede that such a party system affects the 'cohesiveness' of the political centre (which Rajni Kothari considers very important for achievement), and does not correspond positively with the desired rate of 'development'. The breakup of the Janata Party indicated the failure of the party system to support any single group in a party. The Janata system appeared to take the place of the Congress system and acquire a 'one-party-dominance' character, but soon gave way to a coalition system at the centre, reminiscent of the coalition government in the states after 1967. A coalition system reflects the diversity and heterogeneity of Indian society. There is a school that maintains that given the social and economic structure of Indian society, and ideological ambivalence, the politics of manipulation and coalition are inevitable. This is, however, a challenge to political leadership and organization. It is their function to create a political order out of the myriad warring political forces in the country.

7. Bureaucracy, Society and Politics

Political parties and interest groups are chief political agencies in the mobilization of power. Parties aspire to make governments; groups seek to influence government policies. It is however government bureaucracy that makes and implements public policies, often in concert with parties and interest groups. Amidst the fluctuating fortunes of parties and the rivalries of groups, bureaucracy provides administrative expertise and stability. Also with the expansion of government activities, bureaucracy has come to acquire a vital role and enormous power in modern governments that rely heavily on trained civil servants to carry out complicated tasks of administration. Although civil service is not an entirely new institution and was known in ancient times, the most famous being the Chinese, modern bureaucracy is a formally organized institution of great significance and power. Indeed bureaucracy now represents a type and method of organization that is not only confined to government but also extends to private business and industry. As a system characterized by official duties based on formal rules and a hierarchical and stable authority structure, bureaucracy represents functional expertise, and its members are selected on the basis of their merit rather than on that of birth or status.

The best point of departure for understanding bureaucracy is to begin with Max Weber's 'ideal type definition'. Max Weber's characterization of bureaucracy has been summed up in terms of the following:

1. A continuous organization of official functions bound by rules;

2. A specific sphere of competence, and a sphere of obligations to perform functions which have been marked off as part of a systematic division of labour, and the provision of the incumbent with the necessary authority to carry out these functions;
3. The organization of office follows the principle of hierarchy, that is, each lower office is under the control and supervision of a higher one;
4. The rules which regulate the conduct of an office may be technical rules or norms. In such cases, if their application is to be fully rational, specialized training is necessary. It is thus normally true that only a person who has demonstrated an adequate technical training is qualified to be a member of the administrative staff;
5. It is a matter of principle that the members of the administrative staff should be completely separated from ownership of the means of production or administration. There exists, furthermore, in principle, complete separation of property belonging to the organization, which is controlled within the spheres of the office, and the personal property of an official;
6. Administrative acts, decisions and rules are formulated and recorded in writing.[1]

Thus official duties, a specific sphere of competence, hierarchical division of authority, technical rules, separation of management from ownership; official position as incumbency rather than as property or inheritance, and documentary recording of administrative acts, are the elements of bureaucracy. These elements are generally absent from the feudal or traditional forms of administration in which heredity and status, personal relations, and the overlap of personal and public spheres of activities are prominent. In summary form, bureaucracy has the following characteristics: 1. fixed and official jurisdictional areas, which are regularly ordered by rules, that is, by laws or administrative regulations; 2. principles of hierarchy and levels of graded authority that ensure a firmly ordered system in which higher offices supervise lower ones; 3. administration based upon written documents. The body of officials engaged in handling these documents and files, along with other material apparatus, make up a 'bureau' or 'office'; 4. administration by full time officials who are thoroughly and expertly trained; and 5. administration by general rules which are quite stable and comprehensive.[2]

Max Weber's conceptualization of bureaucracy is based on his notion of rationality. Weber classifies authority into three types—traditional, charismatic and rational. Traditional authority is based on birth and status without reference to technical merit. Traditional authority is an inheritance and an ascribed property. In a traditional society, status defines role rather than role determining status. Charismatic authority is inherent in outstanding individuals endowed with extraordinary personal magnetism. Such individuals are rare leaders, generally produced in times of crisis. Rational authority on the other hand is to be found in formal organizations where individuals hold office on merit or expert qualifications for specific jobs, and are judged by their performance rather than by their personal or official status. Rational authority inheres in office rather than in the incumbent as an individual. According to Max Weber, bureaucracy, based as it is on merit or technical qualification, formal duties and impersonal rules and relationships, represents the development of rationality in human organizations.

Weber argues that bureaucracy is not only characterized by rational authority but is also endowed with technical superiority and is therefore conducive to efficiency. As he writes, 'The decisive reason for the advance of bureaucratic organization has always been its technical superiority over any other form of organization. The fully developed bureaucratic mechanism compares with other organizations exactly as does the machine with the non-mechanical modes of production.'[3]

An obvious merit of ideal bureaucracy is a concern for objectivity and impartiality. Bureaucratic decisions are ideally based not on personal considerations but on formal rules. The objective discharge of business primarily means the discharge of business according to calculable rules and 'without regard for persons'.[4]

In Weber's scheme, however, there is a confusion between the elements and the consequences of bureaucratic organization. Blau and Scott rightly point out that Weber's construct of bureaucracy is an admixture of a conceptual scheme and a set of hypotheses.[5] Weber's ideal type comprises the key elements of bureaucratic organization. Whether these consequences follow from the elements of bureaucratic organization or not is an open question and can only have the status of a hypothesis. For example, whether administrative efficiency results from bureaucratic rationality or not, is an empirical, not a logical question. The question regarding the extent to which rationality is an essential or exclusive element in a bureaucratic organization may also be posed here.

The artificiality and confusion of the ideal type are properly exposed by consideration of the dysfunctions of the various elements of bureaucracy, and the conflicts that may arise among these elements. In this connection Merton's exposition of bureaucratic dysfunctions is illuminating.[6] He considers the negative aspects of bureaucracy through the application of Vebler's concept of 'trained incapacity', which refers to the state of affairs in which one's abilities function as inadequacies. For the successful operation of bureaucracy, a high degree of reliability of behaviour and of conformity is necessary. However, Merton points out that as 'adherence to the rules originally conceived as a means becomes transformed into an end in itself, there occurs the familiar process of displacement of goals whereby an instrumental value becomes a terminal value'.[7] Discipline, readily interpreted as conformity with regulations, whatever the situation, is seen not as a measure designed for a specific purpose, but as an immediate value in the life-organization of the bureaucrat.

Such formalism and rigidity, according to Merton, derive from structural sources. There is a need for discipline and devotion to formal rules as a means is turned into the observing of rules as an end. Such rigidity regarding rules interferes with spontaneous adaptation under special conditions. Thus the very elements that are expected to rationalize bureaucratic behaviour and enhance its efficiency in routine matters, may produce inefficiency in special instances and circumstances.

Another dysfunctional aspect of bureaucracy pertains to the rise of defence mechanisms of an informal order which tend to arise whenever there is a threat to the integrity of a group. The bureaucrats tend to develop a sense of a common destiny and an espirit-de-corps. They share and defend their entrenched interests above everything else. The stress and 'depersonalization of relationships' further builds a barrier between the bureaucratic official and the mass of the people. The bureaucratic official representing the power and the prestige of government, with his own image of merit and impartiality, is likely to develop an arrogant and superior attitude in sharp contrast to his theoretical self-description as public servant.

As against Weber's emphasis on formal rules and impersonal conduct in bureaucracy, others have drawn attention to the importance of informal interactions, unofficial transactions, and friendship patterns. These natural elements represent primordial affiliations and mould intellectual behaviour of the members of a bureaucratic organization.

Formal rules and rational matters cannot be separated from the wider social context and cultural milieu of which bureaucracy is a part. For example, the Indian Civil Service was developed by the British on the principles of general competence, integrity and impartiality, and political neutrality. The nature and role of the Indian bureaucracy, however, cannot be meaningfully analyzed and understood without reference to their social and cultural characteristics and those of the wider national environment.

Regardless, however, of the variations in the organization of a specific bureaucracy, the term 'bureaucracy' refers to the organization of management, whether public or private. Indeed, in order to avoid the negative connotation of bureaucracy and also its Weberian associations, increasing use of the term 'organization' in place of 'bureaucracy' is being made. Organizations refer to both public and private sectors, and refer to a group of people engaged in carrying out a task, either public or private in nature, together.

However, the distinctive features of a government bureaucracy are concerned with the public and therefore the political character of its goals and policies. Accordingly, bureaucracy is involved in the process of decision making that is of great political importance. The administrative goals are determined by legislative enactments or executive orders, and as such bureaucratic actions have political origins and ends. Given the primacy of public interest in public administration, one may ask a question about the criteria of public interest. Schubert has made an interesting attempt to classify administrators into three types in terms of their varying perspectives on the criteria of public interest.[8] These three types are labelled rationalists, idealists and realists. Rationalists accept the doctrine of responsibility and seek to find guidance for their decisions in public opinion. Idealists reject the view of the public as an ideal guideline and rely instead upon their own understanding of the social good. Realists seek only to maintain the viability of the administrative system in which policy is adjusted, to meet the demands of competing or rival interests.

Bureaucracy : Rationality and Power

According to Max Weber, bureaucracy is the means of carrying community action over into rationally ordered societal action. For those who control the bureaucratic apparatus, it serves as an instrument of power. Thus bureaucracy as an organization represents rationality and power. Bureaucracy as a machine of expertise and discipline represents rationality and can be placed at the disposal of vested interests in power. Besides being an instrument of power for other interests, bureaucracy itself emerges as a centre of power, and therefore poses serious questions of relationship with other facets of power. Both as an instrument and a centre of power, bureaucracy also raises important questions regarding its relationship with democracy. Bureaucratic power has been perceived as a threat to democracy because bureaucracy is increasingly difficult to control and is not truly accountable to the people; it also precludes or at least minimises the scope and opportunities of popular and political participation in decision making. However, the actual degree of bureaucratic power depends on its position vis-a-vis other elements in a social or political system. As Weber points out,

> Everywhere the modern state is undergoing bureaucratization. But whether the power of bureaucracy within the polity is universally increasing must be an open question.[9]
>
> The fact that bureaucratic organization is technically the most highly developed means of power in the hands of the man who controls it has not determined the weight that bureaucracy as such is capable of having in a particular social structure.[10]
>
> Under normal conditions, the power positions of a fully developed democracy are always overpowering. The political master finds himself in the position of the dilettante who stands opposite the expert, facing the trained official who stands within the management of administration.[11]

Michels, Truman and Lasswell have written about bureaucracy as a social class in the context of industrialization and increasing bureaucratization. However, whether the power of bureaucracy as such increases cannot be decided *a priori* from such reasons, though the increasing power of bureaucracy has been perceived as a threat to democratic values and democratic procedure. There are several versions of this bureaucratic power.

In the first place Roberto Michels put forward his iron law of oligarchy according to which all bureaucratic organizations tend to be oligarchic.[12] The concentration of decision making power in the upper echelons of leadership, the monopoly of information at the top and the obstacles to participation by all the members of an organization in decision making, result in the denial of democracy. Michels demonstrated through his analysis of democratic socialist parties of Germany, that these parties were bureaucratized, and that the members had no opportunity to influence its decisions. If this is true of social democratic parties, it is apparent how much more true this would be of government bureaucracies in which the masses have hardly any influence.

Secondly, the difficulties of controlling an all powerful bureaucracy, even in a democracy, have been emphasized. The surveillance exercised by the legislative bodies or the judicial courts tends to be superficial and nominal. Through the delegated legislation, administration has come to excercise more and more power in actual legislation itself. Likewise, through the process of administrative law and adjudication, even the judicial control of discretionary acts of bureaucracy has lost much of its reality. Through the gradual and insidious bureaucratization of the party as well as the legislative process, it is pointed out, the process of political control over the administration has become attenuated. This problem is becoming acute as bureaucratic power is increasing with the expansion of government regulation of economy, and the welfare services that the modern state seeks to provide to its citizens. Thus

> From its emergence as an important element in the governmental process, public bureaucracy has been an object of continuing concern from the perspective of democratic norms. To many observers, the growth of bureaucratic power has loomed as a serious threat to the responsiveness of the governmental system to public control, and a great deal of attention has been paid to this problem in the work of political scientists.[13]

The democratic defence against bureaucratic power, on the other hand, rests on the following arguments. (*a*) One defence against bureaucratic oligarchy lies in social pluralism, which allows a large number of organizations to compete among themselves as veto groups. The danger to democracy comes from monopoly of power and as long as a large number of organizations operate in a society, they check the arbitrary or excessive power of any one single organization. (*b*) Another defence against oligarchy is the presence of conflict and factionalism within organizations. Internal conflict prevents the concentration of power and presents a challenge to the power of the few. (*c*) It is the democratic ethos that must remain the ultimate check against violations of individual liberties or human rights. The role of mass media, political opposition and voluntary organizations in maintaining a climate of public accountability must be recognized as the ultimate safeguards of democracy. (*d*) Finally, the erstwhile judicial and parliamentary control over the bureaucracy continues to be a last check on the arbitrary exercise of bureaucratic power.

The real control of bureaucracy therefore rests not so much on its own sense of responsibility and commitment, important as these are for good administration, but on the quality of other sectors of the political system and the nature of the regime itself. Bureaucratic authority has increased in response to the nature of modern government as well as economy and society all of which are getting increasingly technological and administratively complex. Thus bureaucratization is a feature of modern society as a whole. The danger arising from bureaucratic power is real, but the answer to this threat lies more in political competition and vigilance, so that the ability and authority of the political leadership can match the competence and skill of the bureaucracy. The remedy against bureaucratic control lies in the vitality of public institutions and political life.

Bureaucracy and Politics

This leads us to an examination of the relationship between politics and bureaucracy. Traditionally, bureaucracy has been conceived of as, and understood to be, politically neutral. The Weberian model emphasized the rationality and objectivity of the bureaucracy. It has been pointed out that the bureaucracy, endowed though it is with administrative ability, is not, and cannot be, neutral. It develops its own group identity and interests, and it develops its organizational objective towards self-protection. Bureaucracy accordingly, must above all be conceived of as a social class with a group solidarity of its own. It may not be monolithic any more than any other social category such as caste, class or nation. The maintenance of its identity and solidarity is its important goal.

It is further observed that individual members of the bureaucracy tend to identify themselves with particular interests or groups and such identity is reflected in the way they conduct government business and influence public policies or programme implementation. Thus the individual officials develop their own social and political links and act as a representative of particular interests. Lobbies and legislators often work in concert with administrators, and together mould public policies.

Given the dominant position of bureaucracy in all societies in general, and in developing societies in particular, the debate regarding the role of bureaucracy vis-a-vis political institutions has continued. Fred W. Riggs has been very vocal in emphasizing the folly of assuming a separatism between bureaucracy and politics. He says,

> This idea of separatism has in my judgement been erroneously equated with the idea that a bureaucracy should serve only administrative functions, and a constitutive system—i.e. legislature, parties and elected politicians—should serve only political functions. This formulation obscures the fact that if bureaucrats are to give priority to managerial and rational-legal criteria in the conduct of their offices, they must have some degree of power. It obscures also the proposition that the administrative effectiveness of a bureaucracy depends in no small measure on its relations with a constitutive system.[14]

It is also pointed out that an excess of bureaucratic power poses not only a danger to individuals, but also threatens to arrest political development. An alternative view however is that given the political instability and even immaturity of developing countries, bureaucracy may provide both stability and efficiency in administration transcending the changing character and composition of political elements. Fritz Morstein Marx has this to say :

> In broadest language, the chief effect of the emerging merit bureacracy may be said to have been in the direction of vastly increasing the viability of institutional government. Popular rule, easily distorted by volatile partisanship, cries out for the counter weight of considered assessment of issues. Representation was strengthened rather than weakened by being linked with the sober insights that originate in the perspective of public management.[15]
>
> The bureaucracy operated as both a source and a manifestation of rationality, to use Max Weber's phrase, even though remaining subject to challenge in the competition of values, attitudes and inferences. To that extent, the workings of the administrative system helped to legitimize governmental authority. Public policy acquired an aura of governmental properiety.[16]

> Moreover, capacity for public management greatly enlarged the range of affective political action. The new administrative profession served as a multiplier in the expeditious discharge of responsibilities assumed by government. It turned into a principal instrumentality for the accommodation of demands made upon the body politic.[17]

On the role of the civil servant as a neutral but not indifferent wing of government, Fritz Marx elaborates his concept of 'prudential neutrality' in the following words:

> The constitutional law of administrative behaviour properly stresses the instrumental character of the career establishment. The arm of the state cannot be permitted to defy the political brain, nor is it free to separate itself from the body politic. The restraining implications of these broad maxims are the test of a bureaucracy's maturity, sophistication and rectitude. On the other hand, administrative neutrality does not mean an ostrich-like withdrawal of the directing cadre from the arena of governmental choice. Policy, programme and management pose countless issues on what the higher civil servant is obliged to come forth with as his best judgement. He fails to do his duty if he avoids these questions. He has no warrant for simply passing them onto the politicians without contributing his special competence for professional analysis.
>
> What administrative neutrality does mean is something else. It means acceptance of the discipline of working without reservation—indeed with devotion for the success of every government lawfully in power. Conversely, it carries with it a prohibition. Permanent officers cannot allow themselves so intimate an identification with a particular policy or programme as to create for them an emotional disability when it comes to turning in the opposite direction under a different government.[18]

Fred W. Riggs provides an opposite view of the nature and role of bureaucracy. He questions the validity of the idea of 'neutral' bureaucracy, and points out the political involvement of civil servants in the decision making process. He says that bureaucrats probably always have some influence in politics. In the developing countries the extent of bureaucratic involvement in politics is exceptionally high.[19]

If we make a quick survey of the transitional societies today, we will be impressed by the weakness of their extra-bureaucratic political institutions in contrast with the burgeoning growth of their bureaucracies. By contrast, parliamentary bodies have in the main proved ineffectual, and even in countries like India and the Philippines their role in basic decision making has been questioned.[20] In the governmental sphere, these principles (technological innovation precedes other changes) means that development in public administration or bureaucratic change, takes place more easily than counterpart changes in politics.

While this proliferation and expansion of bureaucratic machinery was taking place in most of the non-Western countries, no corresponding development of the non-bureaucratic political system occurred.[21] Riggs therefore came to the following view:

> My general thesis is that premature or too rapid expansion of the bureaucracy when the political system lags behind, tends to inhibit the development of effective politics. A corollary thesis holds that separate political institutions have a better chance to grow if bureaucratic institutions are relatively weak.[22] Also, The merit system cuts at the root of one of the strongest props of a nascent political party system, namely spoils.[23]

Finally,

> The existence of career bureaucracy without corresponding strength in the political institutions does not necessarily lead to administrative effectiveness. Without firm political guidance, bureaucrats have weak incentives to provide good service between their formal, pre-entry training and professional qualifications.[24]

These long quotations from both Fritz Marx and Fred Riggs are designed to convey in their own words the apparently contradictory veiws on the nature and role of bureaucracy vis-a-vis political leadership and institutions. There is little doubt that bureaucracy represents expertise and rationality in the Weberian sense, and is therefore an indispensable part of modern government. On the other hand, there is also little doubt that bureaucracy is likely to develop some dysfunctional characteristics and has to be constantly pulled up by political leadership. From this point of view, Riggs has formulated an important thesis that a lag between bureaucratic development and political leadership and institutions is not conducive to political development. The danger arising from such a lag is real precisely because bureaucracy can be developed faster and more easily than political institutions. It may be added that not only political development but also the solution of social and economic problems in the long run cannot be achieved without the development of the political system. It can also be seen from the Indian experience that although the character and calibre of the Indian Administrative Service is by and large the same in all the states, the quality and performance of administration varies from state to state. A major explanation for this probably is the quality and characteristics of state politics which show marked regional differences resulting in differences in state administration. In this connection it is interesting to note that a comparative study of the government and politics of three cities shows that it is the characteristics of the local political system that are the crucial factors in determining the quality and performance of local governments in these three cities.[25]

Bureaucracy and Society

We have discussed the nature of bureaucracy, its increasing power as a vital organ of government and its role vis-a-vis politics. We have also referred briefly to the rise of bureaucracy as a social class, the chief end of which is to maintain its identity and solidarity as a dominant sector of society. This is a somewhat neglected aspect of commentaries on bureaucracy, but one that deserves attention for two reasons. In the first place, bureaucracy is emerging as a special category in modern societies, and second, in a study of political sociology, we are concerned above all with the identity of this very powerful class and its interaction with society as a whole.

On the identity of this class, the most fruitful insights have come from writers such as Lasswell, and the neo-Machiavellians who perceive in bureaucrats or managers the rising class of the future in all modern societies. The bureaucracy represents the elite of merit or meritocracy, which dominates the public and private administration. There are of course different echelons of bureaucracy, but each echelon is a subclass, and its strength derives from the fact that it has a role to play in making or managing government policies. Another important source of their solidarity and power is the fact that they are organized groups, and therefore effective in securing for themselves the benefit of government power and privileges.

Yet another question in this context is the social background of bureaucracy, and the matrix of social relationships. Studies of bureaucracy in the USA have pointed out that American bureaucracy is representative of American society in that both are overwhelmingly middle class. Regardless of whether such identity can help to ensure the instrumentality of American bureaucracy for the benefit of the American people, this identity is supposed to ensure that bureaucracy is in tune with the ethos of the majority of the people, and the bureaucratic class, however influential, is part of the larger society.

In India, on the other hand, studies have shown that the higher bureaucracy has been drawn largely from the upper caste and the upper middle class. In view of the illiteracy and poverty of the majority of the Indian population, the bureaucracy, of course, represents the dominant sections of the society. By its very nature Indian bureaucracy cannot be representative of Indian society.[26]

The reservation of administrative posts initially for the scheduled castes and tribes, and more recently for the backward castes, is likely to make bureaucracy more broad-based and representative of the cross-sections of Indian society. There is little doubt that such reservation of jobs is bound to result in the fragmentation of the bureaucratic mould and in the increase of social penetration of bureaucracy. These results are already in evidence. However, in view of the enormous inequalities in Indian society, the bureaucracy continues to be dominated by the upper class members of all the castes, from which civil servants are recruited. It is observed that even the members of the lower caste or class who join the civil service get increasingly alienated from their own kinship group, and gradually form a new elite with interaction limited to their own caste group in the administration and to the bureaucracy in general. Even so, the basic facts of poverty and deprivation for the masses of the people confer upon the members of bureaucracy privileges unknown to the unorganized masses, especially those of lower castes, outside the charmed circle of government bureaucracy. This is true of the military and the industrial bureaucracy. Officers of the army, navy and air force, engineers and managers, as well as secretaries and commissioners of the government are the top elite in terms of social prestige and power.

Some students of bureaucracy point out a slight reverse trend insofar as the development bureaucracy is closer to the grassroots in their social formation as well as functions. As Pai Panandikar and Kshirsagar point out:

An important finding of the study is that the development bureaucracy in India is not dominated by the upper and upper-middle economic classes of the society, which is the general pattern in many bureaucracies in both developed and developing countries. To that extent again the "representative" character of the development bureaucracy in India seems greater.[27]

It is true that the officials in new departments of planning and development such as community development and Panchayatiraj, extension, education and family planning, are recruited from poorer and rural backgrounds and their lifestyle is not very different from ordinary employed people. However, in terms of real power in the administration, they form a negligible number, and the overall government bureaucracy is still highly elitist.

8. Political Development, Modernization and Political Culture

Whatever the controversy about the meaning and significance of modernization, one can hardly dispute the view that 'the work of modernization is the burden of our age'.[1] This is especially true of the developing countries that acquired independence from Western imperialism after World War II. The third world remained technologically backward and politically dependent and therefore, economically exploited and indigent. The urge for social reform and economic growth was part of the movement for political freedom. The aspiration for national dignity and development as well as independence found a practical basis for the academic concern with modernization and political development.

Modernization

The classical model of modernization in history is provided by the transformation of a feudal Europe into an industrial society. This change was momentous and gigantic, and the cumulative result of a series of events some of which were unique to European history. In trying to understand modernization, it is important to know the long process of change in Western Europe, and to appreciate both what was unique to it and what was potentially universal in the transformation of feudal Europe into a modern industrial community of nations.

European feudalism had certain distinct characteristics. Its economy was predominantly agricultural and rural; its small industrial sector was based on handicrafts; and it was characterized, generally speaking, by self-sufficiency for the bulk of the people. There was little commercial exchange, and most exchange was based on barter. Socially, feudalism was characterized by ascriptive stratification in which the most conspicuous and distinguishing class was that of landed aristocracy which acted as an intermediary between the vast peasantry and the monarch.

Members of the landed aristocracy provided leaders for the society, the army and the Church. The peasants were, for the great part, serfs attached to the knights and barons. They also served as workers and soldiers. Culturally, the Church was very influential and the whole ethos was non-secular. There was extremely limited social or physical mobility. Science was pre-Copernicus, i.e. the earth was believed to be the centre of the universe, and technology was pre-industrial. Politically, the king or emperor was dependent on the lords who wielded real power over their own realms, and the Pope of the Catholic Church was the chief overlord of Christendom. There was no concept of nationalism, democracy or citizenship based on individual rights. It was a traditional society based on hierarchy and heredity, chivalry and loyalty, small groups and face-to-face primary relationships. An individual was an intimate member of his village, guild or group. Thus the society was a diffuse one of cohesive communities. It was, in other words, what Tonnies calls a 'gemeinschaft' society.

A number of events occurred to transform European feudalism. The Italian Renaissance first raised its voice against the constraints and inefficiency of the feudal institutions of the Church and the monarchy. The Renaissance emphasized secular values in politics as well as in other walks of life. There was an assertion of freedom in trade, literature and in morals. The next event was the Reformation led by Martin Luther, the founder of Protestantism. The Reformation led to the establishment of the national Church in Germany, England and Indonesia. The secular attack against the Church was reinforced by the Enlightenment of the eighteenth century, that denounced religious obscurantism and advocated the values of reason, happiness and unlimited progress for mankind. Along with these changes in the cultural field, giant strides were being taken in scientific knowledge and technological inventions.

The new machines laid the foundations for the industrial revolutions that ushered in rapid urbanization as well as industrialization.

In the political field, nationalism had already paved the way for strong national governments. In Western Europe there was a long and bitter, sometimes even bloody, conflict, between the monarchy and aristocracy on the one hand, and the emerging middle class, the pioneers of free enterprise and the champions of a liberal society, economy and polity on the other. The struggle for the supremacy of Parliament in England during the nineteenth century, and the bloody revolution in France, were manifestations of the protest against restrictive, feudal institutions of monarchy and aristocracy.

Thus by the end of the eighteenth century, Western Europe was rid of most of its feudal characteristics. Industrial urbanization had come to stay. People were more mobile, even though initially somewhat insecure. Governments were beginning to be more popular and even representative, even if not fully responsible; political parties, and later trade unions, emerged as important institutions. Life became more secular, and even egalitarian.

Another model of modernization is the case of Soviet Russia. The communist revolution of 1917 changed an economically backward and very feudal Tsarist Russia into a state that deliberately and self-consciously launched a politically directed programme of economic and social change. The rapid economic growth of Soviet Russia within a span of three decades could not fail to impress the new nations of the third world. They were especially impressed by the advantage of a government directed development programme for a better distribution of the fruits of economic development. Thus socialism was seen as a way of bringing about both rapid economic growth and social justice.

The choice before the developing countries was however not an easy one. The Soviet model appealed to the third world's sense of urgency and desperation, but raised doubts about the high cost of political mobilization needed for such a totalitarian programme of economic development. On the other hand, the Western model was bound to be a slow process of change, and the simultaneity of challenges facing the developing countries could not brook much delay. The practical difficulties of the two options allowed for experimentation in optimizing the two basic values of freedom and discipline in the process of achieving modernity. It was clear that forms of civil or political liberties were not enough, and that socioeconomic conditions must be altered so as to sustain freedom. Hence, the importance of a socialist content of democratic freedom that offers choice as regards one's rulers, and also the opportunity to demand accountability from those rulers. Discipline was on the other hand necessary to facilitate concerted and cohesive action to achieve the national goals of ecônomic growth and social justice.

Eisenstadt[2] in his book *Modernization, Protest and Change*, sums up the characteristics of modernization as follows: 1. Social Mobilization: Karl Deutsch uses this term to refer to the socio-demographic aspects of modernization. He describes the process by which major clusters of social, economic and psychological commitments are eroded and broken, and people become available for new patterns of socialism and behaviour. The indices of social mobilization are: (*a*) exposure to aspects of modern life such as machinery and mass media; (*b*) change of residence, urbanization; (*c*) change from agricultural occupations; and (*d*) literacy and the growth of per capita income. 2. Social Differentiation: This characteristic implies the specialization of institutional structures and recruitment based on universal achievement criteria and separatism between the different roles held by an individual and the disposal of rules. 3. Economic Change: The change is with reference to technology and development of secondary and tertiary occupations, and mass consumption. 4. Political Change: This aspect is inclusive of the following: (*a*) the extension of the territorial scope and the intensification of the power of the centre; (*b*) the continued spread of potential power to wider groups; (*c*) populistic and democratic politics and participation; (*d*) fluidity of political support; (*e*) interest oriented politics; and (*f*) political institutions such as political parties and pressure groups.

Eisenstadt points out that 'a very important aspect of the system of stratification in modernization has been the growing disorientation between elite and broad status groups and among the elite themselves. In his book *The Dynamics of Modernization*, C.E. Black[2] attempts to explain the spread of modernization in different countries, and comes to the conclusion that the central problem in political modernization is the process by which a society makes the transition from a political leadership wedded to the traditional system, to one that favours throughgoing modernization. Black identifies four critical problems that all modernizing societies must face. These are: (*a*) a challenge to modernity; (*b*) the consolidation of modernizing leadership; (*c*) economic and social transformation; and (*d*) integration of society.

Barrington Moore[4] attempts to formulate a theory of history pertaining to modernization. Moore points out three basic patterns of modernization: (*a*) the capitalist democratic; (*b*) the communist; and (*c*) the fascist. Moore concentrates on the complex set of interactions among four critical sets of actors in pre-modern society, namely the landed upper classes, the peasantry, the urban bourgeoisie and the government bureaucracy. Moore defines the three patterns of modernization in terms of the social class that sponsors commercialization of agriculture. Thus the capitalist-democratic route either prevails on the bourgeoisie and converts the landed elite to capitalist methods of farming, or it destroys the economic power of the landed elite. The communist route occurs where in the absence of a modernizing urge among the landed elite or the urban bourgeoisie, the peasantry itself takes the initiative. In the fascist route, the landed upper class itself spurs the change before the urban bourgeoisie has a chance to establish its power. Moore also refers to a fourth situation, when the bourgeoisie is weak, the landed upper class sees no incentive to commercialize agriculture, and the peasant community lacks the cohesion necessary for effective political action. In this situation, the probability is high that modernization will simply not occur. This may be called a situation of stagnation.

Samuel Huntington is specially concerned with the prerequisites of political order in times of social change. Unlike other writers, it is to Huntington's credit that he focuses on the institutional dimension of modernization as the political factor of change. He first defines modernization, then argues that modernization may either lead to development or decay depending on whether institutions develop to bridge the gap between social mobilization and political participation.

As far as it can be understood in terms of its various aspects or dimensions one can do no better than quote Samuel Huntington[5] on this:

1. At the psychological level, modernization involves a fundamental shift in values, attitudes and expectations. Modern man accepts the possibility of change and believes in its desirability. (He has a) mobile personality that adjusts to changes in society; broadening of loyalties and identifications, and (he) follows universalistic criteria.

2. Demographically, modernization means changes in the patterns of life, a marked increase in health and life expectancy,

increased mobility and rapid growth of urban population.

3. At the intellectual level modernization involves the tremendous expansion of man's knowledge about his environment and the diffusion of this knowledge throughout this society through literacy, mass communication and education.

4. Socially, modernization tends to supplement the family and other primary groups having diffuse roles with consciously organized secondary associations having much more specific functions.

5. Economically, there is a diversification of activity, the level of occupational skills rises significantly; the ratio of capital to labour increases, subsistence agriculture gives way to market agriculture; and agriculture itself declines in significance compared to secondary and tertiary sectors.

These aspects of modernization most relevant to politics can be broadly grouped into two categories. First, social mobilization is the process by which "major clusters of old social, economic and psychological commitments are eroded and broken, and people become available for new patterns of socialization and behaviour". Secondly, economic development refers to the growth in the total economic activity and output of a society. Social mobilization involves changes in the aspirations of individuals, groups and societies; economic development involves changes in their capabilities, modernization requires both.

Political Development

Political development is often erroneously thought of as a synonym, or at least as an aspect of, modernization. Indeed some writers describing modernization include items of political development as dimensions of modernization. This error is made especially by those who interpret modernization as merely westernization. Such writers make an inventory of all the changes in the modernization of Western Europe and inevitably equate political change of the Western type with political development. An example is Eisenstadt's[6] list of the basic characteristics of modernization: social mobilization; social differentiation; economic change; political change; accountability and democracy; secularization and enlightenment. These are obviously the characteristics of modernization in the West, or characteristics of westernization. About political change, Eisenstadt says that

> In the political sphere modernization has been characterized, first, by the growing extension of the territorial scope, and specially by the intensification of the power of the central, legal, administrative and political agencies of the society.[7]

Eisenstadt further says that 'modern societies are in some sense democratic or at least populistic societies'.

Another approach to the question of political development is found in the analysis of *Alternative Courses of Political Development* by Edward Shils.[8] Shils outlines a model where the criteria of political development are based on the Western value system, but he also offers a typology of political systems that accommodate the non-Western types. These criteria lie in Shils' conception of political development as 'the model regime of civilian rule through representative institutions in the matrix of public liberties'. Shils offers five types of political systems as indicating different courses of political development.

1. Political Democracy, which is characterized by (*a*) the stability, coherence and effectiveness of the ruling elite; (*b*) the practice and acceptance of opposition; (*c*) adequate machinery of authority for the protection of the constitutional order; (*d*) the institutions of public opinion; and (*e*) the civil order, which based on civility, would embrace a sense of nationality, interest in public affairs, legitimacy of the political order, a sense of dignity and of obligations, and a consensus regarding values, institutions and practices.

2. Tutelary Democracy, the traits of which are (*a*) a stronger and more authoritative executive than that in political democracy; (*b*) identity of the party with the government; (*c*) discipline through the influence of personality; (*d*) a diminishing of the powers of the opposition; and (*e*) that the rule of law, however, continues.

3. Modernizing Oligarchy, implying (*a*) an urge to modernity and to unity; (*b*) apprehensions regarding the overwhelming power of traditional elements; (*c*) a higher concentration of authority; (*d*) an organized ruling elite and an elaborate bureaucracy; and (*e*) the lack of an ideology in particular.

4. Totalitarian Oligarchy, constituting (*a*) an ideology as the state doctrine; (*b*) an organized small clique; (*c*) the absence of an opposition; and (*d*) total government control.

5. Traditional Oligarchy, characterized by (*a*) a dynastic constitution and palace rule; (*b*) kinship and a personal choice of advisors;

and (*c*) traditional beliefs and institutions.

Another typology of political change is provided by David Apter, who examines political strategies and their relationship with and impact on, technological change and economic development. Apter refers to three types of states based on a particular political strategy, and calls them the mobilization system, the reconciliation system and the modernizing autocracy.

1. The mobilization system is characterized by (*a*) hierarchical authority; (*b*) total allegiance; (*c*) tactical flexibility; (*d*) militarism; and (*e*) ideological specialization.

2. The reconciliation system is characterized by (*a*) pyramidal authority; (*b*) multiple loyalties; (*c*) the necessity for compromise; (*d*) pluralism; and (*e*) ideological diffuseness.

3. Modernizing autocracy is characterized by (*a*) hierarchical authority; (*b*) exclusivism; (*c*) strategic flexibility; (*d*) unitarism; and (*e*) neo-traditionalism.

Apter analyzes each type with reference to the four process variables goals, costs, coercion and information. His conclusions, briefly, are that the mobilization system can be efficient but that its cost is high in terms of government control and coercion. The reconciliation system tailors its goals to public demands and relies on spontaneous growth, hence its cost of maintenance is low. The modernizing autocracy shares the goals and the costs of the mobilization system but relies on traditional support.

The typology of polity, in either Shils' or Apter's classification refers to different types and can be used to understand political development if the types are considered stages of growth. It is however doubtful if the notion of stages can be applied to these categories or even to the concept of political development in the same sense in which it is applicable to economic growth. These types, however, do offer various options that may be judged as indicators of development if they can be accepted as competent measures of political development.

A valiant effort has been made by Lucian Pye[10] to abstract the different meanings of political development which he sums up as follows.

1. Political development as the political prerequisites of economic development: This is of course too narrow a definition because the criterion of political development would be economic capability. This also means that the problem of political development

would vary according to the particular economic problems in question. There is, on the other hand, a need for independent criteria for political development.

2. Political development as typical of the politics of industrial societies: This is based on an assumption and is not warranted by the differences in the political culture of industrial societies.

3. Political development as political modernization: This is again invalid as it assumes that political modernization is part of the modernization process

4. Political development as the operations of nation states: This is also too sweeping, and it disregards the serious political differences across nations. This may be a necessary condition but cannot be a condition that ensures political development.

5. Political development as administrative, and legal development: This may be part of the concept of political development, but cannot be synonymous with the whole gamut of political development, which includes more than bureaucratic and administrative development.

6. Political development as mass mobilization and participation: This is also narrow and can be misleading in itself.

7. Political development as the building of democracy: But what is democracy?

8. Political development as stability and orderly change: Orderly change is important, but the question that arises is regarding the direction and degree of change.

9. Political development as mobilization of power: It is recognized that political systems should meet some test of performance and must therefore be capable of achieving some useful objectives. Thus the mobilization of power is necessary for the effective execution by a government of its functions.

10. Political development as one aspect of multi-dimensional process of social change: According to this point of view, all forms of development are related. Development is much the same as modernization, and it takes place within a historical context in which influences from outside the society infringe on the process of social change.

Pye, after reviewing these various concepts of political development, seeks 'to isolate these characteristics of political development which seem to be most widely held and most fundamental in the general thinking about problems of development'.[11] He then notes three characteristics—equality, capacity and differentiation.

Equality is implied in mass participation and popular involvement in political activities. Active citizenship calls for equality which also means universalism and achievement.

> Capacity is related to the outputs of a political system and the extent to which the political system can affect the rest of the society and economy. Capacity is also closely associated with governmental performance and the conditions that affect such performance.[12]

Differentiation and specialization of structures refers to the functional specificity of the various political roles within the system. Pye points out that,

> In recognizing these three dimensions of equality, capacity and differentiation as lying at the heart of the development process we do not mean to suggest that they necessarily fit easily together. On the contrary, historically the tendency has usually been that there are acute tensions between the demands for equality, the requirements for capacity and the processes of great differentiation.[13]

Indeed, the crucial test of political development may be the efficiency with which a system absorbs and manages tensions arising from such conflicting demands. Alfred Diament seems to capture the significance of this test when he defines political development as a process by which a political system acquires an increasing capacity to sustain successfully and continuously, new types of goals and demands and the creation of new types of organization.[14] This definition rightly emphasizes, political development as a process, and whatever characteristics may appear to be acceptable must refer to the viability of a political system in effectively responding to the tensions, challenges and demands of its own framework as well as the environment.

Illchman and Uphoff provide a thought provoking critique of the current approaches or theories of political development as well as political analysis. They maintain that

> Analysis based on systems or structures as functional models impose criteria for political action that are not necessarily those of the regime or of political actors. These analyses also fail to illuminate the costs and consequences of concrete short term

political activity. Many macro-analytical models require total knowledge of a system of make judgements about its parts. For the most part they threat government as a variable or as a function of the rest of the system.[15]

Similar problems are presented by other approaches, specially those that treat political and social phenomena as functions of stages or levels of development. Most familiar among them is the analysis of ideal types or of dichotomous characteristics of societies considered 'traditional' or 'modern'. By analyzing societies in terms of traits presumed characteristics of the extremes of conceptualized continua little can usefully be said about the political, social and economic relationships in societies that do not correspond to these ideal types or in societies that may deviate from the ideal type in differing respects and degrees.[16]

This critique is fully applicable to the theories or definitions of political development already mentioned. Illchman and Uphoff point out that

> What is needed is some way of assessing the comparative efficiency of policy alternatives and some means of formulating priorities. The statesman must make his choices under the discipline and penalties of the scarcity of resources. To further his policy objectives, he needs to know how much of what resources can best be used when. Each course of action involves political, social and/or economic costs. He must determine the relative benefit of each.[17]

The authors also very rightly point out that 'the kind of model needed to understand and meet the needs of developing countries must be able to transcend typological analysis'.[18] Also 'a model of politics should not impose a logic external to the system and its participants. It must operate within the assumptions of the polity it is analyzing'.[19]

Illchman and Uphoff offer a different analytical tool based on the concept of political economy. Central to the new political economy is the concept of the productivity of politics. These are five policy areas :

(*a*) choices to cope with social and economic change;
(*b*) choices to induce social and economic change;
(*c*) choices to remain in authority in the present;

(*d*) choices to remain in authority in the future; and
(*e*) choices to construct political and administrative infrastructure.

A sector refers to a group of persons who respond to political issues in a similar fashion. An ideology represents the sector's conception of good society. Propensities are the sector's procedural and resource preferences for political action. The model of political economy can help to suggest what constitutes political solvency.

Illchman and Uphoff make interesting observations on the concept of political development in their book *The Political Economy of Change*. They point out that the new approach of political economy permits a number of definitions of political development. Political development, for example, may be defined as:

(*a*) increasing levels of political solvency;
(*b*) increasing capacity to meet and induce changing and expanding demands;
(*c*) increasing capacity of both generating and processing demands; or
(*d*) increasing capacity to cover an increase in the number of political entrepreneurs.[20]

The authors maintain that political development is a function of the political and administrative infrastructure. Political infrastructure consists of political parties, elections, ideologies and development plans and is used in the mobilization of support and resources for acquiring and maintaining authority. Its primary function is to provide inputs for policy allocations. Administrative infrastructure, on the other hand, is necessary for the exercise of authority; it is responsible for the implementation of policy allocations, in other words, for handling regime outputs.

Modernization and Political Development

Following the conventional dichotomy between traditional and modern politics, Huntington mentions the three following elements of political development:

(*a*) the rationalization of authority; the replacement of a large number of traditional, religious, familial and ethnic political authorities by a single, secular, rational political authority.

(*b*) the differentiation of political functions, and the development of specialized structures to perform these functions; and
(*c*) increased political participation by social groups throughout society.

Amidst the proliferation of concepts and their meanings, Huntington very shrewdly points out that 'a basic distinction exists between political modernization defined as a movement from a traditional to a modern polity and political modernization defined as the political aspects and political effects of social, economic and cultural modernization'.[21] Huntington adds that as a movement, political modernization points the direction in which political change should move theoretically, but as aspects and effects of general modernization, in practice it always involves the disintegration of the traditional political system, and is not necessarily a significant movement towards a modern political system. Indeed the problem is that the rates of social mobilization and the expansion of political participation are high, while the rates of political organization and institutionalization are low. The result is political instability and disorder. The primary problem of political development, therefore, is the lag in the development of political institutions behind social and economic change.

Modernization with its social change and disintegration leads to the proliferation of new social forces and increasing demands for their participation in the political process. The multiplication and diversification of social forces is the heart of the structural aspect of modernization, and there is need for political organization to maintain order, resolve conflicts, select leaders, and maintain a sense of community among the competing social forces. The degree of 'community' in a complex society depends on the strength and scope of its political institutions. Huntington goes on to point out that historically, political institutions have emerged out of interaction and disagreement among social forces, and the gradual development of procedure and organizational devices for resolving these disagreements.

Huntington's famous 'gap hypothesis' states that social mobilization breaks the cognitive and attitudinal barriers of the traditional culture and promotes new levels of aspirations. The ability to satisfy these aspirations increases much more slowly than the aspirations themselves. Hence a gap develops between aspirations and expectations. Huntington points out that economic development lags behinds social mobilization, resulting in social frustrations. Social frustrations and political participation outpace opportunities for social and economic mobility and adaptive political institutions. The result is that 'the absence of mobility opportunities and low level of political institutionalization in most developing countries produce a correlation between social frustration and political instability'.[22] Huntington concludes that 'modernization and social mobilization, in particular, tend to produce political decay unless steps are taken to moderate or to restrict its impact on political consciousness and political invaluement'. Thus modernization leads to expansion of political participation, but it is the degree of institutionalization in relation to participation that determines whether the outcome is political development or decay.

The crux of political development lies in the process of 'institutionalization', that must be developed to match the increasing demands of political participation. Where political institutions are deficient or non-existent, modernization and social mobilization in particular tend to produce political decay, that is disorder and violence. Thus a state may be modern and yet not politically developed. Huntington cities the reverse example of India as politically developed with modern political institutions while still very backward in terms of modernization.

Huntington's distinction between modernization and political development helps to clarify the implications of the two processes. It also focuses on the importance of an autonomous process of political development. Not only is political development autonomous, but underlying even the process of modernization there are political as well as technical factors. The fault of the modernization theory is not merely that it makes political development dependent upon economic and technological change, but also that it ignores the political dimension of such economic change. Studies and experiences of the third world experiment with development leave no doubt that economic change involves policy decisions that affect various sections of the people differently, and that the power structure and the political culture of a country account for the decision making infrastructures and policy outputs. The obstacles to change and growth arise not so much from the conditions themselves but from want of effective political mobilization needed to achieve or promote social change and economic growth. These conditions of backwardness are after all there, and if the removal of these conditions (i.e. modernization) were a prerequisite to development. no political development could take place.

Rajni Kothari concludes that 'for a realistic theory of statebuilding it is necessary to divorce it from the theory of modernization, as conceived so far, and to admit in its framework the primacy of politics in social development'.[23]

Kothari goes on to point out that 'it is by an adequate theoretical approach to problems of statecraft and nationbuilding in the context of world politics of the late twentieth century that this lost perspective of politics and its creative role can be restored. This is a task that remains to be performed'.[24] Kothari argues in favour of a theoretical model that should not only be explanatory but which should provide a basis for action, and suggests the desirability of such a model being 'directly oriented to the specific political tasks of building viable states'. Elaborating on his own preference for the center-periphery model he says:

> There are two levels of theory involved in that model; first there is need for institutionalizing the state in terms of a national community, the establishment of a centre, its outward thrust of permeating the periphery, and its handling the issue of legitimacy through the processes of democratic participation, political conflict and intellectual dissent, and the response of the periphery to these processes by progressively mobilizing its own social structure and moving centreward through both struggle and coalition making.
>
> It provides a perspective in which the building of a political community is considered to be the more basic task, and the important micro problems of technical and economic choice are treated as derivatives of larger institutional and ideological choices.[25]

Kothari undoubtedly provides a forceful corrective to the generally apolitical approaches to the problem of political development. The political task is not only basic but also more difficult to carry out and most governments have found it easier to succumb to the temptation of achieving socioeconomic changes without building political institutions and processes necessary for viable and durable political regimes. It is necessary to recognize the primacy of politics; at the same time it would be realistic to examine the characteristics of a political system and its consequences for development.

The difficulty in Kothari's model is that it involves certain value commitments that may not be universally acceptable, and the governing elites may not be prepared to concede political rights, especially those of dissent and opposition. The practical task is therefore more difficult than the enthusiastic and optimistic formulations would imply. That however is the only model of humane as well as viable political development. The intellectual however is concerned with the model and meaning of things.

Political Culture and Political Development

A novel concept increasingly used nowadays, independently as well as in relation to political development, is the concept of political culture. Political culture has now acquired the status of a heuristic device as a tool of analysis. It has indeed become an important parameter for the analysis of political systems. An example is furnished by a text on *American Political Institutions in the 1970s* in which Part I is entitled 'American Political Culture'.[26]

The way in which this concept has been used shows that it is, an offshoot as it were, of behaviouralism and functionalism, especially of political socialization. Behaviouralism in general and socialization in particular, refer to the attitudes, beliefs and values prevalent in a political system. As Gabriel Almond and Sidney Verba, authors of the most celebrated study of political culture, maintain, culture refers to 'psychological orientation toward social objects, cognitive, affective and evaluational orientations'.[27] With specific reference to political culture, they say that 'the term political culture refers to the specifically political orientations—attitudes towards the political system and its various parts and attitudes towards the role of the self in the system'.[28] Thus 'political culture' refers to the values and norms concerning political life, and the beliefs people entertain about political legitimacy. Such values, norms and beliefs are reflected in people's attitudes and orientations towards political action, institutions and processes.

As Dowse and Hughes point out,

> The focus of political culture studies is less on the formal and informal structure of politics, governments, parties, pressure groups and so on, or on the actual pattern of political behaviour

> observed within a society, but rather on what people believe about these structures and behaviours. It is these beliefs that give the behaviours of men meaning for them and others. These beliefs can be of several kinds, such as cognitive beliefs about what the state of political life is, or they can be values concerning the desirable ends of political life, or attitudes towards some perceived state of the system.[29]

In their book, Almond and Verba deal with political culture as it is found in five different nations—the USA, Britain, West Germany, Italy and Mexico. They identify the people's orientations towards the political life as basically falling into three categories—allegiance, apathy and alienation. Allegiance refers to a positive attitude while apathy shows indifference, and alienation is negative. There is also another dimension employed to measure political culture, and on this dimension we have citizen, subject and parochial political culture. The citizen culture is based on participation, especially in the input functions; the subject culture is aware of the political system but more as an object of the state activities, and the parochial is confined to the local and intimate world of his own family or group, hardly identifying himself with the larger political system.

On the basis of these ideas, Almond and Verba put forward their concept of the civic culture. According to them, 'the civic culture is an allegiant participant culture. The civic culture is a participant political culture in which the political culture and political structure are congruent'.[30] They are however careful to point out that

> In the civic culture participant political orientations combine with and do not replace subject and parochial political orientations. Individuals become participants in the political process but they do not give up their orientations as subjects nor as parochials. Furthermore, not only are these earlier orientations maintained, alongside the participant political orientations, but the subject and parochial orientations are congruent with the participant political orientations.[31]

It is in this sense that the authors assert that 'the civic culture is not a modern culture, but a mixed modernizing traditional one'.[32]

In the bourgeoning literature on modernization and political development, the concept of civic culture as comprising citizen participation, subject beneficiary and parochial roots, is a wholesome one that does away with dichotomous thinking in terms of traditional-modern or any other pure type of culture. Thus civic culture is a syndrome of orientations regarding participation, distribution, and identity, as they cohere together to produce a culture that is congruent with political institutions and performance. In this sense it may be said that the aim of political development is to attain civic culture.

Two very pertinent and momentous questions arise however in connection with the substance of civic culture. The way Almond and Verba, and others following them, have defined civic or political culture, gives the impression that culture is nothing but a set of orientations and attitudes. Culture however is more than, and different from, psychology. Culture is a way of life and refers to the norms and practices that include but transcend individual dispositions. It could be argued that civic culture as defined by Almond and Verba may be treated as an ideal type, and therefore as merely a model to judge the actual political cultures. This would be a fair answer but for the fact that the wholly psychological orientation in the definition of civic or political culture builds into the concept a fundamental limitation and distortion. The distortion smacks of the much discussed ethnocentrism of the Western model pedlars, and seeks to impose an arbitrary and irrelevant model on the non-Western world.

The second question arises with regard to certain trends in the process of modernization followed in most of the third world countries. Attention has been drawn to the fact that a new middle class of bureaucrats, professionals and managers as well as political leaders, has become an elite that seeks the promotion of modernization which is lopsided, unbalanced and discriminatory against the masses of the people. Thus imbalances in development and modernization have aggravated inequalities and created new tensions in the developing countries. This trend has been very ably underlined by Rajni Kothari in the following words:

> Imperceptibly, the class which started as the vanguard of national awakening and reconstruction becomes an exclusive elite, commanding the nerve centres of decision making, enjoying special rights and privileges, and utilizing these for self-aggrandizement and self-perpetuation. It appropriates the nation's resources for maintaining a life style or a pattern of consumption which is the distinguishing feature of all ruling classes at all times in societies characterized by massive inequality and underdevelopment of

> human resources alongside the overdevelopment of the non-human sources of wealth and power.[33]

It is important to note that there is a global discussion of this emergence of an exclusive elite of modernizers. The first world and even the second world set the fashion in intellectual orientations and standard of life; they do help to create a culture of snobbery, and through demonstration tend to create an international fraternity of experts, consultants, advisors and administrators. The myriad international agencies also reinforce this trend and one country's professional becomes another country's saviour, as an international consultant. These have created in many third world countries a state of dependence on the advanced industrial societies and international agencies. The phenomenon has been noted and an alarm raised, particularly against its manifestation as an expression of neocolonialism or imperialism, and the continuing domination of the Western powers over the third world countries. The problem however is of wider dimensions, and it touches the pacesetters of modernization in the West, the East and the North against the poor South. This poverty is not merely economic or technological, but at heart political and cultural. To quote Kothari again,

> For, it is neither the world bourgeoisie nor the world proletariat, but instead, a world middle class which, strictly speaking, cuts across both the relations of production, and the ideological divisions of capitalism and socialism, and which in effect undermines the autonomy of all but a handful of nation states. The Indian middle class elite draws considerable sustenance from its affiliation to the worldwide class. Its alienation from its own people is to no small extent a direct consequence of its links with similar elites elsewhere and its emulation of the techno-economic structure and style of living and thinking of the dominant Western centres (whose dominance is not merely political and economic but, more deeply, cultural).[34]

It is the cultural as well as economic and political subservience to the alien forces that is at the root of the widening gulf between the modernizing elite and the masses of poor people. This gulf is not merely a cultural lag between the elite and the mass, but also an alienation that makes the elite insensitive to the needs and aspirations of the people. Indeed this elite becomes so committed to concepts and methods of modernization that is it unable to appreciate and attend to the real problems of identity, participation and distribution. The elite itself is in danger of fast losing its identity. It favours and follows methods of modernization that hinder popular participation, and neglect the economic interests of the poor.

The above highlights the basic need and importance of indigenous roots for political culture and political development. These indigenous roots must be built around the three dimensions of political development, namely, identity, participation and distribution. The heart of the political culture of modernization is in wholesome development where the elite and the mass share and participate in the building up of a culture of civility and a structure of institutions, that help to solve socio economic problems, and also promote the autonomy of individuals and groups. This is a culture of popular participation and institution building for the sake of solving problems.

9. Political Participation and Electoral Process

Since the publication of Merriam and Gosnell's *Non-voting in 1924*,[1] and the series on citizenship edited by Merriam in the late twenties and early thirties,[2] considerable work has been done on popular participation and non-participation in politics. By now we have considerable literature dealing with how, when, and why, people participate in social and political activities.

Political participation is the involvement of groups and individuals at various levels in the political system. Involvement expresses itself in various kinds of overt or manifest political activities. Nie and Verba's definition includes in the orbit of political participation 'those legal activities by private citizens which are more or less directly aimed at influencing the selection of governmental personnel and/or the actions they take'.[3] Huntington and Nelson's definition refers to political participation 'simply as activity by private citizens designed to influence governmental decision making'.[4] However, behind these apparently simple definitions, there are several issues worthy of serious consideration.

Political participation refers to activity that is designed to affect governmental decision making and actions. In other words, students of political participation are interested in learning about popular attempts to influence 'the authoritative allocations of values' for a society. But such attempts may not always take place through the formal decisions of the government. Much of the distribution of resources among groups in society takes place without interference by the government. Does political participation refer to such activities? According to the notional definition of political participation, a strike designed to influence the management of a private company to increase wages is not political participation because it is not designed to affect governmental decision making. Only when a strike is designed to influence the government, say for example to increase the ceilings on wages, it is political participation. Thus it would appear that the extent of political participation is in some measure a function of the scope of governmental activity.[5]

Another issue is whether we include within the meaning of the term 'political participation' psychological processes leading to it or only the act as such. Some studies of political participation included in their area of inquiry attitudes or orientations towards participation in addition to the actual political behaviour. Almond and Verba devoted particular attention to psychological or subjective components of political participation.[6] Berelson, Lazarsfeld and McPhee in *Voting* used interest in politics as the sole means of measuring participation beyond the vote.[7] This school treats the process of political participation as the continuation of an earlier process, that of political socialization. Political socialization refers to the process by which an individual becomes acquainted with the political system, which determines his perceptions of politics and his reactions to political phenomena. Political participation on the other hand refers as a process to that phase of citizen behaviour when they become actually involved (in varying degrees) in the political system. Rush and Althoff argue that the process of political socialization provides the individual with a perceptual screen through which he receives political stimuli; as a result of these stimuli, individuals involve themselves at various levels in the political system, in the process of political participation.[8]

But the more recent writings on political participation emphasize the latter aspect only. Huntington and Nelson argue:

> Knowledge about politics, interest in politics, feelings of political competence and efficacy, perceptions of the relevance of politics, all these may often be closely related to political action, but at other times they are not. Their study and measurement also require techniques that differ significantly from those needed to study behavior alone.[9]

Therefore, they treat objective political activity and subjective political attitudes as separate variables. Nie and Verba also argue that psychological orientations or attitudes toward participation—one's sense of efficacy or one's civic norms—may be important only as sources of participation,[10] and should not be confused with political participation per se. Thus the recent tendency appears to be to treat only the actual behaviour of citizens in attempting to influence the government through political participation.

From the point of view of forms of participation, there has been a gradual extension of the scope of the term 'political participation'. The earlier concept was quite narrow, with studies usually referring to citizen participation in the electoral process through voting, campaigning and other partisan activities such as discussing politics, convincing another person to vote a particular way, distributing party literature, attending political meetings, contributing money to campaigns and so on. The concept was later broadened to include activities in the period between elections also, when citizens try to influence government decisions. By now the concept of political participation has been widened enough to include a variety of ways in which citizens participate in relation to varied issues. D.R. Matthews and J.W. Protho define political participation as 'all behaviour through which people directly express their political opinions'.[11] Nevertheless it is useful to address ourselves to the question of which forms of political participation we should study. Voting and campaigning are without doubt the most overt and widely studied forms of political participation, which we have treated extensively in an independent section. But many other forms of political participation, largely neglected, need to be explored and studied.

On the basis of the degree or extent of participation, political activities have been arranged hierarchically by Rush and Althoff as the following:[12]

(*i*) holding political or administrative office;
(*ii*) seeking political or administrative office;
(*iii*) active membership in a political organization;
(*iv*) passive membership in a political organization;
(*v*) active membership of a quasi-political organization (interest or pressure group);
(*vi*) passive membership of a quasi-political organization;
(*vii*) participation in public meetings, demonstrations and so on;
(*viii*) participation in informal political discussion;
(*ix*) general interest in politics;
(*x*) voting; and

(*xi*) apathy.

This arrangement disregards a conceptual distinction which Nie and Verba as well as Huntington and Nelson emphasize.[13] They distinguish between professional participation and non professional participation. A political professional is one whose primary calling is politics or government. Holders of political or administrative office, that is party and governmental officials, or even activists such as political candidates and professional lobbyists, are political professionals and they are involved, as a matter of a routine job, in the act of political participation. They exclude their activities from their study and argue that non professional political participation is the true form of political participation. Non professional participation in political activity is intermittent, part time, and usually avocational or secondary to other social roles that the participant simultaneously plays. Only the latter kind of political participation needs to be studied as political participation proper; office holding stands on a different footing and may be studied separately with different perspectives than those required for studying the other kind.

Woodward and Roper suggest that five ways of behaving, taken together, constitute an operational definition of the term political activity.[14] In addition to voting at the polls, they include within their range supporting pressure groups through membership; participation in political party activity and a subsequent claim on legislators; engaging in habitual dissemination of political opinions through word of mouth communications to other citizens and direct personal communication with legislators. Woodward and Roper also do not appear to have made the distinction emphasized by Nie and Verba as well as Huntington and Nelson with regard to professional and non professional participation. Also, their categories are not neat. The distinction between holding an office and performing a function confuses rather than enlightens. A member of a pressure group or political party, like other citizens, indulges in both horizontal and vertical communication to fellow citizens or governmental functionaries. The difference may be of intensity of outcome or effect, but they are not exclusive categories as forms of political participation. Communication is, of course, a very pertinent area of political participation and deserves study in its own right.

Communication through contact is a necessary channel for political participation, since influencing government, that is legislators and officials, is its function. This contact may involve two levels of communication between citizens and citizens (horizontal) and between citizens and government officials (vertical). Citizens through groups and organizations indulge in some kind of cooperative endeavour to deal with social and political problems of common concern.[15] But it must be pointed out here that citizens contact government officials or legislators mainly for personal benefits.[16] In India particularly, the role of 'intermediaries' or 'contact men' for the granting of both legal or illegal benefits, or out-of-turn concessions to individuals, has been most marked. This kind of particularized contacts,[17] in which legislators and political activists generally act as the middle men between decision makers (bureaucrats or political executives) and citizens (the beneficiaries or seekers of favour), deserves to be studied in depth for that is indeed how the contact process operates in between elections, and becomes an issue of individual voting; and in some cases, results in the mobilization of votes by influential persons in favour of or against a particular candidate.

To the list of political participation activities, two recent important though somewhat controversial additions have been made. In 'ceremonial' or support participation, citizens participate by expressing support for the government through parades, developmental projects, and involvement in government-organized youth groups. Political mobilization of citizens in 'supportive' demonstrations are common in the developing societies of the world, and are not uncommon in the developed ones as well.

'Protest' participation, that is political participation through demonstrations or marches, have also assumed significance in recent times. Such activities include riots, assassinations and other forms of civil violence through which citizens try to pressurize or intimidate the government. Nie and Verba consider 'protest' participation outside the orbit of their study because being 'illegal' activities, they regard the origin and impact of 'illegal activities' different from that of legal ones. They argue that efforts to influence governmental decision making may involve persuading or pressurizing existing authorities to act (or refrain from acting) in certain ways.[18] But political participation may also be aimed at changing directions by current authorities, toward replacing or retaining those authorities, or toward changing or defending the existing organization of the political system and the rules of the political game. Sometimes such activities may be 'illegal' according to the established norms of the political system. ut they do not lose thereby their importance as a form of political participation, but on the contrary, tend to enhance it. Thus all activities, whether legal or illegal, constitute political participation if they are made with the end elaborated above. However, 'professional revolutionaries', that is individuals engaged full time in illegal efforts to remove the government belong to a separate category. Huntington and Nelson also regard them as outside the domain of political participation.[19] But one more distinction should be stressed here, namely that we should not be unduly influenced by whether a particular movement succeeds in achieving the end or not. Often 'illegal' activities gain legitimacy after the end has been achieved, because the regime which consequently comes into power sees these activities as not only legitimate, but honourable. But conceptually, we should consider legal and illegal activities on par, regardless of the question of whether the activities lead to the desired consequences or not. After all political participation only aims at influencing the exercise of political power; it is not to be confused with its actual exercise.

Social scientists have recently shown interest in the analysis of certain forms of political participation which actually represent the 'vanishing point' of various forms of political participation. Such forms include apathy and anomie. Some people become apathetic, that is they have no political interest, and do not indulge in political activity. In other words, apathetic individuals lack the sense of political efficacy which is supposed to induce political participation in most cases. This sense of political efficacy has been studied and measured by the authors of *The Voter Decides*.[20] They define a sense of political efficacy as the belief that individual political action does have or can have an impact upon the political process. It is worthwhile then to perform one's civic duties, because political and social change seems possible. The individual citizen is also seen as playing a part in bringing about this change. On the other hand, those who feel otherwise lack a sense of political efficacy and may be non participators. For instance some are uncertain regarding the possible effects of their individual political activity, and are hence not enthusiastic about their political participation.

Apathy may grow both out of a feeling of satisfaction, or out of that of helplessness. Some people feel contented with the social and political system, have faith in their representatives, and see no need for change. Their content tends to be linked with a confidence in the basic stability of their society. But there are other people who feel helpless. Though they favour change they feel that there are no real differences among the major contending parties. The outcome of elections lacks significance for them. But some people do not participate actively also because of the uncertainty of their political conviction. To them politics is confused, complicated and contradictory, and political communication is mere propaganda. Personal reasons may also account for apathy. Some individuals may be too exhausted by the pressure of other activities to pay much attention to it. Certain women feel that political activity is not in keeping with their social role expectation. Some people's reluctance to think about political matters ranges from a certain degree of mental laziness to a phobia toward serious thought. Whatever be the cause or causes, political apathy remains a crucial problem. The necessity of reconciling apathy and democracy, supposedly based on the participation of the people, is an important issue to be dealt with.

Another pathological phenomenon is 'anomie' which refers to a sense of rootlessness, loss of values and lack of direction among individuals. Ever since Durkheim identified the problem of social disintegration and the lack of international and external regulation on an individual, and gave it the term anomie,[21] the concept has captured the imagination of social scientists. Riesman makes the term 'anomic' synonomous with 'maladjusted'.[22] In any case, anomie inhibits political participation because as in the case of apathy it implies a feeling of ineffectiveness, or a feeling that authorities do not care about the person concerned. But the more serious implication is that it involves devaluation of norms and goals. Social disintegration operates more intensely upon a man's values, and as Mayo suggests, this accounts for much of the political phenomena of our time.[23] It may, indeed, be true', observes Robert Lane, that 'the phenomena Durkheim observed have heightened relevance for contemporary society, for the present concentration of all attention and social evaluation upon economic success tends to denigrade other values and leave the intensely competing individual stripped of his culture'.[24] Its effect is intensely felt in the political arena in the shape of abandonment of political ideals and general interests for enjoyment of mundane pleasures and powers on the part of power seeking individuals. The anomic individual, as a reaction, is not only apathetic, but also tends to be politically deviant.

Erich Fromm suggests that anomic individuals may attempt to reintegrate with society, ideologically and socially, through some totalitarian movement.[25] Apparently this was so in Germany in the 1930's, and it has been suggested that immigrant groups in the USA have been more susceptible to communism than the native groups, because American culture has been transmitted to the immigrant in a weak and diluted fashion. We can thus say that among those who for one reason or the other, do not feel integrated with the prevalent social and cultural norms and patterns of a society, some respond with apathy, others with alienation and still others with extremist activities and violence. With violence, the latter derive the vicarious pleasure of avenging themselves upon a society with which they are disgusted and disgruntled. The crucial question is : how far are apathy and anomie pathological in a democracy? While anomic behaviour involving violence and corruption are generally recognized as injurious to any established government, some people see apathy as functional for even a democratic government. The issue of mobilized versus autonomous participation is an important one. Many of the people who vote, demonstrate or take part in such action are mobilized by other actors through coercion, persuasion, or material inducements. This is referred to as mobilized participation as distinguished from autonomous participation, which is voluntary, and not sponsored, manipulated or directed by the government. Myron Weiner says that belonging to organizations or attending mass rallies under government orders for voting in elections where citizens have no choice are not voluntary political participation and therefore, not to be confused with political participation proper.[26] Their main argument is that it is often difficult to distinguish the two kinds of participation. The distinctions drawn between them are arbitrary, and their boundaries are indistinct. Virtually all political systems include a mix of mobilized and autonomous participation.

This point assumes further importance when we stress that political parties, other associations and the organized polity as represented by the state itself, seek to mobilize the nation or sectors of it. In some countries political participation is almost exclusively in the form of groups organized by the ruling apparatus. In that country's politics, the distinction between mobilized and autonomous participation is bound to be immaterial. On the other hand, in some countries, political participation is derived from the membership and functioning of such groups as voluntary associations, professional bodies and fraternal organizations. India stands somewhere between these two extremes, at least in so far as the predominant modes of political participation are concerned. The existence of regional elites, and more particularly, rural elites indeed tends at times to obliterate the thin line of demarcation between participation and mobilization. In any case, mobilized participation, as a significant sector, should not be ignored. The basic distinction between mobilized and autonomous participation, however, ought to be borne in mind in macroanalysis, where the central issue is the extent of democratic norms in a country.

Bases of Political Participation: Political participation, says Robert E. Lane, is a function of age, sex, education and status.[27] He also refers to its complex relation to race, religion and national origin. His conclusions are based on impressive data provided by various empirical studies about the political expression of the American public. In Asia and Africa, one tends to emphasize the role played by class and communal groups in shaping political participation. Indeed, in some societies, class and party identification closely correlate with each other; whereas in others, they cross-cut each other. On a generalized basis, one may say that in different societies, political participation is rooted in different group bases, though it is possible to identify the more common bases among them. Huntington and Nelson identify and define the following common bases of political participation.[28]

(*a*) class—individuals of similar social status, income and occupation;
(*b*) communal group—individuals of similar race, religion, language, or ethnicity;
(*c*) neighbourhood—individuals residing in geographical proximity to each other;
(*d*) party—individuals who identify with the same formal organization attempting to win over or maintain control of the executive and legislative branches of government; and
(*e*) faction—individuals united by sustained or intense personal interaction with each other, one manifestation of which is the patron-client grouping which involves the reciprocal exchange of benefits between individuals of unequal status, wealth, and influence.

Lane makes a monumental effort to identify several socio-psychological and sociological variables to explain various forms of political participation in the USA. The study is valuable in that it provides useful starting points for analyzing political participation of various kinds in other countries. We shall recapitulate some of his important hypotheses here. While dealing specifically with one mode of participation, that is the petitioning of government officials in person, Lane comments that this mode is related to the possession of social skills, the desire to be close to 'greatness', some knowledge (awareness) of political life and also class status.[29]

He elaborates that it is related to class status in the following ways: (1) Those of a lower socioeconomic status are more likely to contact only local officials, while those of a higher socioeconomic status may contact both local and national officials. (2) Those of a lower socioeconomic status require greater organization and effort for an audience with an official, or to secure an equivalent effect upon that official, than those of higher status. (3) Contacting national officials on foreign policy matters is a positively accelerated function of wealth and social position. Similarly, contacting officials through letter writing is related to (*a*) verbal skills and personal familiarity with written expression, (*b*) a capacity to crystallize the desire to unite into a decision to write, (*c*) upper occupational and educational status, (*d*) membership in a subcultural group with appropriate cultural norms (Jews),(*e*) clear-cut economic stakes in specific governmental decisions (businessmen), (*f*) membership in organizations with stakes in legislative policy.[30] Letter writing on policy issues is not associated with the official position in party organizations. Lane also claims that since mail is written at the behest of organized groups, there is a concentration of letters from a given specific 'sociological' area.

Joining associations generally follows the demographic pattern established for voting with the following exceptions: (1) Joining political clubs is not related to income and is more prevalent among Catholics than Jews. (2) Membership in informal associations of unspecified kinds is higher among blacks than among whites. (3) Women are almost as likely to join associations as men are.[31]

Exposure to political material (i.e. reading, viewing and listening to politics) generally increases with status (income, occupation, education). The leaders of society are the most exposed and are therefore, the most likely to be informed on general political developments. Awareness is generally greater in those with personality qualities which make for more effective, self confident social human beings.[32] Each medium has a characteristic audience and effectiveness. The newspaper has the wider coverage, and greater effectiveness in the middle and upper status than in other groups. Television has a wide coverage in the industrial societies of the West, but has very limited audience in the still traditional societies of the third world. Radio reaches both urban and rural regions, to a greater extent than does the press or television. Magazines are most effective with college educated groups in contrast to others, and have a persuasiveness based upon special interests shared with their readers.

About political discussion and conversation, Lane hypothesizes that it is consensual for the most part, because it takes place in homogeneous age, status and religious groups, though it is usually initiated by the lower status partner. Opinion leadership (giving a political orientation to people in personal contact) is related to (*a*) the opportunity to acquire special knowledge and influence, (*b*) role positions which make the leadership appropriate, including, (*c*) a slightly higher education and income within a social stratum, and (*d*) a greater personal interest and feelings of effectiveness.[33]

More recently, some studies associate political participation in general with 'development' or 'modernization' but no general consensus has emerged about the relationship between the two. Higher levels of socioeconomic development and of socioeconomic equality surely lead to higher levels of political participation and its reverse is also true. But Huntington and Nelson point out that while in the earlier phase of development, higher levels of socioeconomic development promote lower levels of socioeconomic equality; in the latter phases of development, higher levels of political participation tend to produce lower rates of economic growth.[34] In all, we can say that though socioeconomic development and participation do, in large measure, go together, the connection between them is more complex and ambiguous than it is often assumed to be. It also appears that there is a tendency to overemphasize the effects of social and economic factors of participation, comparatively ignoring the role of political elites and the policies of the government, which certainly have a significant role in shaping the participation patterns of a society. If we contrast the political participation pattern during the 19 month old emergency rule under Mrs. Indira Gandhi with the pattern soon after it, this point will become clearer. The political participation patterns differ in the countries of the Indian sub-continent more on account of the norms that the elite set, and that the government follow as a part of their political culture than on account of variations in socioeconomic development. This is, however, not a suggestion to ignore the role of socioeconomic development either. A political sociologist, as we have argued elsewhere, will have to look at the problem from an integrated point of view, not an isolated one.

Some studies link political participation with urbanization and argue that citizens in urban settings are likely to be more politically active. There are however, other studies which find little association between urbanization and political participation. Nie and Verba refer to the former as suggesting the 'mobilization' model and to the latter as suggesting the 'decline-of-community model'.[35] They find that conflicting data do not lead to any positive conclusion. The only possible generalization that ensues is that 'cooperative activity' among citizens declines rather drastically as communities become larger and lose their distinctiveness.[36]

Levels of Political Participation: In all societies some people participate in politics, but in some societies, more people participate in politics than in others. In any society, some people participate more than other people. Consider, for instance, the following figures on levels of political participation.[37]

(1) The percentage of the population which engages in one or more political acts beyond voting (1966-1969)

Number of Political Acts Beyond Voting

	1	2	3	4	5	6
United States	64%	40%	26%	16%	9%	5%
Japan	62	35	19	11	5	2
Nigeria	56	30	13	2	1(5+)	(-)
Austria	52	41	17	8	4	2
India	36	18	10	6	4	2

(2) The percentage of the population which is 'politically active', in that it discusses politics once a week or engages in more intense political activity (1959-1960)

United States	46%	Italy	27%
Great Britain	45%	Mexico	25%
Germany	40%		

This cross-national data on participation levels reveals that in many societies, other types of political activity above and beyond voting are also widely engaged in. In industrialized countries, 50% or more of the population participates in ways other than voting. Even in a developing country like India, more than one third

Percentages of Citizens Active in Various Ways in Seven Countries

	Austria	India	Japan	Netherlands	Nigeria	USA	Yogoslavia
Regular Voters	85	48	93	77	56	63	82
Campaign activity of the members of a party or political organization	28	5	4	13	Not	asked	15
					a	8	
Worked for a party	10	6	25	10	a	25	45
Attended a political rally	27	14	50	9	a	19	45
Active member in a community action organization	9	7	50	15	34	32	39
Worked with a local group in a community problem	3	18	15	16	35	30	22
Helped form a local group on a community problem	6	5	5	a	26	14	a
Contacted an official in the community on some social problem	5	4	11	6	2	13	11
Contacted an official outside the community on a problem	3	2	5	7	3	11	a
Particularized contacting—contacted a local official on a personal problem	15	12	7	38	2	6	20
Contacted an official outside the community on a personal problem	10	6	3	10	1799	6	a
Number of cases	1769	2637	2657	1746	1	2544	2995

of the population does more than vote. Citizens in India participate in politics at different levels of the party and governmental hierarchies. Quite a few choose to pressurize government from outside the formal political system, through interest based organizations or ad hoc groups which utilize techniques ranging from lobbying in Parliament to protest of both violent and non violent kinds. Though in most cases such protest cannot by its very nature attract mass participation, occasionally they may do so.[38]

Political activism, however, is not common. In every society, at least one third of the population engages in no political activity beyond voting, and in some countries such as the United States, over one third may not even bother to vote. Nie and Verba suggest that in most societies, and for most kinds of political activity, a person is more likely to be politically active if he is male, middle aged (rather than young or old), relatively wealthy, well educated and perhaps from the dominant ethnic, religious or racial groups.[39] Nie and Verba have drawn up an important table indicating percentages of citizens active in various ways in seven countries.[40]

Electoral Process

Electoral process highlights public issues through its various concomittants such as political participation and recruitment. Elections provide opportunities for the most overt forms of political participation and bring into sharp focus many latent factors to the fore. Charles Hickman Titus points out that because voting records are quantitative and show 'pragmatic recurrence of a situation', and because the large number of votes permit sound numerical summarizations, no other phenomenon seems to possess as many advantages for scientific analysis as does the electoral process.[41] The most important inspiration for electoral studies, however, has come along with the acquisition of an armoury of refined quantitative methods of statistical analysis by social scientists. Electoral studies have in the process of time distinguished themselves through a marked methodological sophistication. Empiricism suited the soil of elections most, because electoral studies are based on the assumption that a large number of people who repeatedly perform voting acts do so with similar motives.

Several studies form milestones in the field of election studies. *The People's Choice* (1944) by Lazarsfeld, Berelson and Gaudet revealed for the first time the utility and power of the interview survey as a tool of voting research. *Voting* (1954) by Berelson, Lazarsfeld and McPhee; *The Voter Decides* (1954) by Campbell, Gurin and Miller, and the most sophisticated study of all, *The American Voter* (1960) by Campbell, Converse and Stokes are among the other prominent studies. Efforts to study elections have been made in other European and Asian countries as well. By now it appears that a new sub-discipline, psephology, has emerged, focusing on the efforts of political scientists, sociologists, social anthropologists and psychologists, with statisticians and technical experts supplying the requisite help.

Psephology has been forging ahead in substantive as well as methodological directions. As Garceau points out, voting studies have not only illuminated regional or particular situations in place or time, and examined voting records to explain political tides or cycles, but have also accomplished much more.[42] Records of participation and the comparison of non-voting ratios have contributed to the understanding of the citizen's perception of political party, the scope and character of citizenship at various levels, of different responses of party organization in different communities, and finally, to gauging the voter's 'capacity to exercise power across the various ranges of political distance'. It has been possible to make correlations between voting preferences and business cycles, ethnic and religious factors, income strata, education and exposure, to mass media panels of respondents through an entire electoral campaign. The process culminating in the voting decisions has been fully traced; the forces contributing to the voting decision have been systematically weighed; and the voters' perception of the party, candidates and issues deeply probed. The undecided or independent voters have been analyzed from the point of view of their integration into, or isolation from, immediate social environment, and their mobility in the social stratification system. Indices have been devised for comparing the degree and effectiveness of party organization in terms of ratios of voting participation and split-ticket versus straight-ticket voting. Case narratives of political machines have highlighted the campaigning and other behind-the-scene techniques, whereby politicians make a meaningful impact upon voters. The linkage between the voter and the local political organization has been explored in depth.

Factors Affecting Electoral Choice: Indian psephologists have paid a great deal of attention to the identification of the factor or factors that affect electoral choice. But in doing so, they have unfortunately relied, for the most part, on sociological and socio-psychological variables. Political variables have not generally received due attention however. There is in this respect a surprising similarity between the studies in the West and our country; they point, in fact, to almost similar factors. The Columbia studies (*The People's Choice* and *Voting*) stressed social and environmental factors; the Michigan studies (*The Voter Decides* and *the American Voter*) stressed the psychological. Likewise the Indian studies also try to explain voting preference in terms of class, factions, kinship, religion, personality of the candidate, role of money and so on. As in the West, political variables such as party organization, party ideology and issues were emphasized subsequently. Voting choice is usually not the product of one factor. Trying to isolate the reasons behind voting either by correlating data on the social composition of the voters and the voting figures, or by tabulating their answers to questions asked through a questionnaire, may not tell us the whole truth. Indigenous and characteristic explanations for voting choice are therefore still to be identified. The categories outlined in Western models need not be unduly favoured.

The most indigeneous and crucial variable in the process of electoral choice in India has been the caste factor. Most studies identify this factor but differ in their assessment of the role that caste actually plays. On the one hand, it has been shown how informal leaders of various castes, or formal organizations of castes, commit support of their entire groups to particular candidates or political parties. It has been argued that inter-party competition, in fact, reflects caste-based cleavages, rather than differences in political identification and party loyalties of the electorate. The studies of the 1962 elections have given us some significant material based on observation and anthropological survey.[43] Rajni Kothari and Tarun Sheth in their paper entitled 'Extent and Limits of Community Voting: The Case of Baroda East' stressed the role of ethnic loyalties and political organization in voting behaviour, though they found that few communities voted as a block. V.M. Sirsikar in 'Party Loyalties versus Caste and Communal Polls: Poona Constituency' pointed out that voters were influenced by caste, and religious and party loyalties, though not by language. Rajni Kothari and Ghanshyam Shah in their study of Modasa Constituency pointed out that caste loyalties proved more important than party affiliations, both the voters and to those most active in politics. These studies, co-edited by Myron Weiner and

Rajni Kothari, are significant in the sense that they deal cogently with the way in which society and politics interact in India through their case studies of assembly and parliamentary constituencies in 1962.

Factors affecting electoral choice have, however, received more specific treatment in studies based on survey research. In his pioneer study of voting in the city of Pune, V.M. Sirsikar pointed out that even in the highly politically conscious constituency of Pune, more than 33% of the voters did not know anything about the political issues involved, and nearly 25% were ignorant of the candidates and the legislatures for which they were contesting.[44] He finds that other residual factors such as instructions of the family head, casteist influence, means of mass manipulation, majority fears and Nehru's charisma influenced the process of election.

Aloo J. Dastur in her study of parliamentary elections (1967) in Bombay (based on interviews of 603 voters in three constituencies taken in three waves) found that the Bombay voters had gained political consciousness and maturity through the passage of years.[45] A high percentage of women, the illiterate, the backward and the scheduled castes, even in rural area, had become conscious of their power to vote. A majority of women voted independently of men. The campaign was subdued, and voters were not easily impressed by propaganda. D.N. Pathak, in his study of Gujarat (based on 698 interviews of voters in three constituencies in two waves), points out that male, young, highly educated and higher caste voters made their voting decisions earlier, while females, old, less educated and lower caste voters delayed their voting decisions. The majority of voters was favourably inclined towards political parties, though only 5.7% of the voters were themselves members of any political party. Exposure to the campaign was quite high, newspapers being the major source of information, and election processions being the most popular and effective of campaign techniques, especially in rural areas. Multiple pressure was higher in urban than in rural areas. Candidate, party and multiple pressure were thus the three chief motivating factors for voting choice.

One important observation was that education tended to encourage non voting. Pathak found that a higher degree of exposure, a rising level of information, awareness and efficacy, a wide acceptance of the party system, and a ready reception of the electoral system, were some of the main features of the voter in Gujarat. B.R. Purohit in his report on Madhya Pradesh, (based on interviews of 983 voters of five booths in five constituencies), puts special emphasis on non voting. He finds that in the urban area, the percentage of non voters is 9.35%, in the rural area 27.50%, and in the rural reserved constituency, 16.00%. As for reasons for voting, Purohit finds that urban voters are guided by the merits of the candidate or by party considerations; whereas rural voters are guided by caste, religion and kinship factors. The impact of the campaign on voting behaviour is found to be negligible. B.S. Khanna and Satya Deva in their report on Punjab and Haryana, (based on interviews of 942 voters in two waves), indicate that the participation of voters in polling have been very large, but personal and religious considerations played an important role in the electoral decision of many voters, especially that of women and the illiterate.

S.P. Verma, Iqbal Narain and their associates probe voting intention in their study of Rajasthan, and correlate it with the voting act, particularly with a view to identifying the consistency pattern and the logic of voting behaviour.[46] The study examines the variations that SES (socioeconomic status) characteristics bring about in the patterns of voting intention and the voting act, and in the correlation between the two. Political information is broadly classified into six categories: (*a*) knowledge of the data of election; (*b*) knowledge of being a voter; (*c*) identification of party symbols and candidates; (*d*) knowledge about sitting MP and/or MLA; (*e*) familiarity with poll verdict; and (*f*) problems pertaining to the nation and the constituency, analyzed in tabular and statistical form. Similarly, the linkage and impact of both categories of communication media—mass media, (newspapers, radio, films, public meetings, posters, handbills and the like) and interpersonal media, (reference groups such as relations, friends, neighbours, party activists and campaigners, trade union workers, local, social and political leaders and candidates) on voting behaviour have been examined. Further, the study examines exposure to, and participation in, campaigning, voting preferences and their determinants. The study leads to the conclusion that the Rajasthan voter, in the wake of the fourth general election, appears reluctant, vacillating and even confused. His psyche is divided between candidate and party-orientation, and the shift, however limited, from the one to the other.[47] The voter has been making efforts to free himself from the bondage of tradition, though his progress in the direction of modernity has been a slow one. The study stresses that what motivates the electorate to become a voter is its sense of political efficacy. A weak sense of political efficacy and a poor image of the system's performance have according to them led to the alienation and apathy of voters.

V.M. Sirsikar in his book *Sovereigns without Crowns*, repeats a survey of the Pune parliamentary constituency, this time in the context of the 1967 elections.[48] He tests six general hypotheses about voting behaviour in that particular area, and wholly or partly confirms them. The hypotheses were:[49]

(1) Highly educated voters tend to vote for the opposition parties.
(2) Minority voters, linguistic or religious, tend to support Congress.
(3) The lower the level of education of the family, the higher the influences of the family head on the voting of other members of the family.
(4) Caste loyalties influence voting preferences.
(5) The occupation and income of voters do not influence their voting.
(6) The age of the voter has no association with his vote preference.

The comparative study of elite and mass electoral behaviour, and the use of value scales to probe the values of voters, are novelties of the study. The discussion of value orientations of elites and masses, ascertained with the help of certain scales, brings out the conclusion that the elite strata is more authoritarian than the common voter. Another conclusion of the study is that the voters are still dominated by regional and parochial considerations.

R.C. Prasad, has worked on the rather unusual theme of whether the repeated electoral experiences in the country have acted as instruments of political socialization. To measure this, he accepts electoral maturity as an indicator.[50] The concept of electoral maturity has been built around four dimensions—political awareness, political involvement, political judgement, and political adjustment. Several empirical measures have been employed to operationalize the various indices of maturity within each dimension. His conclusion is that conversation is the only source of political information in rural India, and whatever political maturity is due to conversation brings to light an important fact of rural life.

Local elections at the municipal or village level, and Panchayati Raj elections, have attracted the attention of scholars. The municipal elections held in October 1970 in Rajasthan form the subject matter of a full length study by C.P. Bhambhri and S.P. Verma.[51] While they had started with the hypothesis that heterogeneity, together with improvement in levels of communication, articulation, participation and modernization, would help the breakdown of traditional order, they found that primordial sentiments, the poor extent of participation (except in terms of voting) and persistence of candidate-orientation are the factors which point to the continuing hold of the traditional order.

The Hyderabad study of Panchayati Raj electoral behaviour made by K. Seshadri and S.P. Jain, examines the political perceptions of the people, their awareness of contemporary problems confronting the nation, the various media that played significant roles in the process of politicization of the masses and, finally the role played by the leaders of the Panchayati Raj institutions in linking national policies and their implementation.[52] An analysis of the perception of the electorate in the urban area has been made to explore the differentials between the urban and the rural electorate. The tables have not been prepared statistically. However, the study explains the role the Panchayati Raj institutions have played, in the process of political socialization of the masses in the rural areas.

The Warangal study made by G. Ram Reddy and K. Seshadri, aims at (*a*) assessing the image of Panchayati Raj in the minds of the people; (*b*) gauging the perception of the people of the ideas, work, achievements and failures of Panchayati Raj bodies; and (*c*) investigating the factors that influence the voters in their choice—social, economic, political.[53] The authors have relied on direct observation. The study shows that while leaders believe that the voters' choice is determined by caste and wealth, voters admit to having been prompted by the requirement of general welfare and ideological considerations. The emergence of younger leaders indicates the decline of historical leadership. Factional conflicts, in both the Congress and CPI (M), had an impact on their electoral fate and this helped the Jana Sangh to consolidate its position.

We may also refer to an interesting study of voting behaviour at the village level.[54] Somjee conducted this study in a Gujarat village on the basis of participant-observation and interview (talking and later noting) of 321 of the 4000 voters in the village. He came to the conclusion that so far as the second general election in this village was concerned, local leadership played a more important part than the forces of 'falia', and caste; and economic consideration played a decisive part in the voting decision of the village electorate. This study was, however, made at an elementary level. A recent study of rural elites by Iqbal Narain and others has highlighted some new facts.[55] For instance, they point out that the Panchayati Raj leaders who are likely to lend their support because of the candidate's caste make up merely 4.6%, and that the P.R. leaders are vote banks in a very modest sense.

If we try to draw final conclusions about the factors affecting electoral choice in India, we are at a loss. This feeling is justified to an extent because India is a big sub-continent and survey researches require not only research skill and techniques of a high order, but also proper pre-planning and adequate funds. Yet it is staggering to find the paucity of substantive conclusions even on a broad matter such as the influence of caste on elections. Whereas some studies unduly emphasize and confirm this as the most important factor affecting electoral choice in India, other studies show how caste loyalties and caste identities are often undermined by political factors such as party loyalties of the electorate, ideological appeals of political parties and issue orientation of voters.[56] Instances of split voting in the same castes, and of factional alignment between and across castes, are cited by them in support of this argument. The position that emerges is that caste appears to be an important factor at some places, and in some elections, and not so at some other places and at other times. On the basis of the studies made, no country-wide generalization can be made. Moreover, it is doubtful whether the correlation between caste composition and votes cast can at all give us the true position about caste voting. It is regrettable that personal dispositions and individual characteristics of voters have been by and large ignored, and that psephologists have been guided by the simplistic notion that voters do not act as individuals but as members of a group or caste alone.

Studies on electoral process have however one merit. They do not only enrich our information about the social and economic composition of voters, but also contribute significantly to political sociology by examining whether elections have caused desirable changes in the relationship between governmental institutions and social and economic structures in the country. B.D. Graham finds that Indian studies have contributed to two kinds of theories in this regard.[57] The first is what he calls the enlightenment theory, which maintains that elections, combined with other factors such as improved educational standards and the growth of national feeling, have made Indian society more open, more liberal, more demanding and more discriminating in the electoral choice. The old barriers of caste are falling down and the government is becoming conscious of popular pressures and demands.

The second theory, which he calls the transactional theory, maintains that there are coalitions of leaders and sub-leaders, and groups which are fed by informal contacts, favours and change, if need be, to suit each other. Electors are governed by such groups and relationships rather than by political parties. Thus Indian society remains oligarchic. Both these explanations bring to focus very important issues before Indian political sociologists for analytical purposes. Graham warns however that psephologists should not confuse the combination of the twin roles of empirical analysis and normative concerns about their society and politics. Perhaps it is not out of place to point out here that having borrowed the methods and even some of the concerns of sociology or psychology, political science proper has drifted away from some of its major concerns. If psychology only seeks to probe into the reasons why people vote for a particular candidate, sociologists or psychologists can do better in answering such questions regarding motive with the help of the variables crucial to their discipline and the methods developed in their disciplines. Political scientists, on the other hand. may do better in examining the impact of performance, development, constitutional constraints and the nature of the electoral system or party system, on voting. The election is to be viewed in the context of the working of the system as a whole. And it is here that the political scientists may step in and succeed but unfortunately, it is here that they have yet to succeed in spite of some pioneering efforts in this direction.

Electoral Process, Social Change and the Political System: Some works of insight try to link electoral process to important socio-political variables such as social change and political system. In this connection, we can name N.G.S. Kini, who after producing two mimoegraphed volumes (in collaboration with his colleagues) on women's voting behaviour, and the non-voter, brought out independently a notable book on the city voter in India. This study focuses on the political and theoretical dimension of social change.[58] According to Kini, issues in elections (which determine attitudes of voting populations) are related to the rate of social change. Group alignments and rivalries in elections proceed from the consequences which follow from the behaviour of individuals acting through groups, and seeking to modify the rate of change and to improve one's value position. To use his words, 'voting behaviour of individuals acting through groups is not only a consequence of the impact of the rate of social change but in its own turn is directed to modify this rate of change.[59]

He also points out that voting behavioural responses of individuals and sub-classes of individuals are not only responses to, and in this sense consequences of change. They also seek to modify, accelerate, or otherwise control the rate of change and its direction. The central hypothesis of Kini's study is drawn in terms of the polarization of two political sub-cultures which differ in their degree of modernization. The explanation of the voting act has been provided in a time perspective, from the immediately related to the remotely relevant. The scale of political awareness seeks to measure the amount of voters' political knowledge, and is related to the voting choice. Other distinguishing features include an explanation of the split-vote in terms of conflict of images about parties within the psychological awareness of the voters, an analysis of the shift in the original voting intention in terms of heavy exposure to propaganda, an exploration of the stability of vote intention in terms of high political involvements, and the method of finding out the proportion of votes that can be attributed to campaign strategies of candidates.

Some other works seek to link elections not only with variables such as political parties or the party system, but also with the performance of the political system as a whole and with its developmental goals in particular. Mention in this connection may be made also of a working paper on 'Voting Behaviour in a Developing Society'.[60] In addition to the attempt to examine the patterns of voting behaviour and the social, psychological, and political context in which the voter expresses his political choices, the paper aims at exploring the functional inter-relationship between this behaviour and the achievement of development, and cultural change. The promise contained in the working paper is yet to be fulfilled. But following the promise, some works of rare insight have been written though they fall short of the promises made. An essay by Gopal Krishna, attempts to show statistically how elections are helping the minority groups to get assimilated into the national mainstream.[61]

He examines the impact of electoral politics on political integration. Rajni Kothari, in a survey of election results is mostly concerned with the pattern of elite turn-over.[62]

A successful attempt in this connection is Ramashray Roy's *The Uncertain Verdict*, which while focusing on the midterm elections in 1969, seeks to grapple with the relationship between the functioning of the electoral system, the developing patterns of the party system and the performance capability of the political system.[63] According to the author, the performance capability of a political system is dependent not only on how parties are organized and on how they function and interact among themselves, but also on how parties themselves are shaped by the interaction between the dynamic components of the society reflecting themselves in electoral competition. Hence, in order to get the voter's intentions and actions, one must take into account all relevant forces that impinge on it; it is here, says the author, that the panel survey research does not help us. The book makes two worthwhile suggestions. First, it challenges the assumption of sample survey research that treats individuals as the basic universe of observation and considers the universe undifferentiated and free from the influences emanating from varying contexts.

Alternatively, Roy's approach emphasizes the profound influences of contextual variations on the attitudes and behaviour of individuals. Second, this study suggests that the roots of democratic stability should not be linked only with the type of party system and the quality of leadership. Rather, they should be sought in the complex interaction patterns among socioeconomic conditions, individual characteristics, political processes and public policies. One may doubt whether emphasis on contextual variation is enough and whether it should not be combined with personality traits. Non-emphasis on elites is in itself a doubtful proposition. But the author has given a new perspective, and with this perspective, he studies the mid-term elections held in 1969 in four of the Indian states viz. West Bengal, Bihar, Uttar Pradesh and Punjab. His work is based on a representative random probability sample of all voters. Along with finding out the correlation of socioeconomic variables with the vote, the study identifies the partisans, and shifted and indifferent voters, and ascertains their attributes. Further, it probes into the extent to which voters are interested in and engage in political activities, and the legitimacy of democratic institutions as seen through the voters' eyes and their sense of efficacy. In the last chapter, certain implications have been drawn for the political system in these four states.

In a bid to explain the political change of 1967, Rajni Kothari initiated 'the developmental model' of Indian politics, visualizing a sequential relationship between electoral behaviour, party system and political development.[64] In this theoretical context, the Centre for the Study of Developing Societies made a study of a national sample based on a stratified random probability sample of all voters.[65] The data was used to study electoral behaviour in terms of 'regularity and change' in the Indian political system, along with three indicators: voting trends, party identification and issue orientation (both objective and subjective). They treated political variables as autonomous of socioeconomic and demographic factors in political choice, and thus expressed their resolve to move from 'the sociology of politics' to 'political sociology'. The data have been used for developing a typology of 'political stratification' of the Indian electorate, for examining the implications of secular identities for political development of the voter, and for drawing the socioeconomic map of different parties and partisan groups.

Methods of Electoral Research: Even a casual student of the electoral process will not miss noting that in this area, survey methods and statistical techniques dominate the scene. Indian psephologists have brought methodological rigour to their studies and some of them deserve credit for it. One such pioneering contributor is V.M. Sirsikar, who produced the first panel study of voting behaviour in the 1962 elections in India making use of statistical data, interview techniques and the content analysis method to which we have already referred in an earlier section.[66] This study was based on the random sampling method, and the actual sample was 9.5% of the universe which comes to 1457. This is a three-wave study. However, it is no use comparing it to the Elmira enquiry which had four waves of interviews with 175 questions and a supplementary questionnaire sent by mail.[67] But considering the point in time when Sirsikar worked on the study, the attempt was creditable in the Indian context. It is even more creditable that he has continued studying the same constituency, i.e. Pune, in subsequent elections with greater methodological sophistication and rigour. In 1967, Sirsikar made a survey of 45 out of a total of 549 polling booths and then drew a sample of 1050 electors, of whom 913 were canvassed.[68] Further, the purposive selection of elite voters (for ten groups viz.

doctors, lawyers, businessmen, secondary teachers, post-graduate students, salaried graduates, Lions and Rotarians) was made from lists provided by professional organizations. The total of the elite voters sample came to 450 out of whom 395 were canvassed. Besides structured interviews of these 1308 voters, the candidates were also interviewed both before and after the elections. Moreover, an effort was made to interview party-workers. A separate questionnaire was used for different categories of the sample: two for the voters, two for the candidates, one for the 'rejects' of the Congress nomination and one for the party workers, i.e. the militants. Whereas in the 1962 study, three waves of questionnaires were used, this time, two waves were used—the first about one month before the elections and the second in the week after the election. The analysis of the answers is presented in a large number of neatly drawn tables which also indicate the stages in the conduct of the survey.

Kini's work, discussed in the last section, uses the chi-square test for testing hypotheses and factor analysis for substantiating theory.[69] Thomas Pantham's study of voting behaviour in Baroda city is based on interviews of the candidates and campaign workers of a city constituency for parliamentary and three Assembly seats, and content analysis of local newspapers.[70] His located sample is 416 which is less than 30% of the total population, and which has been randomly chosen by the use of random tables. Based on the multi-staged stratified sample design prepared by the ICSSR, B. Ganguly and Mira Ganguly undertook a study of West Bengal Assembly election of 1972.[71] They collected data from structured interviews with 504 respondents in twelve polling stations just after the Assembly election. A novelty of this study is the use of factor analysis—a multivariate statistical technique for identification and measurement of basic variables associated with the victory of the Congress-dominated Progressive Democratic Alliance and the defeat of the left in West Bengal in 1972. They listed 27 variables and then divided them into two groups: (*i*) those relating to the social characteristics of the voters, and (*ii*) those concerning campaign, interest in election, and the psychological dimensions of the voters. They applied the chi-square test to measure the association between the dependent variable and each one of the independent variables. The 0.5 level of probability (P) was accepted as the standard of significance. While the conclusions of the study are not substantially significant, its conscious attempt to maintain methodological rigour is noteworthy.

We have said earlier that the strength of psephology lies more in methodological sophistication than in reaching substantive conclusions. This point should be made with some reservations in India; a preoccupation with the niceties of methodology should in no case be allowed to become an end in itself. We ought to keep in mind that methodology as employed in the social sciences in India has not been constructed in the process of analyzing problems arising out of Indian politics, society or culture, but has been taken over from a very different social and cultural milieu. Under such circumstances, there is at times disproportion between the problems to be studied and the apparatus mobilized. Karl Mannheim had referred to 'a very marked and painful disproportion between the vastness of the scientific machinery employed and the value of the ultimate results.[72] A poor country like India cannot afford the luxury of expensive research projects in social sciences if they do not lead to substantive conclusions. After all, methodology is only the process of finding an appropriate tool to reach substantial conclusions. This fact is more glaring in the case of psephology which is indeed a fertile field for worthwhile conclusions, particularly in India, which is a good laboratory for research because of the distinctiveness of its socio-economic structure and levels of culture. It seems that the majority of Indian psephologists have yet to become conscious of this.

Though it is recognized that the goal of psephology is to contribute towards the development of general theories of politics, not many of the contributions have so far been in this direction. In many cases, election studies have lacked a theoretical perspective. Consequently election studies by Indian social scientists lack in most cases significant conclusions with potential for theory-building. It is, however, a happy sign that this need is being realized, particularly by psephologists such as Rajni Kothari, Iqbal Narain and V.M. Sirsikar.[73] If their suggestions, coupled with those made in various books and articles by the Centre for the Study of Developing Societies are seriously attended to, we can be hopeful of a richer literature on electoral politics in India in the next decade to come. But there is also an alternate viewpoint which we shall only casually refer to at the end of this book. This is the recent American trend—a move from behaviouralism to policy science. This would perhaps suit us if we do not copy it as a matter of fashion but with the serious intention which this new perspective demands and deserves.

10. Public Opinion and Political Socialization

With the growth of democracy, the consent of the governed is recognized as a basic principle of governance. There is also the pragmatic consideration that the cost of maintaining a regime can be reduced if the views of the citizenry and the acts of its rulers are made to match. Modern mass media of communication have served to bridge the gap between the rulers and the ruled. Even dictatorships today take note of the prevailing public opinion before taking action. The imperative that government heed the opinion of the public stems not only from democratic ideology, but from the practical necessity that government obtain popular support in order to gain stability. Public opinion, Bailey says, 'has a giant's strength, and (we) may use it with frightful effect'.[1]

There are, however, writers who do not place too high a value on the importance of public opinion. Writing in 1922, Walter Lippmann in his famous book *Public Opinion*, maintained that 'the public cannot be regarded as an omnicompetent and omniscient collectivity equipped to decide the affairs of the state.[2] The average person, he argued, had neither time, talent nor taste, for indulging in debate over weighty matters concerning the state. Even if he were willing to spare his time for the study of public issues, the information available to him would be inadequate and unenlightening. Moreover, the amorphous' public, even if informed, was not capable of taking initiative in any public action. New theories of psychology emphasize the conception of a non-rational man acting under the influence of subconscious urges and external suggestions. Graham

Wallas highlighted the role of instincts and impulses in politics.[3] Further reinforcement came in the wake of the media explosion—when people began being manipulated by mass communication through media such as newspapers, radio and television. Eventually, the concept of public opinion as a knowledgeable and influential giant was replaced by the notion of hidden persuaders, opinion manipulators, and engineers of consent.

A variant of the latter viewpoint is a forthright exposition in the 1950s by C. Wright Mills who found that the group of 'power elites' in America—the corporation heads, the political leaders and the military chiefs—fixes the principal lines of national policy through consultations among its members and through constant manoeuvres.[4] The press, the radio, television and the corps of sub-leaders trail behind the power elites, and in due course, the public tags along. Mills refuted the idea of any organized public to which the power elite was responsible for its decisions. Indeed, this version was a deadly blow to the earlier idealized vision of public opinion.

It is true that as governments expand their functions and become more technical and complex, the average man feels more bewildered and repelled by questions of public policy. With the extension of the curtain of secrecy over wider areas, the public is denied information and thereby the opportunity for meaningful criticism of public policy. Yet, it cannot be denied that policy innovations in various countries are inversely connected with mass sentiments. The impact of the 'politics of equality' has been noted by writers such as Lloyd Fallers.[8] The growth in populist tendencies in various countries in recent times points to the growing desire among the rulers to seek the identification of their programmes with the underdogs in society, who are invariably the most numerous. The fate of rulers who have become unpopular and the weight of public opinion in determining their fate is writ large on the face of contemporary history. Public opinion in a democracy makes and remakes a government. Even an authoritarian regime consult public opinion and tries to maintain an equation between the government and the public through a process of adaptation and adjustment. We may agree with the double proposition that if the public is ignorant the voter is no fool.

Some Conceptions of Public Opinion: Some speculators on public opinion see the public as a semi-organized entity that in some way or another moves through stages of initiation and debate, and reaches a recognizable collective decision on an issue. To them, the public is an organic entity linked together either by means of mass communication or through something like a city-state or town-hall meeting. To Young '. . . a public is a transitory, amorphous, and relatively unstructured association of individuals with certain interests in common'.[6] However, in a mass society, there are hardly any questions on which the entire public can have an opinion. But on the other hand, as V.O. Key argues, when public opinion is regarded as those opinions that may influence government, the 'public' does not exist as any specific sort of loosely structured association or ghostly sociological entity.[7] On a given question, the operative public may consist of a highly structured association, while on another matter, opinions may be diffused through a wide public that lacks any special organization. On one issue, the public may consist of one sector of the population; on another, of a quite different sector.

It is often found that sectional or group interests operate independently sometimes and sometimes in close interaction with each other. so that there are in fact special 'publics'. The question, however, is as to how the interests of special publics may be reconciled with the idea of public interest or the interest of the general public. Blumer tries to resolve this problem by remarking that public opinion may be

> . . . different from the opinion of any of the groups in public. It can be thought of, perhaps, as a composite opinion formed out of the several opinions that are held in the public, or better, as the central tendency set by the striving of these separate opinions and, consequently as being shaped by the relative strength and play of opposition among them.[8]

Public opinion is thus an aggregation of certain types of attitudes across some kind of affect toward public object of cognition.[9] In this connection, Almond's distinction between 'mass public' and the 'attentive public' is notable.[10] The mass public, informed by the mass media, pays heed to the tone of discussion of issues and responds through moods of apprehension or complacency. The attentive public, a far smaller group, follows public issues in an analytical manner, is relatively well informed, and constitutes a critical audience for the discussion of public affairs. However, the size of the attentive public varies from time to time as new issues and new problems arise. Again, at times, the attentive public may be large and quickly responsive to events and actions. At other times and on other questions, public discontent may be generated rather slowly. It may require years or decades for a public sentiment to develop. However, it is surprising to find, as the surveys in the US suggest, that the opinions of the most attentive or the better informed people on issues analyzed, resemble those of the group with only a marginal attention to politics, that is the less informed.[11] Public opinion, even in a country like the USA with a very high rate of literacy, is portrayed as both wretchedly informed and feebly structured.[12]

Patterns of Distribution of Public Opinion: Earlier, a distribution of opinion meant merely the division of the people into the defendants or critics of a proposal, a candidate, or a party. The psychometricians found fault with such categorization as it concealed wide gradations in opinion. They therefore contrived scales to measure opinion in its dimension of direction.[13]

Some other social scientists examine public opinion from the point of view of its structural distribution. Opinions about issues and political objects are distributed among different kinds of people in different ways. Hence it has been found worthwhile to examine their distribution among various geographical areas, occupations and classes. In America, geographical distribution plays a significant role. The attitude of the South on the Negro question is in sharp contrast with the attitude of the North on the same question. The 1977 elections in India and the Chikmagalur bye-election highlight regional variation in political attitudes and party affiliations in India. Even smaller regions, reflecting the heterogeniety of populations, may be contrasted to show differences in public opinion. In the American setting, as in other capitalist societies, a major opinion cleavage along occupational lines is also visible, particularly on social welfare policy and other bread and butter questions. But while differences of opinion exist among occupational groups, considerable overlapping of opinion also prevails among them. In part, such deviations from the occupational norm are accounted for by class identifications which may depart from the objective occupational status. Manual workers who regard themselves as members of the middle class, on an average, differ in their opinions from those manual workers who place themselves in the working class. Richard Centers demonstrates the existence of these relationships in the population at large.[14] In India, we find a poor peasant of a higher caste identifying himself with the rich peasantry of the lower castes. However, the class relationship may show variation through time. As Converse has shown, class identification is a more important determinant of policy opinions in times of depression than it would be in periods of prosperity.[15] Similarly, other variables may also have an effect.

Properties of Public Opinion: The properties or qualities of opinion are of prime importance in the governing process. Opinions vary in their intensity and hence in their effect. On some questions, opinions may be so lightly held by the citizenry that they have only the slightest impact upon public action. In other instances, even a small part of the population may hold a position so tenaciously that it may block, if not direct, public action. Daniel Katz, Hadley Cantril and Reuban Mehling have attempted to measure the intensity of public opinion on various issues in the USA.[16] The intensity or depth of concern indeed rests on most varied foundations. It is intimately connected with ego involvement. But it is also the product of group identification, self-interest, attachment to community values, knowledge, threat to security and so on. By and large, intensity of opinion develops when persons are confronted by issues or circumstances that arouse their concern most deeply. Therefore, in a society characterized to a large extent by consensus, intensity of opinion on most issues will be relatively low. Intensity of opinion leads to heightened political participation generally, but in some cases its reverse is also true. At times, intensity has been found leading to a low sense of political efficacy, and even to apathy and alienation.

Another quality of public opinion is its stability. An individual, for example, may have a view, expressed on the basis of little or no information, which may readily be changed. On the other hand, an opinion may be so firmly held that it is not easily altered. The stability is connected with the changes in external stimuli. Issues that relate to opinions of high stability widely held within the population present radically different problems for government than do those matters on which opinion is unstable.

Political Socialization and Opinion Formation: Political socialization as an aspect of communicating attitudes, norms, knowledge, and above all, behaviour patterns, is a basic antecedent of opinion formation. 'Political socialization', to cite a recent survey of the ICSSR 'is concerned with the learning of political response, of absorbing preferences, and in a sense with the wide problems of allegiance to and alienation from the body politic'.[17]

Political socialization is an earlier phase of opinion formation—a phase in which individuals acquire knowledge, information, values and attitudes towards the political system. Following this process, individuals develop political preferences and are inducted into citizenship roles and orientations. Rush and Althoff describe it as 'the process' by which an individual becomes acquainted with the political system and which determines his perceptions of politics and his reactions to political phenomena.[18] Easton and Dennis define it as 'those developing processes through which persons acquire political orientations and patterns of behaviour'.[19] The end product of political socialization is a set of attributes—cognitions, value standards and feelings—towards the political system, its various roles, and role incumbents. It also includes knowledge of values and feelings affecting the inputs of demands and claims, and the authoritative outputs.[20]

Political socialization is also important as a means of inter-generational and inter-continental transmission of culture. It is the way society transmits its political culture from generation to generation and from one continent to another. This process helps societies to achieve cohesion through a shared understanding of values, norms and symbols.

The crucial period of 'induction into the political culture'[21] is said to be during childhood, but in India, early adolescence appears to be the more crucial period in which not only primary socializing institutions like the family, but also secondary groups, tend to transmit culture. The secondary structures influence individuals as they grow older, and these seem to be more important in the Indian case.

It is more accurate to say therefore, that political socialization is a lifelong experience. Induction into a new profession, migration to new cultures and social or political upheavals entail the learning of new patterns and norms. This point has been very well brought out by Hyman in his pioneering work in which he examines both the latent and manifest components of political socialization.[22] The psychologists, psychiatrists and anthropologists stress the latent aspects of socialization. They perceive that people develop their political attitudes unconsciously in the family.

But other schools such as the national voluntarists and supporters of the enlightenment, and liberalism, emphasize the significance of political and social history as well as formal, educational and propaganda practices in the development of political attitudes and civic norms of nations and peoples. Hyman's study correctly stresses the importance of both cognition or emotional learning during childhood, and subsequent political indoctrination as elements of political socialization. He studies the influence of both the primary and the secondary groups. We would do well to recall that Plato, Aristotle, Rousseau and Locke have also emphasized education as an important variable for the training of both the rulers and the ruled.

We must appreciate the fact that during adolescence and even later, socializing influences are received, and at times they result in marked changes in earlier dispositions. Political systems in their bid to perpetuate their cultures and structures, through time indoctrinate the young to no less extent than the child, and the young in turn transmit it to the child.[23] Both aspects of political socialization are important in that they lead to the formation of attitudes of attachment, allegiance or apathy, and opinions about the political system and its various role takers as well as their activities.

The principal agencies and institutions influential in the formation of attitudes and opinion, or what we call 'political socialization', are the family, the school, the church, the club, occupational unions, and the mass media. In developed countries, newspapers, radio and television play a tremendous role in influencing public opinion, but in a developing country like India, the influence of mass media is limited. Only 4% read newspapers in India and they are generally residents of urban areas.[24] India stands near the bottom in audience coverage. According to the UNESCO, for every thousand persons in a developing country, there are fifty radio receivers, twenty cinema seats and hundred newspapers. In India, for every thousand persons there are thirteen newspapers, seventeen radios, and seven cinema seats.[25] The difference in coverage is reflected in the difference in the impact that mass media has. An attempt is made to bridge this gap in developing countries by organizing mass meetings, public speeches and public demonstrations. Opposition leaders organize mass movements, rallies and demonstrations to highlight their points of view. Through strikes, pressure groups also try to bring their demands to public view. Talking habits and the tradition of long open air conversation to while away the leisure hours also constitute an informal means of communication and political education in India. The fact is that in a society like India, the primary agencies of the family, the caste and the community, cultural associations and ethnic organizations based on regional, linguistic and religious affinities play a dominant role in moulding attitudes and opinions. Informal communication by word of mouth is still the most common and potent channel of communication. Even mass media such as newspapers, radio and television are community affairs. One copy of the newspaper is read by a large number of people and likewise, radio and television programmes are generally shared by the entire neighbourhood. Thus the primary group and neighbourhood contribute to the crystallization of opinion.

Political socialization and opinion formation induce the individual to act in various ways in the political life and process. Almond describes political socialization as the first important input from the environment into the political system. Certainly, socialization is a necessary precondition not only of public opinion formation, but also of myriad overt societal and political activities and behaviour.

Structural and institutional factors are however, not to be ignored as important factors in political behaviour, and individuals do interact with those factors almost incessantly. Another crucial question, therefore, is to what extent and in which form the individual's personality, as opposed to other variables, affects behaviour. One view of political socialization, emanating from Freud and the psychoanalytic tradition, views socialization as a process of curbing potentially disruptive drives by channelling them in socially acceptable directions. This view is derived from the Platonic ideal which sees the problem of order as one of devising means whereby a human being's innate drives can be controlled, or from Rousseau's idea that private and personal drives ('particular will') can be transferred to the public will ('general will'). For the psychologist, political involvement is one of the ways in which individuals meet certain drives and release personal tensions. But for political sociologists, the interest does not lie so much in the fact of psychological release. Rather, they bring in other factors such as the environment, personality and response to explain the phenomenon of the interaction between personality and politics. These factors characterize the works of Kurt Lewin as well as those of Lasswell and Kaplan who introduced the E-P-R paradigm to explain the basic antecedents of political behaviour. Greenstein has explained the process in his paper 'Personality and Politics'.[26]

The Environment of the Political Actor

Perceptions of the Environment

Conscious political and politically relevant orientations (political and politically) relevant cognitive, affective, and conative dispositions- e.g., opinions, attitudes, beliefs, values, ideology, identifications, stereotypes, etc.

Functional bases of conscious orientations—basic personality structures 1. Cognition and needs 2. Mediation, self-other relationships 3. Ego defences	Political responses
Biological underpinnings of personality, temperament, physiological state, genetic inheritance, etc.	

We find then that political sociologists regard personality as a basic variable, the environment as the next basic variable and political socialization as a product of the interaction of the variables of personality and experience. Their stand is that notwithstanding psychological problems, politicians and political structures are pressurized to behave in ways congruent with social expectations and norms. They take into account the total social, economic and cultural environment which determine political socialization and political involvement.

Various agents transmit the elements of political socialization through three ways or mechanisms: imitation, instruction and motivation.[27] Robert Le Vine suggests that these are the mechanisms of political socialization in childhood, but Rush and Althoff point out that these mechanisms are applicable to the whole socialization process.[28] Imitation is generally found among children, but in the case of adolescents and adults, imitation is mixed up with both instruction and motivation. Vocational training or discussion groups are examples of instruction. Both imitation and instruction are specific types of experience but motivation is most closely identified with experience in general. Motivation is the learning of what Le Vine has called appropriate behaviour, through a process of trial and error. The individual learns directly from his experience actions that are most congruent with his attitudes and opinions. The term appropriate refers not to the extent to which the individual is led to conform to some norm of group behaviour (though this may well be the result), but to the process by which the individual relates action to attitudes and opinions formed through experience.

There are two key variables in political socialization, experience and personality. An individual's politically relevant experience arises out of, and is contributory to, the process of political socialization. The individual's conception of political problems is seen through the variety of his experiences. If experiences are shared by a number of individuals, they acquire greater significance in the formation of values and attitudes. Group experiences reinforce commonly held values and attitudes, while experiences often assume considerable political significance. Robert Lane notes this point in his famous work, *Political Ideology : Why the American Common Man Believes What He Does* (1962). Widespread economic prosperity or deprivation, the rapidity of social change, frequent violence or prolonged peace, the existence or absence of social tension and so on provide an experiential environment which contributes to the individual's orientations towards political behaviour.

It is apt to note here that political socialization constitutes an important dimension of opinion formation, particularly in the Indian context, where modernity and tradition coexist, and where agricultural culture is giving way to bureaucratic and industrial culture, creating in effect a transitional culture of ambiguity and even anomie. In urban or cosmopolitan areas, we come across symbols and patterns of behaviour drawn from Western culture. Messages are received with an extraordinary rapidity from alien societies and large segments of upper class youth receive such influences directly. Messages are also received at the other end of the pole, that is, the poor semi-literate public with strong muscles, and their behaviour pattern is characterized by political disloyalty and disaffection.

Prerequisites for the Existence of Public Opinion: Apart from freedom of speech and discussion, and the free availability of information about public issues and public questions, democratic theorists place emphasis on the existence of a consensus on fundamentals as a prerequisite for the existence of public opinion. A consensus on fundamentals is claimed to be the only basis for the settlement of the differences involved in the development of a prevailing opinion on transient issues. Park argued that there needs to be with the public 'a general understanding and a community of interest among all parties sufficient to make discussion possible'.[29] Public opinion Lowell thought, need not be a unanimous opinion, but it should create an obligation, moral or political, on the part of the minority to submit at least under certain conditions.[30] According to him 'a body of men are politically capable of a public opinion only so far as they are agreed upon the ends and aims of government and upon the principles by which those ends shall be attained'. 'No public opinion can exist in nations with large minorities unwilling to abide by the majority decision'. Moreover, public opinion can exist only when 'the bulk of the people are in a position to determine their own knowledge or by weighing a substantial part of the facts required for a rational decision', or when the question involves an issue of 'apparent harmony or contradiction with settled convictions'. Thus consensus implies two things: an overwhelming public agreement upon a question of public policy after rational discussion, and the willingness of sections of the people to abide by decisions or actions based on consensus. The rise of popular consensus on a particular issue may involve the development of simultaneous concurrence by several groups within the public. In the language of political theory, this is called a 'concurrent majority'.

Government and Public Opinion: Governments may move towards action in deference to public opinion or they may even anticipate it before they act. In either case they keep in mind the expectations as well as demands of public opinion. The government communicates to the people the necessity of ascertaining and obtaining consent, and also receives communications from the people, thus creating a two way process of receiving and influencing opinions.[31] The government can ignore public opinion only at its risk. But the range of opinions that enter into the calculations of governors varies among societies with their political norms and customs. Nevertheless public opinion is important operationally only in terms of its impact on the actions, personnel or structure of the government. Varying properties or qualities of opinions are communicated to the government. Governments take into account settled matters such as mores, enduring attitudes and customs; and even lightly held views, transient anxieties, prejudices, preferences, demands, and convictions. It is commonly assumed that public opinion concerns issues of substantive policy; but governments have to pay heed even to lightly held views or complaints which contribute to the development of the prime parameters of opinions and behaviour. A contented or discontented people may have opinions that are most relevant politically, though they are not concrete policy issues. For instance, they may have opinions about economic conditions or the threat of riot or war. They may feel concerned about the issue of inequality of incomes or privileges, corruption among ministers and civil servants, scarcity of goods in the market or their rising prices. All such questions are of direct relevance for governmental consideration and action, though they may not be considered policy agendas or controversial issue areas.

Although all regimes pay heed to the opinions of their peoples, opinions play a more important role in democratic states than they do in dictatorial states. For the maximum participation of the public (or publics), deceleration of prospective actions, along with the arguments and the considerations underlying such proposals, is practiced through party manifestos and leadership statements. This is followed by the free expression of views by associations, groups and individuals, that is, various publics. The government is expected to give weight to latent opinion in advance of action. It estimates the kinds of opinions that may be expressed if a given course is proposed or followed and in the event of unexpected opposition, withdraws or substantially modifies the proposals; or sometimes delays or postpones their implementation. However, we must admit that the formal give and take between government and public opinion at any given time is difficult to perceive and appraise.

Cleavages or conflicts involving the mass public are generally not in terms of conflicting attachments to issues, but of loyalties to competing groups, and the most inclusive of such groups are political parties. Groups try to induce conforming behaviour or a common outlook among their members. In this process, the role of leadership is important. Patterns of action at the leadership level affect the distribution of popular opinion which has repercussions upon the behaviour of the governing apparatus. It is in the set of complex interactions, among leadership components and between them and clusters of mass opinion, that the role of public opinion in popular government can be found.

It is true that a government's response to public opinion depends on the nature of issues and the intensity of feeling about the issue concerned. The government's response is also mediated by a number of agencies such as political parties, pressure groups, and other interested organizations. In the ultimate analysis, governments act on the basis of their calculations about the likely effects of alternative courses of action. Governments are not only followers but also moulders of public opinion. It is the crucial interaction between government media of communication and the social structure that determines the nature and role of public opinion in the political process.

Notes and References

1. Political Sociology, Nature, Scope and Emergence

1 In the words of Marx and Engels, '... the economic structure of society always furnishes the real basis, starting from which alone we can work out the ultimate explanation of the whole superstructure of juridicial and political institutions as well as of the religious, philosophical, and other ideas of a given historical period.' MARX and ENGELS, *Selected Works*, Vol. 2, Moscow, 1962, p. 134

2 Ibn Khaldun, who lived in the fourteenth century, may have been the earliest scientific exponent of the economic conception of history. He believed that the leading thread of history lay not in military or political vicissitudes, but in man's social state. By social state, he meant man's degree of civilization, and his casual or concurrent conditions such as barbarism, the improvement of manners, the formation of families, tribes, and all the various elements of superiority that people acquire in the course of one event or the other. From there oiginate dynasties and empires, social differentiations and lucrative professional occupations, the trades, the sciences, and the arts. Moreover, he insisted on the essential thesis that differences in customs and institutions depend on the various ways in which man procures for himself the means of subsistence. See MICHELS, R. *First Lectures in Political Sociology*, New York, Harper and Row, 1949, p. 10

3 Madison, Federalist Paper No. X in BENDIX, R. and LIPSET, S.M. (eds.), *Class, Status and Power*, Glencoe, Illinois, Free Press, 1953, p. 22

4 CRICK, B. *In Defense of Politics*, London, Penguin, 1964, p. 30

5 GREER, S. and ORLEANS, P. 'Political Sociology' in FARIS, R.L. (ed.), *Handbook of Modern Sociology*, Chicago, Rand McNally, 1964, p. 810

6 WEBER, M. 'Class, Status and Party' in GERTH, H.H. and MILLS, C.W. (trs. and eds.), *From Max Weber*, London, Routledge and Kegan Paul, 1948, p. 810

7 LASSWELL, H.D. *Politics: Who Gets What, When, How*, New York, Meridian Books, 1958, p. 23

8 DAHL, R.A. *Modern Political Analysis*, New Jersey, Prentice-Hall, 1963, p. 6

9 BENDIX, R. (ed.), *State and Society: A Reader In Comparative Political Sociology*, Boston, Little Brown, 1968, p.6

10 WOLIN, SHELDON S. *Politics and Vision*, London, George Allen and Unwin Ltd., 1960, pp. 10-11

11 BENTLEY, ARTHUR F. *The Process of Government*: *A Study of Social Pressures*, Bloomington, The Principia Press, 1935, p. 216

12 GREER and ORLEANS, *op. cit.*

13 EFFRAT, A. (ed.), *Perspectives in Political Sociology*, New York, Bobbs-Merrill Company, 1973, p. 3

14 LIPSET, S.M. and BENDIX, R. 'The Field of Political Sociology' in COSER, LEWIS A. (ed.), *Political Sociology*, New York, Harper and Row, 1966, p. 10

15 DOWSE, ROBERT E. and HUGHES, JOHN A. *Political Sociology*, London, John Wiley and Sons, 1972, p. 13

16 BRAUNGART, RICHARD G. (ed.), *Society and Politics: Readings in Political Sociology*, New Jersey, Prentice-Hall, 1976, Introductory Essay, p. 2

17 LIPSET, S.M. *Political Man: The Social Bases of Politics*, New York, Doubleday and Company, 1960

18 BENDIX, R. and LIPSET, S.M. 'Political Sociology' in FARIS, R.L. (ed.), *Handbook of Modern Sociology*, *op. cit.*

19 COSER, LEWIS A. (ed.), *Political Sociology*, *op. cit.*, p.1

20 SARTORI, G. 'From Sociology of Politics to Political Sociology' in LIPSET, S.M. (ed.), *Politics and Social Sciences*, Delhi, Wiley Easstrn, 1972

21 LIPSET, S.M. and ROKKAN, S. 'Cleavage Structures, Party Systems, and Voter Alignments: An Introduction' in LIPSET and ROKKAN (eds.), *Party Systems and Voter Alignments*: *Cross-National Perspectives*, New York, Free Press, 1967, p. 300

22 A good illustration of this approach is the book cited above, particularly the sub-section entitled 'Implications for Comparative Political Sociology' *ibid.*, pp. 50-6

23 This point has been emphasized in ROSENAU, JAMES N. *The Dramas of Politics*, Boston, Little Brown, 1973, p. 171; and PALMER, NORMAN D. *Elections and Political Development*: *The South Asian Experience*, Delhi, Vikas Publishing House, 1976, p. 2

24 DOWSE and HUGHES, *op. cit.*, p. 7

25 Robert E. Lane's comment is worth recapitulating in this connection. He writes that 'If any single lesson has been driven home by the investigations of the behavioural sciences in the past twenty years, it is the idea that all social acts are determined by multiple forces. In studying the genesis of neuroses Freud referred to a similar principle as "overdetermination" meaning that a symptom was the product of the culmination of influences; rarely if ever, only one.' See LANE *Political Life*: *Why People Get Involved in Politics*, Glencoe, Illinois, Free Press, 1961, p. 131

26 ARON, R. 'Social Structure and the Ruling Class' extracted in COSER (ed.), *Political Sociology*, *op. cit.*, pp. 48-100

27 For this concept of political power, see DAHL, ROBERT A. *Who Governs*: *Democracy and Power in an American City*, New Haven, Yale University Press, 1961, p. 7

28 MERTON, ROBERT K., BROOM, L. and COTTRELL, L.S. Jr. (eds.), *Sociology Today*, New York, Basic Books, 1959, p. VII

29 RUNCIMAN, W.G. *Social Science and Political Theory*, London, Cambridge University Press, 1963

30 GERTH and MILLS, *From Max Weber*, *op. cit.*

31 ALMOND, GABRIEL A. and BINGHAM POWELL, G. Jr. *Comparative Politics: A Developmental Approach*, Delhi, Amerind Publishing Company, Indian edition, 1972, p. 5

32 See HERRING, E.P. *Group Representation Before Congress*, New York, McGraw Hill, 1929; SCHATTSCHNEIDER, E. *Politics, Pressures, and the Tariff*, New Jersey, Prentice-Hall, 1937; ODEGARD, P. *Pressure Politics: The Story of the Anti-Saloon League*, New York Columbia University Press, 1928

33 For a good exposition of this viewpoint, see SHILS, E. 'On the Comparative Study of the New States' in GEERTZ, C. (ed.), *Old Societies and New States: The Quest for Modernity in Asia and Africa*, Delhi, Amerind Publishing Company, Indian edition, 1971, pp. 1-26

34 See APTER, DAVID E. *The Politics of Modernization*, Chicago, University of Chicago Press, 1965; and DEUTSCH, KARL W. and FOLTZ, WILLIAM J. (eds.), *Nation Building*, New York, Artherton, 1963

35 RIGGS, FRED W. 'The Theory of Political Development' in CHARLESWORTH, J.C. (ed.), *Contemporary Political Analysis*, New York, Free Press, 1967, p. 319

36 *Ibid.*, p. 322

37 SHILS, E. *op. cit.*, p. 20

38 ALMOND, G.A. 'Comparative Political Systems' *Journal of Politics*, Vol. XVIII, No. 3, August 1956, pp. 391-409

39 Almond's Introduction to ALMOND, G.A. and COLEMAN, J.S. (eds.), *The Politics of the Developing Areas*, New Jersey, Princeton University Press, 1960. It may be noted here that though Almond is the most popular figure in the application of the functional approach, the first two attempts in this direction were: EASTON, D. in 'An Approach to the Analysis of Political Systems' *World Politics*, Vol. IX, No. 3, April 1957; and LASSWELL, H.D. in *The Decision Process*, Bureau of Governmental Research, University of Maryland, 1956

40 Representative examples include COLEMAN, J.C. *Nigeria: Background to Nationalism*, Berkeley, University of California Press, 1959; WRIGGINS, W.H. *Ceylon: Dilemmas of a New Nation*, New Jersey, Princeton University Press, 1960; *The Political Kingdom of Uganda: A Study in Bureaucratic Nationalism*, New Jersey, Princeton University Press, 1961; *Religion and Politics in Pakistan* Berkeley, University of California Press, 1961; BINDER, L. *Iran: Political Development in a Changing Society*, Berkeley, University of California Press, 1962; FEITH, H. *The Decline of Constitutional Democracy in Indonesia*, Ithaca, Cornell University Press, 1962; PYE, LUCIAN W. *Politics, Personality and Nation Building: Burma's Search for Identity*, New Haven, Yale University Press, 1962; WEINER, M. *The Politics of Scarcity: Public Pressure and Political Response in India*, Chicago, University of Chicago Press, 1962; APTER, D. *Ghana in Transition*, New York, Atheneum, revised edition, 1963; LA PALOMBARA, J. *Interest Groups in Italian Politics*, New Jersey, Princeton University Press, 1964; and RIGGS, F.W. *Thailand: The Modernization of a Bureaucrat Polity*, Honolulu, East-West Centre Press, 1966

41 DUVERGER, MAURICE (ed.), *The Study of Politics*, translated by Robert Wagoner, London, Nelson 1972, p. 11

42 For the distinction, see DOWSE, R.E. 'Political Behaviour: Parties, Groups, and Elections' in WISEMAN, H.V. (ed.), *Political Science: An Outline for the Intending Student of Government, Politics and Political Science*, London, Routledge and Kegan Paul, 1967, p. 131

43 ALMOND and POWELL, *Comparative Politics, op. cit.*, p. 6

44 For a useful inventory and introduction of survey analysis, see ROKKAN, S., VERBA, S., VIET, J. and ALMASY, E. *Comparative Survey Analysis*, Paris, Mouton, 1969

2. Approaches in Political Analysis

1 APTER, DAVID E. *Introduction to Political Analysis*, Massachusetts, Winthrop Publishers, 1977, p. 7

2 For characteristics of behaviouralism, see among others: EULAU, H., ELDERSVELD, S.J. and JANOWITZ, M. (eds.), *Political Behaviour: A Reader in Theory and Research*, Delhi, Amerind Publishing Company, Indian edition, 1972, p.8; the three essays in CHARLESWORTH, J.C. (ed.), *Contemporary Political Analysis*, New York, Free Press, 1967; ELCOCK, H. *Political Behaviour: An Assessment*, London, Methuen, 1967; and WALDO, D. 'Political Science: Tradition, Discipline, Profession, Science, Enterprise' in GREENSTEIN, F. and POLSBY, N.W. (eds.), *Handbook of Political Science*, Vol. I, Massachusetts, Addison-Wesley Publishing Company, 1967; and SHARMA, L.N. Behaviouralism and Post-behaviouralism' *Journal of Social and Economic Studies*, Vol. VII, No. 1, 1979, pp. 123-47

3 EULAU, H. *The Behavioural Persuasion in Politics*, New York, Random House, 1963, p. 161

4 For a full-length study of behavioural techniques, see among others: ACKOFF, R.L. *The Design of Social Research*, Chicago, University of Chicago Press, 1953; and LAZARSFELD, P.F. and ROSENBERG, M. (eds.), *The Language of Social Research*, Glencoe, Illinois, Free Press, 1955

5 WALLAS, G. *Human Nature in Politics*, London, Constable and Company, 1908

6 Harold Lasswell summed up the 'political type' in this book through the formula of *rdp* i.e. rationalization of the displacement of private motives on public objects in terms of public interest; See EULAU et. al. (eds.), *op. cit.* pp. 90-103. For an introduction to the long range of Lasswell's massive writings, see MARVICK (ed.), *Harold D Lasswell on Political Sociology*, Chicago, University of Chicago Press, 1977, particularly pp. 279-319 LASSWELL 'The Psychology of Hitlerism' *Political Quarterly*, Vol. IV, 1933, pp. 372-84 is an excellent piece of study incorporating both psychological and sociological insights in politics

7 PYE, LUCIAN W. *Politics, Personality and Nation Building: Burma's Search for Identity*, New Haven, Yale University Press, 1962

8 WALLACE, ANATONY F.C. *Culture and Personality*, New York, Random House, 1961, pp. 42-3

9 ELDERSVELD S.J. 'Theory and Method in Voting Behaviour Research' in EULAU et. al., *op. cit.*, p. 271

10 For the post-behavioural viewpoint, see EASTON, D. 'The New Revolution in Political Science' epilogue to the Indian edition of *The Political System: An Inquiry into the State of Political Science*, Calcutta, Scientific Book Agency, 1971, pp. 323-77

11 Oakeshott brilliantly argues against 'the scientific experiences' in his *Experience and Its Modes*, London, Cambridge University Press, 1933, p. 354 and against 'the sovereignty of technique' in *Rationalism in Politics and Other Essays*, London, Metheun, 1962, pp. 192-247

12 SUSSER, B. 'The Behavioural Ideology: A Review and a Retrospect' *Journal of Political Studies*, January 1979, pp. 271-88

13 DURKHEIM, E. *Suicide: A Study in Sociology*, translated by Spandling and Simpson, Glencoe, Illinois, Free Press, 1951

14 WEBER, M. *Protestant Ethic and the Spirit of Capitalism*, translated by Parsons, London, Unwin University Books, 1970

15 MARX, K. 'Critique of the Gotha Programme' in MARX and ENGELS, *Selected Works*, Vol. 2, Moscow, 1962, p. 26

16 APTER, DAVID E. *Introduction to Political Analysis*, *op. cit.*, p. 381

17 SPIRO, HERBERT J., 'An Evaluation of Systems Theory' in CHARLESWORTH, J.C. (ed.), *op. cit.*, p. 166

18 For elucidation of systems analysis, see the essays in CHARLESWORTH (ed.), *op. cit.* For authoritative works of systems analysis, see EASTON, D. 'An Approach to the Analysis of Political Systems' *World Politics* Vol. 9, 1956-57; and *A Systems Analysis of Political Life*, New York, John Wiley and Sons, 1965; ALMOND, G.A. and COLEMAN, J. *The Politics of the Developing Areas*, New Jersey, Princeton University Press, 1970; ALMOND, G.A. and BINGHAM POWELL, Jr. *Comparative Politics: A Developmental Approach*, Delhi, Amerind Publishing Company, Indian edition, 1972, p. 19; and *Comparative Politics: System, Process and Policy*, Boston, Little Brown, second edition, 1978; DEUTSCH, KARL W. *The Nerves of Government*, New York, Free Press, 1963; and KAPLAN, MORTON A. *System and Process in International Politics*, New York, John Wiley and Sons, 1957

19 BERTALANFFY, LUDWIG VON *General Systems Theory*, New York, George Braziller, 1968

20 LASZLO, E. *Philosophy of Systems Analysis*, New York, Harper Torchbooks, 1973, p. 3

21 EASTON, D. 'Systems Analysis in Political Science Today' *Political Science Review*, January-March 1980, pp. 1-25

22 *Ibid*

23 LASZLO, *op. cit.*, p. 6

24 KAPLAN, MORTON A. 'Systems Theory' in CHARLESWORTH, JAMES C. (ed.), *op. cit.*, pp. 150 and 155-7

25 SPIRO, *op. cit.*, p. 166

26 YOUNG, O. *Systems of Political Science*, New Jersey, Prentice-Hall, 1968, p. 24

27 KAPLAN, *op. cit.*, p. 156

28 RADCLIFFE-BROWN, A.R. *Structure and Function in Primitive Society*, Glencoe, Illinois, Free Press, 1957; and MALINOWSKI, B. *Magic, Sciences, Religion and Other Essays*, New York, Doubleday and Company, 1954

29 MERTON, R. *The Social Theory and Social Structure*, Glencoe, Illinois, Free Press, 1957

30 PARSONS, T. *The Structure of Social Action*, Illinois, Free Press, 1957

31 Almond's Introduction to ALMOND and COLEMEN (eds.), *The Politics of the Developing Areas, op. cit.*, p. 16

32 HOLT, ROBERT T. and TURNER, JOHN E. *The Political Basis of Economic Development*, Delhi, Affiliated East-West Press, 1966

33 *Ibid.*, p. 34

34 For such an argument see KOTHARI, R. (ed.), *State and Nation Building: A Third World Perspective*, Delhi, Allied Publishers, 1976

35 SHETH, D.L. 'Comparative Political Analysis and Nation Building' *ibid.*, pp. 67-92

36 ENGELS, F. *Anti Duhring*, Moscow, 1959; and Stalin, J. *Dialectical and Historical Materialism*, Moscow, 1936

37 *Ibid.*

38 *Ibid.*

39 *Ibid.*

40 MARX, K. and ENGELS, F. *Communist Manifesto*, English edition, 1888

41 *Ibid.*

42 KAPLAN, *op. cit.*

43 GOULDNER, ALVIN W. *The Coming Crisis of Western Sociology*, New York, Basic Books, 1970

44 LASZLO, *op. cit.*, p. 13

45 *Ibid.*

46 HOLT, R.T. and RICHARDSON, J. *The State of Theory in Comparative Politics*, Minneapolis, University of Minnesota, 1968

47 *Ibid.*, p. 79

48 *Ibid.*, p. 79

49 DEUTSCH, K. and WILDENMANN, R. *Social Science Year Book for Politics*, Bond 5, 1976

50 IRLE, H. et. al., *Social Science Year Book for Politics*, Gunter Olzog Verlog, 8 Murchen 22, 1976

51 HOLT and RICHARDSON, *op. cit.*, p. 79

52 See among others ROBERTS, C. *The Scientific Conscience*, New York, George Braziller, 1967; and ANDRESKI, S. *Social Science as Sorcery*, New York, St. Martin's Press, 1972

53 For this argument, see COHEN, M.R. *Reason and Nature: An Essay in the Meaning of the Scientific Method*, New York, Harcourt Brace and Company, 1931, p. 351

54 For such discussion, see excerpts of Eugene Meehan in BALL, H. and LAUTH, T.P. Jr. (eds.), *Changing Perspective in Contemporary Political Analysis*, New Jersey, Prentice-Hall, 1971, p. 21

55 WEBER, M. *Basic Concepts in Sociology*, New York, The Citadel Press, 1964, p.29

56 LEFF, G. *History and Social Theory*, New York, Doubleday and Company, 1971

57 SALMON, L. 'Comparative History and the Theory of Modernization', *World Politics*, Vol. 23, No.1, October 1970, pp. 83-103

3. Political Power and Social Stratification : Class and Caste

1 MARX, K. and ENGELS, F. *Selected Works*, Vol. 2, Moscow, Progress Publishers, 1962, p. 65

2 BENDIX, R. and LIPSET, S.M. (eds.), *Class, Status and Power: Factions in American Society*, Glencoe, Illinois, Free Press, 1953, p. 29

3 PAPPENHEIM, F. *The Alienation of Modern Man*, New York, Modern Reader Paperbacks, 1969, p. 81

4 GERTH and MILLS, *From Max Weber: Essays in Sociology*, New York, Oxford University Press, 1958, p. 181

5 *Ibid.*, p. 181

6 LEFF, G. *History and Social Sciences*, New York, Doubleday and Company, 1971, p. 165

7 MICHELS, R. *First Lectures in Political Sociology*, translated by Alfred de Grazia, New York, Harper and Row, 1949, p. 20

8 WEBER, M. *op. cit.*, p. 194

9 LEFF, G. *op. cit.*, p. 158

10 *Ibid.*, p. 158

11 DAHRENDORF, R. *Class and Class Conflict in Industrial Society*, London, Routledge and Kegan Paul, 1976

12 CAMPBELL, CONVERSE, MILLER and STOKES, *The American Voter*, New York, John Wiley and Sons, 1960, p. 334

13 MADISON, 'Federalist Paper' in BENDIX and LIPSET (eds.), *Class, Status and Power: Factions in American Society*, Glencoe, Illinois, Free Press, 1953, p.22

14 CENTERS, R. *The Psychology of Social Classes*, New Jersey, Princeton University Press, 1949, p. 206

15 KEY, V.O. *Public Opinion and American Democracy*, New York, Alfred A. Knopf, 1961, p. 138

16 See the next chapter

17 ARON, R. 'Social Structure and the Ruling Class' in BENDIX and LIPSET, *op. cit.*, pp. 567-77

18 LASSWELL, H.D. 'Who Gets What, When, How' collected in the *Political Writings of Harold D Lasswell*, Illinois, Free Press, 1951

19 CAMPBELL et. al. *op. cit.*, p. 335

20 PRESTHUS, R. *The Organizational Society*, New York,, Alfred A Knopf, 1962, pp. 59-92

21 For a pointer towards prevalence of caste system among Muslims, see AHMED, IMTIAZ (ed.), *Caste and Social Stratification Among Muslims in India*, Delhi, Manohar, 1972

22 MANDELBAUM, D.G. *Society in India*, Bombay, Popular Prakashan, Indian edition, 1972, p. 3

23 GHURYE, G.S. *Class, Caste and Occupation*, Bombay, Popular Book Depot, 1961, pp. 42-111

24 MARX, K. 'The British Rule in India' in *Selected Works*, Vol. 2, pp. 652-61

25 WEBER, M. *The Religion of India: The Sociology of Hinduism and Buddhism*, translated and edited by Gerth and Martindale, Glencoe, Illinois, Free Press, 1958

26 The concept of Sanskritization was first used by Srinivas in his book, *Religion and Society Among the Coorgs of South India*, London, Oxford University Press, 1952; this concept is discussed in detail in his *Caste in Modern India and Other Essays*, Bombay, Asia Publishing House, p. 23

27 The concept of 'dominant caste' was developed by M N Srinivas in his studies of village social structure. He held that each Indian village was 'multi-caste' usually containing a dominant caste. He has specially used this concept in 'The Dominant Caste in Rampura', *American Anthropologist*, Vol. 61, No. 1, February 1959

28 BETEILLE, A. *Castes: Old and New*, Bombay, Asia Publishing House, 1969, p. 70

29 RUDOLPH, LLOYD I. and RUDOLPH, SUSANNE H. 'The Political Role of India's Caste Associations' *Pacific Affairs*, Vol. 32, No. 1, March 1960; and *The Modernity of Tradition*, Chicago, University of Chicago Press, 1967

30 BAVISKAR, B.S. 'Co-operatives and Politics' *Economic and Political Weekly*, Vol. 3, No. 12, March 1968

31 NARAIN, I. 'Politics and Panchayati Raj' *Indian Journal of Political Science*, Vol. 23, No.4, October-December 1962

32 NARAIN, I. *State Politics in India*, Meerut, Meenakshi Prakashan, 1967

33 ROY, R. 'Caste and Political Recruitment in Bihar' in KOTHARI, R. (ed.), *Caste in Indian Politics*, Delhi, Orient Longman, 1973, pp. 228-58

34 Some important studies of the Indian Cabinet: NORTH, R.C. 'The Indian Council of Ministers, A Study of Origins' in PARK, R.L. and TINKER, I. (eds.), *Leadership and Political Institutions in India*, London, Oxford University Press, 1960; ARORA, S.K. 'Social Background of the Indian Cabinet' *Economic and Political Weekly*, Vol. VII, Nos. 31-33, 1972, pp. 1523-5; and SHARMA, L.N. 'The Prime Minister and Cabinet' in his book *The Indian Prime Minister* Delhi, Macmillan Company of India, 1976

35 SADASIVAN, S.N. *Party and Democracy in India*, Delhi, Tata Mcgraw-Hill Publishing Company, 1977, p. 474

36 *Ibid.*

37 WEINER, M. and KOTHARI, R. *Indian Voting Behaviour: Studies of the 1962 General Elections*, Calcutta, Mukhopadhyaya, 1965

38 *Ibid.*

39 See Centre for the Study of Developing Societies, *Party System and Election Studies*, Delhi, Allied Publishers, 1967

40 WEINER and KOTHARI, *Indian Voting Behaviour, op. cit.*
41 *Ibid.*
42 KOTHARI, R. 'The Political Change of 1967' *Economic and Political Weekly*, Annual Issue, January 1971
43 See GOYAL, O.P. 'Caste and Politics—A Conceptual Framework' *Asian Survey*, Vol. 5, No. 10, 1965
44 This view is also expressed by Philips in his introduction to PHILIPS, C.H. (ed.), *Politics and Society in India*, London, George Allen and Unwin, 1963, p. 7
45 SHETH, D.L. 'Caste and Politics: A Trend Report' *Political Science in India : A Trend Report*, Indian Council of Social Science Research, Delhi, March 1971. (Mimeographed and circulated among the members of the Committee)

4. The Elite Theory of Political Power

1 SCHUMPETER, *Capitalism, Socialism and Democracy*, New York, Harper, 1950
2 MEISEL, J.H. *The Myth of the Ruling Class: Gaetano Mosca and the Elite*, Ann Arbor, University of Michigan Press, 1956 p. 4
3 The propositions constituting Vilfredo Pareto's theory of the elites are found mainly in these sources (*i*) A monograph written in Italian in 1901 translated into English under the title *The Rise and Fall of the Elites: An Application of Theoretical Society*, New Jersey, The Bedminton Press, 1968; (*ii*) His major work is a 3000 page treatise written in Italian in 1916. Its English translation was first called *Mind and Society*, 4 Vols., New York, Harcourt, Brace and Company, 1935; but a more appropriate title has been given in another reprint, *The Mind and Society: A Treatise on General Sociology*, New York, 1963. We shall hereinafter refer to the 1963 edition; (*iii*) Two other works not translated are *Les Systems Socialistes*, 2 Vols., Paris, Giard, 1902-03; and *Manule Di Economic Political*, 1906
4 For sub-classification of residues, see Pareto, *A Treatise on General Sociology*, pp. 516-9
5 *Ibid.*, p. 899
6 *Ibid.*, pp. 1515 and 1561-2
7 PARETO, *The Rise & Fall of the Elites*, p. 36
8 See ZETTERBERG, HANS *Introduction, ibid.*, p. 9
9 PARETO, *A Treatise on General Sociology*, p. 1431
10 PARETO, *The Rise and Fall of the Elites*, p. 59
11 *Ibid.*, p. 36
12 *Ibid.*, p. 86
13 MOSCA, G. *The Ruling Class*, first published in Italian in 1896, New York, McGraw-Hill, English edition, 1939, p. 50
14 *Ibid*
15 *Ibid.*, pp. 50-1

16 *Ibid.*, p. 53
17 *Ibid.*, pp. 57-60
18 *Ibid.*, pp. 60-2
19 *Ibid.*, p. 65
20 *Ibid*
21 MICHELS, R. *First Lectures in Political Sociology*, translated by Alfred de Grazia, New York, Harper and Row, 1949, pp. 141-2
22 MICHELS, R. *Political Parties: A Sociological Study of The Oligarchical Tendencies of Modern Democracy*, Illinois, Free Press, 1915, p. 418
23 *Ibid.*, p. 417
24 *Ibid.*, p. 418
25 *Ibid.*, p. 288
26 *Ibid.*, p. 58
27 BURNHAM, J. *The Managerial Revolution*, London, Putnam, 1942, pp. 27-28 and 72-3
28 VEBLEN, T. *The Engineers and the Price System*, New York, The Viking Press, 1921, p. 74
29 DJILAS, M. *The New Class*, London, Thames and Hudson, 1957, p. 38
30 *Ibid.*, p. 40
31 *Ibid.*, p. 45
32 *Ibid.*, p. 69
33 MILLS, C.W. *The Power Elites*, London, Oxford University Press, 1959, p. 4
34 LASSWELL, H.D. 'Politics: Who Gets What, When, How', collected in the *Political Writings of Harold D Lasswell*, Illinois, Free Press, 1951, p. 259
35 *Ibid.*, p. 311
36 *Ibid.*, p. 392
37 *Ibid.*, p. 409
38 For a good summary of elitist views as well as criticisms, see PARRY, G. *Political Elites*, London, George Allen and Unwin, 1969, p. 30
39 SCHUMPETER, *Capitalism, Socialism and Democracy*, p. 269
40 KAUFMAN, H. *Politics in State and Local Governments*, New Jersey, Prentice-Hall, 1963, p. 89
41 DAHL, R.A. *Polyarchy: Participation and Opposition*, New Haven, Yale University Press, 1971, p. 1
42 PLAMENATZ, J. *Democracy and Illusion*, London, Longman, 1973, p. 187
43 DAHL, R.A. *Who Governs?* New Haven, Yale University Press, 1961, p. 90
44 *Ibid.*, p. 102
45 POLSBY, NELSON W. *Community Power and Political Theory*, New Haven, Yale University Press, 1963, p. 128
46 Lipset uses this word in Introduction to MICHELS, R. *Political Parties*, New York, Collier, 1962, p. 33
47 MOSCA, *The Ruling Class*, p. 292
48 *Ibid.*, p. 286
49 Cited in BOTTOMORE, T.B. *Elites and Society*, Middlesex, Penguin, 1964, p. 15
50 ARON, R. 'Social Structure and the Ruling Class' in EISENSTADT, S.N. (ed.), *Political Sociology: A Reader*, New York, Basic Books, 1971, pp. 418-20

5. The Group Theory of Politics

1 Each discipline however, has a varied frame of reference. When sociology, for instance, devotes itself to the study of groups and groupings (social groupings such as economic and social class, are analytically prior to social groups in the sense that the activity and even the interpretation of goals of a formal organization reflect the fundamental groupings from which the members of the groups are drawn), its focus is on the forms of group structure and behaviour, the role of the individual in the group and his relation to it, the internal organization of the group, the development of functional norms of behaviour, the tendency of informal groups to sift themselves into leadership and the led, the relation of the subgroups to a central body, and so on.

2 The pluralists who reached their zenith by the first quarter of this century recognized multiple patterns of group affiliations of loyalities; nevertheless, they failed to recognize in them the functional basis of the institution of government. They were bent upon discrediting the state and hence, could not substantially make out a reasonable case for correlation between the functioning of groups and that of the government.

3 WOOTON, G. *Interest Groups*, New Jersey, Prentice-Hall, 1969

4 BENTLEY, ARTHUR F. *The Process of Government: A Study of Social Pressures*, Bloomington, The Principia Press, 1908, pp. 208-9

5 *Ibid.*, p. 211

6 *Ibid.*, p. 3

7 *Ibid.*, p. 163

8 *Ibid*

9 *Ibid.*, p. 176

10 *Ibid.*, p. 209

11 *Ibid.*, p. 190

12 *Ibid.*, p. 200

13 *Ibid.*, pp. 218-22

14 *Ibid.*, p. 259

15 *Ibid.*, see pp. 260 and 273-6

16 TRUMAN, DAVID B. *The Governmental Process*, New York, Alfred A Knopf, 1957, p. 24

17 *Ibid.*, p. 27

18 *Ibid.*, pp. 33-7

19 *Ibid.*, p. 40

20 *Ibid.*, p. 45

21 LATHAM, E. 'The Group Basis of Politics: Notes for a Theory' reprinted in EULAU et. al. (eds.), *Political Behaviour: A Reader in Theory and Research*, Delhi, Amerind Publishing Company, Indian edition, 1972, pp. 232-42

22 MORRIS-JONES, W.H. *The Government and Politics of India*, London, Hutchinson, 1964, p. 185

23 For an account of interest groups in the USA, see CORRY and HODGETS *Democratic Government and Politics*, Ch. 10; GROSS *Legislative Struggle*, Ch. 3; BANNEY *The Governing of Man*, Ch. 16; and ODEGARD et. al., *American Government*, Ch. 7

24 PHILIPS, C.H. *Politics and Society in India*, London, George Allen and Unwin, 1963

25 ALMOND, *op. cit.*

26 For this line of argument, see KOCHANEK, STANLEY A. 'Group Formation and Interest Group Theory' *Political Science Review*, Jaipur, January-March 1980

6. Political Parties and Political System

1 DUVERGER, M. *Political Parties—Their Organization and Activity in the Modern State*, London, Methuen, 1954, pp. 24-5

2 SCHUMPETER, J.A. *Capitalism, Socialism and Democracy*, New York, Harper, 1950, p. 283

3 WEBER, M. *The Theory of Social and Economic Organization*, London, William Hodge and Company, 1947, pp. 373-4

4 Giovanni Sartori prefers this 'minimal definition' of party. See his *Parties and Party Systems*, Vol. I, London, Cambridge University Press, 1976, p. 63

5 HENNESSY, B. 'On the Study of Party Organization' in CROTTY, WIILLIAM D. (ed.), *Approaches to the Study of Party Organization*, Allyn and Bacon, 1968, p. 1

6 See LEISERSON, A. *Parties and Politics: An Institutional and Behavioural Approach*, New York, Alfred A Knopf, 1958

7 DUVERGER, *op. cit.*, p. 15

8 *Ibid.*, p. 17

9 Duverger's study is, however, monumental and provides a wide comparative perspective

10 BRYCE, J. *The American Commonwealth*, 2 Vols., New York, Macmillan, 1916

11 OSTROGORSKI, M. Y. *Democracy and Organization of Political Parties*, 2 Vols., Chicago, Quadrangle, 1964, p. 102

12 MICHELS, R. *Political Parties: A Sociological Study of the Oligarchical Tendencies of Modern Democracy*, Illinois, Free Press, 1915

13 NEUMANN, S. (ed.), *Modern Political Parties*, Chicago, University of Chicago Press, 1956, p. 407

14 MACKENZIE, R.T. *British Political Parties*, London, Heinemann, 1963, p. 635

15 For details of this episode, see MORRISON, H. *Government and Parliament*, London, Oxford University Press, 1950, pp. 140-1; and MACKENZIE, R.T. *op. cit.*, p. 330. For further discussion on the point, see BEER, S.H. *Modern British Politics*, London, Faber and Faber, 1955, p. 89; CROSSMAN, R. *Inside View*, London, Jonathan Cape, 1965; and SHARMA, L.N. *The Indian Prime Minister*, Delhi, Macmillan, 1976

16 DUVERGER, *op. cit.*, pp. 5-16
17 See *ibid.*, pp. 63-78
18 MICHELS, R. *op. cit.*
19 NEUMANN, S. 'Toward a Comparative Study of Political Parties' in NEUMANN (ed.), *Modern Political Parties*, Chicago, University of Chicago Press, 1956, p. 407
20 *Ibid.*, p. 410
21 ELDERSVELD, S. J. *Political Parties: A Behavioural Analysis*, Bombay, Vora and Co., 1971
22 See WEBER, M. *The Theory of Social and Economic Organization*, Illinois, Free Press, 1947, p. 407; and NEUMANN, *op. cit.*, p. 412
23 ELDERSVELD, *op. cit.*, p. 135
24 LEISERSON, *op. cit.*
25 Rejecting the numerical criterion, La Palombara and Weiner propose for the competitive party systems, the following fourfold typology (*i*) hegemonic ideological (*ii*) hegemonic pragmatic (*iii*) turnover ideological (*iv*) turnover pragmatic. See their *Political Parties and Political Development*, New Jersey, Princeton University Press, pp. 34-6. Though this classification is suggestive, the numerical criterion has relevance and with elucidations of its variations can be put to better use. From this point of view, Sartori's classification is worth consideration. He examines seven classes of political parties—one party, hegemonic party, predominant party, two party, limited pluralism, extreme pluralism, atomized (i.e. when it has no noticeable effect and has no structural consolidation). However, for purposes of our discussion, we have taken here the numerical division above
26 See SARTORI, *op. cit.*, p. 125
27 *Ibid.*, p. 4
28 *Ibid.*, p. 29
29 *Ibid.*, p. 26
30 *Ibid.*, p. 36
31 HUNTINGTON, SAMUEL P. *Political Order in Changing Societies*, New Haven, Yale University Press, 1968, p. 407
32 SARTORI, *op. cit.*, p. 40
33 *Ibid.*, p. 42
34 *Ibid.*, p. 28
35 KEY, V.O. *Politics, Parties and Pressure Groups*, New York, Thomas Y Gowsell Company, 1958, p. 184
36 *Ibid.*, p. 12
37 LOWI, T. 'Toward Functionalism in Political Science, The Case of Innovation in Party System' *American Political Science Review*, Vol. LVII, No. 3, September 1963, p. 571
38 KEY, V.O. *op. cit.*, pp. 227-30
39 See SADASIVAN, S.N. *Party and Democracy in India*, Delhi, Tata McGraw-Hill Publishing Company, 1977
40 *Ibid.*, p. 462
41 Various terms like 'one party dominant system' or 'one party dominance' or 'one dominant party system' have been used to connote the same meaning

42 MORRIS-JONES, W.H. 'Dominance and Dissent' *Government and Opposition*, Vol. I, July-September 1958; 'The Indian Congress Party, A Dilemma of Dominance' *Modern Asian Studies*, Vol. 1, April 1967; and KOTHARI, R. 'Form and Substance in Indian Politics, Union and State Relations' *The Economic Weekly*, Vol. XIII, 29 April and 6 May 1961; 'The Congress System in India' *Asian Survey*, Vol. IV, December 1964; 'India: The Congress System on Trial' *Asian Survey*, Vol. VII, February 1967

43 DUVERGER, M. *Party Politics and Pressure Groups*, translated by Robert Wagoner, London, Nelson, 1972

44 KEY, V.O. Jr. *Southern Politics in State and Nation*, New York, Alfred A Knopf, 1949, pp. 298-311

45 DUVERGER, M. *op. cit.*, p. 36

46 WHITE, G. 'One Party Dominance and Third Parties: The Pinnard Theory Reconsidered' *Canadian Journal of Political Science*, Vol. 3, September 1973, pp. 400-1

47 The Central Government was always Congress Government and it has substantial following in the Lok Sabha. The following figures indicating the strength of the Central Government after each general election, will illustrate this point.

Year	Total No. of Seats	No. of Congress Members in L.S.
1952	489	364
1957	494	371
1962	491	358
1967	518	284
1971	518	352

See JAIN H.M. 'Minority Government: Indian Experience' in *Studies in Political Science*, Delhi, Research Publications, p. 139 (not dated)
The figures for the seats in state legislatures roughly correspond to these till 1967 but there were variations in different states in 1967 elections

48 See *ibid.*, pp. 139-48

49 In the elections to the Lok Sabha, it secured 44.99% of votes cast in 1952, 47.78% in 1962 and 40.72% in 1967. See the table in CHANDIDAS, R. *The Electoral System and Political Development in Elections and Electoral Reforms in India*, Delhi, 1971, p. 129. In 1971 Parliamentary election, it secured 43.06% valid votes polled

50 PALMER, NORMAN D. *The Indian Political System*, Boston, Houghton Mifflin Company, 1971, p. 205

51 In a recent study, it is pointed out that political pressure groups in the form of political pragmatic dissenters exist in one party system as well. See SHAPIRO, L. *Political Opposition in One Party State*, London, Macmillan Press, 1972, pp. 5-14

52 For the differences in party relationships and characteristics between a democratic and a totalitarian party, see VERNEY, D.V. *An Analysis of Political System*, London, Routledge and Kegan Paul, 1969, p. 329

53 KOTHARI, R. *Politics in India, op. cit.*, pp. 160-1. It is obvious by this analysis that political parties do not perform in India the function of identification with one group and differentiation from another which Neumann and Apter think essential for a political party to perform
54 *Ibid.*, p. 161
55 See also JOSHI and DESAI, 'Dominance with a Difference, Strains and Challenges' *Economic and Political Weekly*, Annual Number, February 1973
56 KOTHARI, R. *Politics in India, op. cit.*, p. 166
57 Cited in GRAHAM, B.D. 'Congress as a Rally: An Image of Leadership' *South Asian Review*, Vol. 6, January 1973, p. 117
58 For Nehru's own statement on the subject, see *Congress Bulletin*, April 1955, pp. 249-51
59 For an analysis, see KOCHANEK, STANLEY A. *The Congress Party of India: The Dynamics of One Party Democracy*, New Jersey, Princeton University Press, 1968, pp. 417-8
60 MORRIS-JONES, W.H. *The Government and Politics of India*, London, Hutchinson University Library, 1971, p. 213

7. Bureaucracy, Society and Politics

1 WEBER, M. 'Bureaucracy' in GERTH and MILLS (eds.), *From Max Weber, Essays in Sociology*, New York, Oxford University Press, 1958, pp. 196-204
2 WEBER, M. *Theory of Social and Economic Organization*, New York, Oxford University Press, 1947, pp. 333-6
3 WEBER, M. 'Bureaucracy', *op. cit.*, p. 214
4 *Ibid.*, p. 215
5 BALAU, P.M. and SCOTT, W.R. *Formal Organization*, San Francisco, Chandler, 1962
6 MERTON, R.K. *Social Theory and Social Structure*, Glencoe, Illinois, Free Press, 1957, pp. 253-4
7 *Ibid.*, p. 254
8 SCHUBERT Jr. *The Public Interest*, Glencoe, Illinois, Free Press, 1960
9 WEBER, M., 'Bureaucracy', *op. cit.*, p. 228
10 *Ibid.*, p. 231
11 *Ibid.*, p. 231
12 MICHELS, R. *Political Parties, A Sociological Study of The Oligarchial Tendencies of Modern Democracy*, Illinois, Free Press, 1956
13 PEABODY, R.L. and REURKE, F.E. 'Public Bureaucratics' in MARCH, J.G. (ed.), *Handbook of Organizations*, Chicago, Rand McNally and Company, 1965, p. 828
14 RIGGS, F.W. 'The Context of Development Administrator' in RIGGS, F.W. (ed.), *Frontiers of Development Administration*, Durham, Duke University Press, 1970, p. 80

15 MARX, F.M. 'The Higher Civil Service As An Action Group in Western Political Development' in LA PALOMBARA (ed.), *Bureaucracy and Political Development*, New Jersey, Princeton University Press, 1963, p. 64
16 *Ibid.*, p. 64
17 *Ibid.*, p. 64
18 *Ibid.*, p. 93
19 RIGGS, 'Bureaucracy and Political Development: A Paradoxical View' in LA PALOMBARA (ed.), *op. cit.*, p. 121
20 *Ibid.*, p. 121
21 *Ibid.*, p. 124
22 *Ibid.*, p. 126
23 *Ibid.*, p. 127
24 *Ibid.*, p. 129
25 ASHRAF, A. *Government and Politics of Big Cities: An Indian Case Study*, Delhi, Concept Publishers, 1977
26 SUBRAMANIAM V. 'Representative Bureaucracy' *American Political Science Review*, Vol. 61, No. 4, pp. 1010-9
27 PANANDIKER and KSHIRSAGAR, *Bureaucracy and Development*, New Delhi, Administrative Centre for Policy Research, 1978, p. 46

8. Political Development, Modernization and Political Culture

1 APTER, D. *The Politics of Modernization*, Chicago, University of Chicago Press, 1965, p. 1
2 EISENSTADT, S.N. *Modernization, Protest and Change*, Delhi, Prentice-Hall of India, 1969, p. 11
3 BLACK, C.E. *The Dynamics of Modernization*, New York, 1966
4 MOORE, B. *Social Origins of Dictatorship and Democracy: Lord and Peasant in the Making of the Modern World*, London, Allen Lane, 1967
5 HUNTINGTON, S. *Political Order in Changing Societies*, New Haven, Yale University Press, 1968, p. 32
6 EISENSTADT, S.N. *Modernization, Protest and Change*, Delhi, Prentice-Hall of India, 1969, p. 1
7 *Ibid.*, p. 1
8 SHILS, E. *Political Development in the New State*, The Hague, Mouton, 1962
9 APTER, D. *The Politics of Modernization*, Chicago, University of Chicago Press, 1965
10 PYE, L.W. *Aspects of Political Development*, Delhi, Amerind Publishing Company, Indian edition, 1972, p. 31
11 *Ibid.*, p. 45
12 *Ibid.*, p. 46

13 *Ibid.*, p. 47
14 DIAMENT, A. 'The Nature of Political Development' in FINKLE and GABLE (eds.), *Political Development and Social Change*, New York, John Wiley and Sons, 1968, pp. 91-118
15 ILLCHMAN, W. and UPHOFF, N. *The Political Economy of Change*, Berkeley, University of California Press, 1969, p. 8
16 *Ibid.*, p. 8
17 *Ibid.*, p. 11
18 *Ibid.*, p. 15
19 *Ibid.*, p. 17
20 *Ibid.*, p. 47
21 HUNTINGTON, *op. cit.*, p. 35
22 *Ibid.*, p. 49
23 KOTHARI, R. (ed.), *State and Nation Building: A Third World Perspective*, Delhi, Allied Publishers, 1976, p. 6
24 *Ibid.*, p. 7
25 *Ibid.*, p. 12
26 CAZALEY, D. (ed.), *American Political Institutions in the 1970s*, New York, Columbia University Press, 1976
27 ALMOND and VERBA, *The Civic Culture*, New Jersey, Princeton University Press, 1963, p. 14
28 *Ibid.*, p. 13
29 DOWSE, R. and HUGHES, JOHN A. *Political Sociology*, London, John Wiley and Sons, 1972, p. 227
30 ALMOND and VERBA, *op. cit.*, p. 31
31 *Ibid.*, p. 32
32 *Ibid.*, p. 6
33 KOTHARI, R. *Democratic Polity and Social Change in India*, Bombay, Allied Publishers, 1976, p. 22
34 *Ibid.*, p. 23

9. Political Participation and Electoral Process

1 MERRIAM, CHARLES E. and GOSNELL, HAROLD F. *Non-Voting*, Chicago, University of Chicago Press, 1924
2 MERRIAM, CHARLES E. *The Making of Citizens: A Comparative Study of the Methods of Civic Training*, Chicago, University of Chicago Press, 1931
3 NIE, NORMAN H. and VERBA, S. 'Political Participation' in GREENSTEIN, F.I. and POLSBY N.W. (eds.), *Handbook of Political Science*, Vol. 4, Massachusetts, Addison-Wesley Publishing Company, 1975, p. 1
4 HUNTINGTON, SAMUEL P. and NELSON, JOAN M. *No Easy Choice*, Cambridge, Harvard University Press, 1976, p. 4
5 *Ibid.*, p. 5

6 ALMOND and VERBA, *The Civic Culture*, New Jersey, Princeton University Press, 1963
7 BERELSON, B., LAZARSFELD, PAUL F. and MCPHES, W.N. *Voting*, Chicago, University of Chicago Press, 1954
8 RUSH, M. and ALTHOFF, P. *An Introduction to Political Sociology*, London, Nelson, 1971
9 HUNTINGTON and NELSON, *op. cit.*, pp. 4-5
10 NIE and VERBA, *op. cit.*, p. 3
11 MATHEWS, D.R. and PROTHO, J.W. *Negroes and the New Southern Politics*, New York, Harcourt, Brace and World, 1966, p. 37
12 RUSH and ALTHOFF, *op. cit.*
13 NIE and VERBA, *op. cit.*, p. 3; HUNTINGTON and NELSON, *op. cit.*, p. 5
14 WOODWARD, JULIAN L. and ROPER, E. 'Political Activity of American Citizens' in EULAU et. al. (eds.), *Political Behaviour: A Reader in Theory and Research*, Delhi, American Publication Company, p. 133
15 NIE and VERBA (*op. cit.*, p. 10) term them as 'co-operative activity' and HUNTINGTON and NELSON (*op. cit.*, p. 12) as 'lobbying'
16 NIE and VERBA (*op. cit.*, p. 9) term them as 'citizen-initiated contacts'
17 VERBA, S., NIE, N.H. and KIM, JAE-ON in *The Modes of Democratic Participation: A Cross-National Comparison*, California, Sage Publications, 1971, pp. 41-3 and 57-9, regard 'particularized contacting' as a mode of political participation separate from and almost wholly unrelated to other modes
18 NIE and VERBA, *op. cit.*, p. 3
19 HUNTINGTON and NELSON, *op. cit.*, p. 6
20 CAMPBELL et. al., *The Voter Decides*, Evanston, Row, Peterson and Company, 1954, p. 187. Also see ROSENBERG, MORRIS 'Some Determination of Political Apathy' in EULAU et. al. (eds.), *op. cit.*, pp. 160-9, for further enlightenment on the subject
21 DURKHEIM, E. *Suicide: A Study in Sociology*, translated by Spandling and Simpson, Glencoe, Illinois, Free Press, 1951, pp. 246-54
22 RIESMAN, D. *The Lonely Crowd*, New Haven, Yale University Press, 1950, p. 287
23 MAYO, E. *The Human Problems of an Industrial Civilization*, New York, Macmillan, 1933, pp. 131-2
24 LANE, ROBERT E. *Political Life*, Glencoe, Illinois, Free Press, 1959, p. 167
25 FROMM, E. *The Sane Society*, New York, Rinehart, 1955, pp. 120-208
26 WEINER, M. 'Political Participation: Crisis of the Political Process' in BINDER, L., COLEMAN, J.S., LA PALOMBARA, J., PYE, L., VERBA, S. and WEINER, M. (eds.), *Crisis and Sequences in Political Development*, New Jersey, Princeton University Press, 1971
27 LANE, *op. cit.*, p. 94
28 HUNTINGTON and NELSON, *op. cit.*, p. 15
29 LANE, *op. cit.*, p. 67
30 *Ibid.*, p. 73
31 *Ibid.*, p. 79
32 *Ibid.*, p. 85
33 *Ibid.*, p. 92
34 HUNTINGTON and NELSON, *op. cit.*, p. 42
35 NIE and VERBA, *op. cit.*, p. 33

36 *Ibid.*, p. 38
37 Cited in HUNTINGTON and NELSON, *op. cit.*, p. 11
38 One study, conducted in the United States during the height of the Vietnam War protests, found only eight citizens (out of 1500 interviewed) who had even taken part in a demonstration about Vietnam, about one half of a per cent. See VERBA and RICHARD, 'Participation, Preferences and the War in Vietnam' *Public Opinion Quarterly*, Vol. 34, 1970, pp. 325-32. For a theoretical, cross-national exploration of the type of individuals who tend to participate in demonstrations and protests, see ARORA, S.K. 'Political Participation: Deprivation and Protest' *Economic and Political Weekly*, Vol. 6, Annual Number, 1971, pp. 341-50
39 NIE and VERBA, *op. cit.*, p. 38
40 *Ibid.*, pp. 24-5
41 TITUS, CHARLES H. *Voting Behaviour in the United States*, Berkeley, University of California Press, pp. 1-2
42 GARCEAU, OLIVER 'Research in the Political Process' in EULAU et. al. (eds.), *Political Behaviour*, Glencoe, Free Press, pp. 44-5
43 WEINER, M. and KOTHARI, R. *Indian Voting Behaviour: Studies of the 1962 General Elections*, Calcutta, Mukhopadhyay, 1965
44 SIRSIKAR, V.M. *Political Behaviour in India: A Case Study of the 1962 General Elections*, Bombay, Manaktalas, 1965
45 A summary of the ICSSR sponsored studies of the 1967 elections in several states is available in ICSSR, *Studies in the Fourth General Election*, Delhi, Allied Publishers, 1972
46 VERMA, S.P., NARAIN, I. et. al., *Voting Behaviour in A Changing Society*, Delhi, National, 1973
47 *Ibid.*, p. 365
48 SIRSIKAR, V.M. *Sovereigns Without Crowns*, Bombay, Popular Prakashan, 1973
49 See *ibid.*, p. 22
50 PRASAD, R.C. *The Mature Electorate*, Delhi, Ashish Publishing House, 1975
51 BHAMBHRI, C.P. and VERMA, S.P. *The Urban Voter: Municipal Elections in Rajasthan*, Delhi, National, 1973
52 SESHADRI, K. and JAIN, S.P. *Panchayati Raj and Political Perceptions of Electorate*, Hyderabad, National Institute of Community Development, not dated
53 REDDY and SESHADRI, *The Voter and Panchayati Raj: A Study of the Electoral Behaviour During Panchayati Elections in Warangal District, Andhra Pradesh*, Hyderabad, National Institute of Community Development, 1972
54 SOMJEE, A.H. *Voting Behaviour in an Indian Village*, Baroda, 1969
55 NARAIN, I., PANDA, K.C. and SHARMA, M.L. *The Rural Elite and Elections*, Delhi, National, 1976
56 This argument forms the hub of a few papers in Centre for the Study of Developing Societies, *Party System and Election Studies*, Delhi, Allied Publishers, 1967
57 GRAHAM, B.D. 'Studies of Indian Elections—A Review Article' *Journal of Commonwealth and Comparative Politics*, July 1975, pp. 193-205
58 KINI, N.G.S. *The City Voter in India*, Delhi, Abhinav Publications, 1974

59 *Ibid.*, p. 21
60 See last part of Centre for the Study of Developing Societies, *Party System and Election Studies, op. cit.*
61 See *Context of Electoral Change in India*; *General Elections 1967*, Bombay, Academic Books, 1969
62 *Ibid.*
63 ROY, R. *The Uncertain Verdict: A Study of the 1969 Elections in Four States*, Delhi, Orient Longman, 1972
64 KOTHARI, R. 'The Political Change of 1967' *Economic and Political Weekly*, Annual Number, January 1971
65 The findings are published in a series of articles entitled 'Voting in India: Competitive Politics and Electoral Change' *Economic and Political Weekly*, Annual Number, February 1971
66 SIRSIKAR, *Political Behaviour in India. op. cit.*
67 The reference is to BERELSON, LAZARSFELD and MCPHEE'S *Voting: A Study of Opinion Formation in a Presidential Campaign*, Chicago, University of Chicago Press, 1954
68 SIRSIKAR, *Sovereigns Without Crowns op. cit.*
69 KINI, *The City Voter in India, op. cit.*
70 PANTHAM, T. *Voting Behaviour in Baroda City: A 1967 General Election Study*, Baroda, M S University of Baroda, 1968
71 GANGULY, B. and GANGULY, M. *Voting Behaviour in a Developing Society West Bengal: A Case Study*, Delhi, Sterling, 1975
72 MANNHEIM, K. 'American Sociology' in his *Essays on Sociology and Social Psychology*, London, 1953, p. 187
73 See SIRSIKAR, V.M. 'The Study of Voting Behaviour in India' *Political Science Review*, Vol. 2, No. 1, March 1963. Iqbal Narain has drawn attention to this fact in a forthcoming publication, *Election Studies in India: An Evaluation.* A summary of the findings of this book is available in *Teaching Politics*, Delhi, Vol. III, Nos. 1 and 2, 1977, pp. 47-57. Also see in the same issue KAUSHIK, S. 'Election Studies in India —Wanted a Theoretical Perspective' pp. 59-60

10. Public Opinion and Political Stabilization

1 BAILEY, THOMAS A. *The Man in the Street*, New York, Macmillan, 1948, p.1
2 LIPPMAN, WALTER *Public Opinion*, New York, Macmillan, 1954
3 WALLAS, GRAHAM *Human Nature in Politics*, London, Constable and Company, 1908
4 MILLS, C.W *The Power Elites*, London, Oxford University Press, 1969
5 FALLERS, L. 'Equality, Modernity and Democracy in the New States' in GEERTZ, C. (ed.), *Old Societies and New States*, Delhi, Amerind Publishing Company, Indian edition, 1971, pp. 204-7

6 Cited in KEY, Jr., *Public Opinion and American Democracy*, New York, Alfred A Knoff, 1961, p. 9

7 *Ibid.*, p. 15

8 BLUMER, H. 'The Mass, the Public, and Public Opinion' in BERELSON, B. and JANOWITZ, M. *Reader in Public Opinion and Communication*, Glencoe, Illinois, Free Press, 1953, pp. 46-8

9 CONVERSE, P.E. 'Public Opinion and Voting Behaviour' in GREENSTEIN, F.I. and POLSBY, N.W. *Handbook of Political Science*, Vol. 4, Cambridge, Addison-Wesley Publishing Company, p. 78

10 ALMOND, 'Public Opinion and National Security Policy' *Public Opinion Quarterly*, Vol. XX, 1956, pp. 371-8

11 KEY, V.O. *op. cit.* p. 89; for detailed exposition, see REMMERS, H.H. *Introduction to Opinion and Attitude Measurement*, New York, Harper, 1954; GREEN, BERT F. 'Attitude Measurement' in LINDZEY, G. (ed.), *Handbook of Social Psychology* Vol. I, Cambridge, Addison-Wesley Publishing Company, 1954, pp. 335-69 and TORGERSON, WARREN S. *Theory and Methods of Scaling*, New York, Wiley, 1956

12 *Handbook of Political Science*, Vol. 4, *op. cit.*, p. 78

13 These scales have made possible measurement of attitudes towards a public issue by ranging them along a scale through a series of different ways of dealing with the question. For example, views on economic policy may be arranged along a scale from the extreme left to the extreme right. The opinion of an individual may be located at any one of the many points along such a scale. One person may favour governmental ownership of all the means of production, another may be satisfied with a large dose of governmental regulation, still another may prefer only the most limited control of the economy, and others may wish to abolish whatever controls exist. Such scaling makes possible a more informed estimate of the nature of public opinion

14 CENTERS, R. *The Psychology of Social Classes*, New Jersey, Princeton University Press, 1949

15 CONVERSE, 'The Shifting Role of Class in Political Attitudes and Behaviour' in MACCOBY, E., NEWCOMB, T. and HARTLAY, E. *Reading in Social Psychology*, New York, Holt, Reinhart and Winston, 1958

16 See KATZ, D. 'The Measurement of Intensity' in CANTRIL H., *Gauging Public Opinion*, New Jersey, Princeton University Press, 1944, Ch. 8.

17 Indian Council of Social Science Research sponsored project, *A Survey of Research in Political Science*, Vol. 2, Delhi, Allied Publishers, 1981, p. 2

18 RUSH and ALTHOFF, *An Introduction to Political Sociology*, London, Nelson, 1971, p. 1

19 EASTON, D. and DENNIS, J. *Children in the Political System: Origins of Political Legitimacy*, New York, McGraw-Hill, 1969 p. 7; for a detailed and fine discussion, see RENSHON, S.A. (ed.), *Handbook of Political Socialization: Theory and Research*, New York, Free Press, 1977

20 ALMOND, G.A. and COLEMEN, J.S. *The Politics of the Developing Areas*, New Jersey, Princeton University Press, 1960. See particularly the Introduction to this book by G. Almond, p. 16

21 *Ibid.*

22 HYMAN, H.H. *Political Socialization: A Study in the Psychology of Political Behaviour*, Glencoe, Illinois, Free Press, 1959

23 ALMOND and COLEMAN, *op. cit.*

24 Revealed by a survey referred to in GUJRAL, J.K. 'Planning for Television' *The States*, 28 April 1973, p. 7

25 CHANDER, R. 'TV Challenge' in *ibid.*, p. 6

26 *Handbook of Political Science*, Vol. 4, *op. cit.*

27 Cited in RUSH and ALTHOFF, *An Introduction to Politicial Sociology, op. cit.*

28 *Ibid.*

29 PARK, ROBERT E. 'News and the Power of the Press', *American Journal of Sociology*, Vol. XLVII

30 LOWELL, A.L. *Public Opinion and Popular Government*, New York, Longmans Green, 1931, Chs. 1 and 2

31 Students of comparative politics deal with political communications as one of the most important variables and Almond mentions it as an important input of the political system. For a succinct and brief treatment of political communication in the Indian context, see ICSSR project, *op. cit.*, pp. 4-16

Glossary

Important Thinkers

This chronological compilation of important thinkers and the following glossary of terms is of immense value for students because it clearly unfolds the developments taking place in the field of political sociology over the years. The glossary provides simple and accessible guidelines to the thinkers and intellectuals who have helped to give the discipline concrete shape, and the terms which have developed into an indispensible part of the language of political sociology.

Niccolo Machiavelli (1469-1527), Italy. *The Prince* (1513); *The Discourses* (1518). A representative of the Renaissance movement in Italy and the first modern political thinker, Machiavelli considered virtue to lie in greatness, fame and power rather than in dedicating one's life to the pursuit of the salvation of the soul. Holding a realistic and objective perception of human nature, he suggested that a prince (ruler) should possess the qualities of both a lion and a fox in order to keep off enemies and to avoid getting trapped. Though critical of the church, he did not rule out the possibility of the use of religion for political purposes. Conventionally regarded as an advocate of immoral politics, he was in fact amoral in his approach, holding the view that a ruler should practise morality but must feel free to disregard it if the state so demanded. His advocacy of the strength and independence of the ruler implying the autonomy and creativity of politics—marks him out as the precursor of elitism and leadership role as against economic or sociological determinism.

Alexis de Tocqueville (1805-1859), France. *Democracy in America* (1835); *The Old Regime and the French Revolution* (1856). His analysis of the French Revolution of 1789 as marking not a complete break, but maintaining some continuity with the past anticipates many later ideas regarding the process and nature of social change. Though he studied the social conditions in America and France his observations regarding the nature of mass society and the dangers of conformity are of general significance. The problems of democracy in mass society focus on the concentration of power in the government and the atomization of the individual. As a safeguard against these dangers, he emphasized the usefulness of voluntary organizations and autonomous local bodies, advocated social pluralism and stressed the importance of the dispersal of power as a necessary condition of individual freedom.

Karl Marx (1818-1883), Germany. *The Economic and Philosophical Manuscripts of 1844* (1932, English edition 1953); *The German Ideology* (1845-46); *The Poverty of Philosophy* (1847); *The Communist Manifesto* (1858); *Grudrisse, Foundations of the Critique of Political Economy* (1857-58, German edition 1939-41, English edition 1973); *A Critique of Political Economy* (1859); *Das Kapital* Vol. 1 (1867); *Selected Works* authored with Engels (1962). The greatest revolutionary thinker and proponent of a revolutionary ideology and movement, Marx analyzed the capitalist society and exposed its inner contradictions highlighting the resulting alienation, exploitation and pauperization of workers. Dialectical materialism forms the basis of his philosophy of history which emphasizes the role of conflict between classes. Conflict, in its most intense form, characterizes the relationship between the proletariat and the bourgeoisie in the contemporary society that Marx analyzed. He perceives the state as a party to this conflict and not as a neutral medium or reconciliator, portraying it as a tool of the class that owns the means of production and exchange. By analyzing politics as a superstructure of the economic substructure, he laid the foundation of the sociology of politics. He is regarded as the father of scientific socialism because he based his conclusion of the inevitability of socialistic turnover on laws of history and movement of dialectical process. As a philosopher, he saw the vision and actively participated in the workers' movement and helped the realization of the 'dictatorship of the proletariat' as a prelude to the establishment of the ideal of communism—free from class distinctions, state on the road of withering away and government of people replaced by administration of things. His claim to objectivity is disputed.

Vilfredo Pareto (1848-1923), Italy. *Mind and Society: A Treatise on General Sociology* 4 vols (1916-17, English edition 1935); *The Rise and Fall of the Elites* (1901, English edition 1968). A major figure in political economy and political sociology seeking experimental reality by applying the established methods of the natural sciences. His outstanding contribution to political sociology is his concept of logical and non-logical action, residues and derivatives, and his theory of elites and circulation of elites. Pareto maintained that the elite is a universal phenomenon seen even in a democratic or socialist society. He unravelled the non-logical or residual categories underlying the logical derivatives, highlighted the role of irrational and personal qualities of leadership in politics. He followed the neo-Machiavellian tradition to which Mosca, Michels and Lasswell belong.

Sigmund Freud (1856-1939), Austria. *On Dreams* (1901); *Beyond the Pleasure Principle* (1920); *The Ego and the Id* (1923); *Inhibitions, Symptoms and Anxiety* (1926); *Collected Works* 4 vols (English edition 1924). What Karl Marx was to social sciences in general, Freud has been to psychology, anthropology and religion. He laid the foundations of psychoanalysis. Although Freud never applied his mind in a systematic way to the study of politics, his theories have influenced political thought in several ways. He opened new vistas in the study of personality and indirectly influenced the role of personality factors in politics. His theory of unconscious determination has given additional impetus to the thought that the real motives of political action are to be found elsewhere than in the conscious reasons that might be given for it. Some political theories have been built upon his theory of repression, according to which important instincts are denied direct expression by social pressures and consequently submerge to re-emerge in new and surprising forms. Repression is also regarded as a process whereby primordial instincts are transformed into the motivating force of civilization. Freud's emphasis is on fundamental instincts such as the sexual libido, and the death instinct or death wish as providing the ultimate explanation of human conduct. Like Rousseau, he criticized civilization for suppressing spontaneity and natural gratification.

Max Weber (1864-1920), Germany. Translation of basic writings in *From Max Weber* (1948); *The Methodology of the Social Sciences* (1949); *The Protestant Ethic and the Spirit of Capitalism* (1905, English edition 1970); *Wirtschaft and Gesellschaft* (*Economy and Society*) 3 vols (1925). His basic contribution to political sociology is the introduction of the concept of ideal type (which may not correspond to concrete reality but is a significant conceptual device to measure empirical reality) such as the Western City, the Protestant Ethic, modern capitalism, feudalism and bureaucracy. His identification of the three modes of claiming legitimacy or bases of authority such as traditional, rational and charismatic is a major landmark which enables him to portray bureaucracy as possessing legal-rational authority anchored in impersonal rules and sustained by the hierarchical structure. His fame also rests on his major modifications of Marxian analysis. His emphasis on the influence of religious ideas on the emergence of modern capitalism and denial to perceive ideas as simple reflections of economic interests are in direct contrast with Marxian conceptions. By relating class to status and party, he views class from a wider perspective than Marx. His definition of power as the chance of a man, or a number of men to realize their own will in communal action, even against the resistance of others, is significant. He argued that the emergence of economic power may be the consequence of power existing on other grounds and men do not strive for power only to become rich but often for the sake of honour—these are modifications of Marxian concern with economic categories. He also emphasized cultural dimensions of social change. By delineating the interdependence between political phenomena and socio-cultural or organizational factors, he laid the foundation of political sociology.

Emile Durkheim (1858-1917), France. *The Rules of Sociological Method*; *The Division of Labour in Society* (1893); *Suicide* (1897, English edition 1951); *Individual and Collective Representations*: *The Elementary Forms of the Religious Life* (1912). A structuralist, Durkheim attached great importance to the phemomena of social cohesion, integration or solidarity. Rapid social change or mobility leads to a breakdown of social regulations and the controlling influence of society on individual propensities is no longer effective. The breakdown of social norms leaves the individual to his own devices. Durkheim conceptualizes such a state of affairs as 'anomie' a term that refers to a condition of relative normlessness. His concepts of social solidarity and anomie are highly useful in understanding the consequences of social change and political development.

Robert Michels (1876-1936), Italy. *Political Parties*: *A Sociological*

Study of the Oligarchical Tendencies of Modern Democracy (1911, English edition 1915); *First Lectures in Political Sociology* (English edition 1949). Michels' contribution lies in his application and improvement of the Marxist categories of thought to political analysis. His unique accomplishment, however, lies in the identification of the organization as a significant and independent variable underlying the structure of power. His study of political parties led him to conclude that regardless of their sociology or ideology, they tend to centralize the power of decision making in an active minority. This is due to the fact that parties are also organizations in which a minority of leaders enjoy authority and influence over the rank and file of members—this led him to propound the famous law: organization spells oligarchy. His 'iron law of oligarchy' has far reaching consequences for the understanding of political process and reinforces the neo-Machiavellian projection of elitism.

Walter Lippmann (1889-1974), America. *Public Opinion* (1922). He argued that modern communications have the effect of condensing all information into brief slogans. These slogans, he thought, create a wall of stereotypes between the citizen and the issues to which he is expected to respond.

Harold D Lasswell (1902-1980), America. *Propaganda Technique in the World War* (1927); *Psychopathology and Politics* (1930); *Psychology of Hitlerism* (1933); *World Politics and Personal Insecurity* (1935); *Politics: Who Gets What, When and How* (1936); *Democracy Through Public Opinion* (1941). A prodigious writer, Lasswell is the author of several books and articles. Since 1923, he has contributed a series of offbeat and pathbreaking concepts and methodologies and has thus given effective expression to Charles Merriam's call for a new science of politics. His formulations that people everywhere strive for conditions of welfare (health, knowledge, skill, wealth) and deference (respect, affection, power and rectitude); that politics is related to the power aspects of any situation; and that people displace their private frustration onto public causes and thus become politicians, are in common currency in political studies. In his analysis of extremism he introduces the thesis that insecure people are receptive to revolutionary propaganda which is guided by professional specialists in violence and symbol manipulation. His suggestion that modern intellectuals can best serve the cause of human dignity by becoming competent and imaginative policy scientists worth consulting by decision makers, marks his march from behaviouralism to post behaviouralism much before either became prevalent in American universities. He has enriched five fields—elite analysis, developmental constructs, communications, personality dynamics and policy-making. As a scientist, he sees a stake in the future and therefore advocates adoption of both contemplative and manipulative standpoints. His influence on his contemporaries such as Key, Truman, Simon, Almond, Leites, Shils, Janowitz, Eulau, Barrington Moore and Abraham Kaplan is immense.

Talcott Parsons (1902-), America. *The Structure of Social Action* (1937); *The Social System* (1951); with Shils *Toward a General Theory of Action* (1951). One of the most prominent figures in modern sociology, Parsons identified the typology of systems—biological, physiological, social and personality, and held that the political system was not an autonomous body but a part of the social system. The leading proponent of the functional approach to which Merton and Levy belong, he upheld the view that a system seeks to achieve particular goals and all behaviour and phenomena are related to this end. His identification of functional prerequisites (goal-attainment, adaptation, integration and pattern maintenance) and contrasting modes and styles of functions (universalistic-particularistic, specific-diffuse, achievement-ascriptive, affective-affective neutral and collectivity vs self-oriented) have been applied subsequently by scholars and have far reaching consequences.

Robert Merton (1910-), America. *Social Theory and Social Structure* (1949). A prominent writer on sociological theory, functionalism and bureaucracy, Merton holds that the same social institution or item may have multiple functions and the same function can be diversely fulfilled by alternative items. He also introduced the concept of dysfunctions and non-functions—indicating that some structures or institutions may produce consequences harmful to society. Just as there are observed consequences which make for the adaptation or adjustment of a system, similarly there are some consequences which lessen this adaptation.

David Easton (1917-), America. *The Political System: An Inquiry into the State of Political Science* (1953); *A Framework for Political Analysis* (1965); *A Systems Analysis of Political Life* (1965); *Systems Analysis in Political Science Today* (1980). Introduced the input-output framework in systems analysis. Identified demand and support to the community, regime or government, as entering from the environment into the system (inputs) and analyzed the manner in which these inputs are converted into 'authoritative allocation of values' through policies and decisions (outputs) and how part of the output enter through feedback in the form of new inputs again and produce effect or consequences. Basically he stressed the process of transformation from inputs to outputs of a political system.

Gabriel A Almond America. Along with James Coleman edited *Politics of the Developing Areas* and wrote its famous Introduction (1960); authored with Sidney Verba, *The Civic Culture: Political Attitudes and Democracy in Five Nations* (1963); *Comparative Politics A Developmental Approach: An Analytic Study* (1972); *Comparative Politics: System, Process and Policy* (1978). Adapting Lasswell's and Easton's approach to a structural-functional framework, he introduced a developmental approach to politics. His significant contributions to comparative politics include the identification of structures and styles of modern and traditional political systems and the introduction of three types of political culture—subject, parochial and civic. He emphasized the capability of a political system to cope with the challenges so as to survive.

Hanah Arendt (1906-1975), America. *On Revolution* (1963). A philosopher and social critic, Arendt argued that all revolutions are united by the straining of subject peoples towards liberty, and the search for a constitution that will guarantee liberty. She also argued that the phrase 'the people' is the key to the understanding of the French Revolution, and its connotations determined by those who were exposed to the spectacle of the people's sufferings which they themselves did not share.

Seymour Martin Lipset (1922-), America. *Political Man* (1960); *The First New Nation: The US in Historical and Comparative Perspective* (1963). A lucid writer on the condition of political participation, and the social basis of democracy, he has contributed to the articulation of issues in sociology of politics by focusing upon the function of conflict, bureaucracy and democracy.

Erich Fromm (1900-), America. *Escape from Freedom* (1942). A psychologist concerned with the adverse psychological consequences of modernization, he emphasizes the loneliness and homelessness of the individual resulting from the disruption of community life in modern industrial society.

William Kornhauser America. *The Politics of Mass Society* (1959). Kornhauser studied the erosion of social institutions and the atomization of individuals in what he describes as the 'mass society'. The mass society exposes the individual and makes him a target for manipulation by leaders, organizations and mass media.

Raymond Aron France. *The Opium of the Intellectuals* (English edition 1957); *Social Structure and the Ruling Class* (1966). A sociologist, intellectual and journalist, Aron has written several widely read books on contemporary social and political issues. He has adopted a balanced middle position between the Machiavellian and the Marxist interpretation of social structure and political power.

Giovanni Sartori Italy. *Democratic Theory* (1962); *From Sociology of Politics to Political Sociology* (1964). An incisive thinker and writer on politics, his theory of democracy is provocative and of profound importance. His paper on political sociology is of seminal value in restoring the autonomous status to politics.

Karl W Deutsch (1912-), America. *Political Community at the International Level: Problems of Definition and Measurement* (1954); *Political Analysis and the Nerves of Government : Models of Political Communication and Control* (1962). He has done path breaking work in the field of political communication, control and development. The application of cybernetics owes much to his ideas.

Robert A Dahl (1915-), America. *Who Governs: Democracy and Power in An American City* (1961). Professor of politics at Yale University, Dahl is famous for his study of a university town, focusing on its power structure and the changing patterns of local elites. This is not only a landmark in the study of community power structure but also a major contribution to the study of democratic theory.

Fred W Riggs America. *Bureaucracy and Political Development: A Paradoxical View* (1963). An acknowledged authority in the field of public administration, especially in developing countries, Riggs is known for his advocacy of understanding administration as part of the political process and of the need to integrate administration with political development.

M Narasimhachar Srinivas India. *Caste in Modern India and Other Essays* (1962); *Social Change in Modern India* (1966). An anthropologist, he is a doyen among Indian social scientists. Srinivas is famous for his contribution towards increased understanding of caste and social change, and for his concept of 'Sanskritization' as opposed to 'Westernization'.

Rajni Kothari, (1928-), India. *Congress System* (1964); *Politics in India* (1970); *Footstep into the Future : Diagnosis of the Present World and a Design for an Alternative* (1975). A leading political scientist of the third world, Kothari has done original and imaginative analysis of Indian politics and is well known for his interpretation of the Indian party system and the Congress system. He takes an architechtonic view of politics, his quest for alternative models of civilization and political development is inspiring and stimulating.

Terms and Concepts

Acculturation the process whereby an individual or group acquires the cultural characteristics of another through direct contact.

Alienation a state of mind reflecting man's estrangement from himself and from his social and natural environment. Rousseau used the concept to signify man's separation from his nature. According to him, man is good by nature but society or civilization put him in chains and thereby deprave him. Social man is an alienated being because he tries to be what he is not. Hegel believed that man's true and ideal state emerges when transcending himself, he identifies with the Absolute Idea. In the absence of such objectification, he stands alienated. In his early writings (published as *Economic and Philosophical Manuscripts of 1844*) Marx refers to four aspects of the workers' alienation (*i*) the relationship of the worker to the product of labour; (*ii*) the relationship of the worker to the process of production; (*iii*) the alienation of man from himself as a 'species-being'; and (*iv*) the alienation of man from other men. Marx borrowed the term 'species-being' from Feuerbach who had secularized some of the theological ideas of Hegel and thus paved the way for Marx's views. Marx's distinctive contribution, however lay in the fact that he saw this state of alienation as associated with private property and technology which compels the division of labour, and the institution of the wage contract. In Freudian and post-Freudian psychology, alienation is seen as a condition in which man is placed by civilization, through the necessity to conform to roles and expectations, and to repress and transform vital instincts and impulses, so that in becoming acceptable to others he becomes a stranger to himself.

Marcuse and Erich Fromm attempted to synthesize the Marxian and Freudian ideas and believed that the 'capitalist man' is a being—crippled through the degeneration of the will, driven to see himself always as an object and never as the originator of his acts, a person who is no longer a true person because he cannot be what he really is: he loses interest in life because it is not he who lives his life. In none of the usages is the notion very precise, but in all of them it expresses the condition of the modern consicousness, and its being separated from the human way of being.

Allegiance is a feeling of loyalty and commitment to a political regime.

Alternative society a form of liberalism (prevalent in the US and other highly developed urban-industrial societies during the 1960s), according to which the aim of individual life is to follow an 'authentic life style', achieved through independent personal choice. There is no reason to conform to the 'structures of the system' into which one is born. More compelling is the impetus to enact the authentic life style of one's own devising, and so to create, in community with one's fellows, the alternative society and its associated *counter-culture.* This counter-culture tends to offend the guardians of the establishment, since it threatens the easy solution by which they have chosen to live. This idea of alternative society is derived in part from Sartre's existentialism, in part from psychotheraputic doctrines of Wilhem Reich and R.D. Laing, and in part from the radical social criticism of Marcuse.

Anomie a state of mind resulting from the loss of norms or guiding principles of life and social action due to a series of rapid, traumatic changes in one's life situation.

Apathy indifference to or lack of interest in or withdrawal from the political process.

Assimilation a process by which one culture is absorbed by another.

Association a formal organization of people who share common interests.

Authority that feature of a person, role, office or government which makes legitimate (either in reality or in appearance) the acts and commands exercised in its name. Authority must be distinguished from power, being a relation *de jure* and not necessarily *de facto* :

authority is the right to act, rather than the power to act. It may be accompanied by power and so upheld, or without power and so ignored. One of the most important powers that upheld authority is the power of the people's belief in it.

Bureaucracy is rule by administrative offices. In a bureaucracy actual power is vested in those who are, from the legal point of view, administrative intermediaries between sovereign and subject. They (normally the civil servants, although there can also be military and religious bureaucracies) can delay or advance the causes of both sovereign and subject to an extent that gives them *de facto* control over major political transformations. Now the term bureaucracy refers to formal organizations where authority is hierarchical and office is based on merit and tasks are governed by formal rules.

Caste the hereditary division of society in India. Traditionally, based on hierarchy and functional identity, members of a caste are supposed to follow the occupation, social customs and religious rites of their caste. The original Vedic fourfold division has, in course of time, proliferated into thousands of castes and sub-castes. Caste identities still persist, but caste relationships have undergone radical change under the impact of modernization, democratization, secularization and socialism. Caste has been politicized, it is an important factor in politics and administration, and performs modern functions of social groups.

Class a general term subsuming all those distinctions between people which involve unequal but systematic distribution of privileges, thus covering distinctions of rank, caste, estate, status, degree, but not distinctions of group, role or office. Some sociologists find that the essence of class resides in life changes, while others believe that it lies in separate social or economic functions. Marx uses this as a technical term to denote positions in the system of production relations—such as master and slave, patrician and plebian, lord and serf (in feudalism), and bourgeoisie and proletarian (in capitalism). It is not unusual to speak of the lower class, the lower middle class, the middle middle class, the upper middle class, and the upper class, and also to conceive of classes or individuals in the class to move upwards or backwards. Some noted authorities in the field believe that both class and status are equally important variables for explaining social inequalities or social stratification.

Class consciousness a term used to denote either (*i*) the individual's sense of himself as belonging to a social class, or (*ii*) those features of the individual's outlook and understanding which can be explained on basis of his membership of a social class.

Class struggle According to the socialist theory, class conflict is the driving force of history, being at the root of all major changes in law, institutions, morality and religion. Marxists believe that class struggle will intensify under capitalism resulting in a revolution, when the whole social order is overturned in the interest of a rising class. Lenin argued that the capitalist proletariat may achieve trade-union consciousness but never true class consciousness, unless led by the 'professional revolutionaries'. For Weber the principal class struggle was between creditors and debtors and for him, the conflict under capitalist conditions between employers and workers was merely a special case.

Coalition a temporary working political alliance of distinct parties or persons, who preserve their separate political identities.

Collectivity a large number of unorganized people sharing a common interest.

Communication the transmission of information, ideas, emotions, values and attitudes. Political communication is a two way process, between the government and citizens, though the actual forms and degrees of communication vary with the political system.

Community denotes a social group, usually identified in terms of a common habitat (such as a town, village, or district), and implies both a body of common interest, a degree of social cohesion, co-operation and interaction, and a sense of belonging among the members. The concept may be extended to include any self-identifying group of people with similar interests who attempt to advance those interests by establishing themselves in a common place.

Concept an abstraction deduced from numerous sense impressions on the basis of which one is able to generalize and communicate.

Conflict social condition depicting a clash or opposition of ideas, views or interests. It is commonly perceived as a disease of society but it plays a useful part in the articulation of diversity and reconciliation or consensus of a higher order. The aim of politics is not to eliminate but to manage conflict through the accommodation of differences.

Culture depicts a way of life; it refers to the learned patterns of thought, behaviour and feeling that distinguish one race from another.

Cybernetics the study of communication, control and internal governance of systems (i.e. organisms and machines exhibiting artificial intelligence), where the various operations interact reciprocally and systematically. Political sociologists regard cybernetics as a useful tool in explaining social and political processes as it makes possible the scientific study of processing and monitoring of information.

Differentiation division of labour and specialization leading to differentiation of roles and structures whereby roles are separated and performed by different individuals and structures.

Diffusion spread of cultural traits by means of contact between cultures.

Elite and elitism an elite is an active minority that represents higher status, excellence or power in society. Elitism advocates the belief that the special role of the elite is both desirable and inevitable.

Empirical method the methodology used for making generalizations on the basis of sensory experience, observation and experiment.

Equilibrium model of society contrasts with the conflict model of society—it states that societies have a natural tendency towards equilibrium or balance, and political institutions and processes develop partly in order to facilitate the return to equilibrium in times of strain or conflict.

Ethnicity racial and cultural similarities that are shared by a population.

Ethnocentrism attitude that one's own race and culture are superior to all others.

Faction any group organized within a political party, institution or government, defined partly by its opposition to some rival group or leader, acting in personal or group interest.

Feedback a technical term of systems theory or cybernetics, but is widely misused to indicate a response to a question, action or policy. It refers instead to the transformation of part of the output into new inputs. Positive feedback increases the input, negative feedback decreases it. Negative feedback leads to stability since it acts to reduce activity, while positive feedback may be inherently destructive.

Function is that activity which must be performed for the survival or continued existence of an organism, institution or society. Respiration and circulation of blood are in this sense vital functions of an organism. Likewise, reproduction, socialization and goal achievement are vital social functions. Similarly, political recruitment and socialization, interest-articulation, interest-aggregation, political communication, are vital political functions. Functions are universal, though they may be performed in diverse styles and through different structures. For example, reproduction is a necessary function, it is usually performed through the institution of marriage but marriage systems vary and may even be abolished.

Group a number of individuals having a stable relationship (whether or not formally associated) for the pursuit of common interests. Groups vary according to size, organization and intensity of interest, and many contain sub-groups and factions. Usually classified into primary groups (Gemeinschaft) based on face-to-face relationships involving kinship and marriage, and secondary groups (Gesellschaft) based on formal relationships. Ferdinand Tonnies wrote a famous book on the subject entitled *Gemeinschaft* and *Gesellschaft*.

Hypothesis refers to a statement of related conditions and expected relationships between phenomena under study.

Ideology a set of ideas, policies or programmes used to defend and justify a political system, regime or action. Marx considered ideology to reflect 'false consciousness' and 'inversion' of reality since like the state it is a mere 'reflex' of the material mode of production. Several intellectual movements claiming to be scientific conceal an ideology within themselves. Ideology is distinguished from utopia, which is a projection of the future, whereas ideology is a defence of the status quo.

Institutionalization process by which a social pattern becomes a norm, enforced by sanction.

Integration different groups within a jurisdiction may have the same legal rights, but nevertheless enjoy unequal privileges, and include disparate social, educational, cultural and recreational institutions. Political integration is the process whereby all such separate groups are united by a common purpose and community feeling. They have access to institutions, regardless of creed, race, religion, language and origin. The aim is to form a unified civil society within the jurisdiction of a unified state.

Interest aggregation is the amalgamation and organizing of numerous views and opinions into larger issues so as to facilitate their conversion into viable policies and programmes in tune with public interest.

Interest articulation refers to the expression of ideas, views and interests—public or sectional, and to the formulation of issues with a view to win public support and governmental acceptance.

Interest group a group, united by common interests, having sufficient identity of purpose to act on its own behalf (i.e. by electing officers and representatives, generating funds, establishing associations and engaging in active propaganda) and which therefore has some influence either on public opinion or on government. An interest group may have sufficient political access to become a pressure group, alternatively its political influence may be only indirect, i.e. through the mobilization of popular support. Pressure groups in recent times have emerged to give expression to public interests and are known as public interest groups.

Leadership signifies the role of providing guidance, direction and cordination to a group, organization or country. It also refers to the capacity to inspire confidence in the rightness of one's purpose, courage in their collective execution, and obedience in the threat of resistance. Leadership is a question of degree, and is determined by the extent to which a single person can build control on the basis of influence. A few sociologists perceive leadership to be the inevitable outcome of irresistible and impersonal forces while others explain it in terms of the personal characteristics of the leader. Survival is of immense value in perpetuating the myth of a great leader.

Legitimacy like virtue or justice, is more easily recognized in its negative than in its positive form. A power is exercised illegitimately if there is no right to its exercise. The vital concepts in understanding legitimacy are those of power and right and the questions often asked are: Is the exercise of power by the state of government right? What is the sanction behind the law? Why must one obey the state? But a crucial question in political sociology relates to the acceptance of power by the people and the process whereby power gains acceptance by the people which essentially includes the process of mobilization of support through ideology, institution-building, system of rewards and punishment, performance or manipulation. There is a significant relationship between legitimacy and stability.

Marginal man is a person participating partially in two ethnic populations, or living at the periphery of a society or culture.

Modernization a widely but imprecisely used word. Briefly it can be understood as the process of socioeconomic and cultural change from feudal to industrial, from rural to urban, and from community based on primary relationships to society based on secondary relationships.

Norm signifies both the normal and the normative. Biologists and psychologists use the term to denote normal while for social scientists it implies the normative—a principle or standard of conduct.

Participation is the involvement and consultation of those affected by decisions in the process of decision making. Involvement may include a right to elect representatives, to vote on issues, to campaign and canvass, to decide matters, to veto, etc. Participation is related to one's status, education, occupation, income and membership of organization.

Political culture is a set of values, norms and attitudes pertaining to politics and political processes. The assumption is that these values, norms and attitudes are predispositions that condition the style of political behaviour.

Political development is the capability of a political system to maintain its stability, to solve problems and meet demands, encourage popular participation and avoid disorder.

Political parties are political institutions or organizations, inspired by ideology or power or both to acquire control over government. They perform essential functions of mobilizing and transforming public opinion into parliamentary and even extra-parliamentary groups.

Politicization the process by which an activity or institution, seemingly non-political, is transformed into one that is consciously directed towards political ends.

Power the ability to achieve the desired effect, even in the face of resistance from others. Stemming from either consent or coercion, it may be exercised either through persuasion or through control. It refers specifically to influence that may be exerted through control. Political power means the ability to influence or control the institutions, actions, behaviour or processes pertaining to decision making in society.

Pressure group an interest group which exerts sufficient influence on government to be able to put pressure on behalf of its interests. Pressure groups differ from interest groups in terms of both organization and power.

Public opinion is opinion pertaining to public issues, active and effective in the realm to which it belongs. The agencies and processes in public opinion formation and the extent of its impact on government are of importance in political sociology in that they indicate the relationship between society and polity.

Reference group is one with which an individual identifies and whose perspectives and views he assumes. It serves as a model of behaviour for the individual.

Regime denotes the actual office-bearers within the government, independently of the offices they hold.

Regionalism the phenomenon which permits and encourages the development of indigenous culture and institutions within separate areas or regions of the jurisdiction, and involves the delegation of substantial political and legal power to local regional authorities with less than full sovereignty but more than merely administrative function.

Role is a customary and identifiable way of doing things for a specific purpose in society. Roles are conventionally recognized as there are known expectations about the conditions, forms and etiquette of social behaviour.

Social mobility is the upward or downward movement of individuals, families and groups from one class or status group to another.

Social mobilization is the process of deep social change that results in the loss of roots and weakening of traditions.

Secularization is the process by which man's orientation is changed from the other-wordly to this-worldly. Achievement, success or happiness in this world rather than salvation in the next lies at the root of secularization. It is opposed to the sacred or religious preoccupation with matters of the other-world or hereafter. In the European context, secularization has been a mark of modernization and represents the emergence of a pragmatic and empirical orientation. In the Indian context, secularism connotes not rejection but equal treatment of all religions as well as separation between the state and the religious order, and as such misses the original attribute of secularization.

Social stratification the development of systematic inequalities of wealth, power, influence, education and privilege within a society and the consequent division of society into a higher and a lower order.

Socialization in political science signifies transfer of an object from private to social ownership. In sociology, it refers to the process whereby the individual acquires the norms, roles and rules pertaining to social relations that enable him to be an effective member of society. Political sociologists however refer to political socialization as a process whereby political attitudes and beliefs are transmitted from one generation or regime to another, latently or manifestly, through various agencies.

Society any aggregate of individuals who interact in a systematic way, so as to determine the criteria of membership. A civil society is a social system which bears the marks of a political organization, and is ordered according to the constitution and legislation of a state. Such a society might precede and survive the state. Relations between state and society can be described as those between matter and form. Civil society denotes a society identified through its political order.

Solidarity attachment which is strong enough to create a solid resistance to attack. Durkheim used this term to denote the internal forces of social cohesion.

Stability political stability implies the security of a regime from the threat of subversion, revolution, rebellion and eventual overthrow. Such security may be obtained on the basis of military or economic power but in the long run legitimacy and popular support are required to sustain it. Conventionally speaking, ideology, language, religion and culture are considered contributary factors to social cohesion and eventually to stability. But experience shows that the culture of consensus, open political institutions and avoidance of extreme inequality are important prerequisites for stability. Countries undergoing rapid social and economic change, particularly require viable political institutions and processes to regulate and channelize the pressures of change and prevent anomic effects and outbreak of violence.

Status refers to one's position in the social hierarchy, determined by wealth, prestige and power. Education, occupation, skill, income and caste are the usual determinants of status in India.

Value used both in a positive as well as a normative sense. In the positive sense, it is applied to all objects thought to be worthy of human pursuit. In the normative sense, it denotes a norm or principle of conduct. Value judgements involve judgements of what is good, right or worthy.

Westernization the import of customs and institutions thought to be characteristic of the West.

Index

Alienation, 3, 42-3, 137, 139-40, 147, 158, 171, 179
Almond, 15, 136-8, 141, 169, 174
anomie/anomic, 22-3, 83, 86, 145-7, 176, 180
Aron, 11, 48
apathy, 145-7, 158, 171, 173, 180
Aristotle, 2-4, 12, 41, 173
articulation, 1, 29, 50, 86, 90, 159, 185
association, 6, 80-1, 85, 89-90, 126, 147, 149, 169, 178, 180
authority, 1, 7, 46, 96, 107-9, 114, 116, 127-8, 132-3, 180-1
behaviour, 13, 19-20, 137, 141, 163, 171-2, 174-8, 186
behaviouralism, 1, 16, 18, 19-21, 23, 36, 91, 95, 136
Bentley, 6, 76-80
Beteille, 52, 54, 56
caste, 41, 51-60, 155, 160-1, 170, 181
caste : backward, 53-4; dominant, 53, 55-6, 58-9; higher, 53, 55; intermediate, 53-5; leader, 58; scheduled, 53, 55
change, 7, 22, 31, 33-6, 39, 57, 67, 70, 74, 81, 84, 97, 105, 121, 123-30, 132-6, 145-6, 161-2, 164, 176
class, 2, 5, 6, 8, 9, 11, 22-3, 32, 34, 41-53, 65, 67, 69-70, 73, 91, 97, 99-100, 104, 112, 114, 118-9, 123-5, 139, 170, 181
communication, 16, 29, 97, 99, 143, 146, 157, 159, 167, 173, 177, 181
community, 43, 52, 92, 94, 133, 135, 151, 154-5, 171, 181
conflict, 1, 3-4, 10, 16, 31, 41, 55, 67-8, 77, 90, 100, 104, 110, 113, 123, 133, 135, 148-9, 151, 159, 162, 178, 181, 183
consensus, 4, 7, 104-6

Dahl, 6, 71
democracy/democratic, 61, 72-5, 95-6, 102, 104-5, 112-4, 124, 127-9, 135, 146, 148, 163, 167-8
derivatives, 63-5
dominant party, 103-5
Durkheim, 13, 22, 146
Duverger, 90, 92-4, 102-3
dysfunction, 28-9, 110
economic, 1, 7-8, 11, 47, 126, 129, 131-5, 150, 157, 163-4, 177
education, 54-5, 91, 126, 149-50, 154, 156, 161, 173
efficacy, 145, 156, 158, 164, 171
Eldersveld, 95-7
election, 57, 90, 95, 101, 104, 132, 146, 152-66
environment, 1, 23-5, 96, 111, 126, 130, 154-55, 175-6
equality, 130, 150, 168
equilibrium, 25, 35, 79-83, 183
faction/factionalism, 46-7, 55-7, 59, 74, 89-90, 102, 105-6, 113, 136, 148, 159, 183
FICCI, 6, 84
freedom, 102, 105-6, 113, 136
function/functional, 29-30, 41, 95-100, 107-8, 110, 131, 133, 141, 144, 147-8, 162-3, 168
functionalism, 25-6, 28-32
Hegel, 12
history/historical, 33-4, 36, 40, 64, 67, 69-70, 96, 121, 125, 129-30, 134, 168
Hobbes, 4, 12
Huntington, 98, 125, 133, 141, 143, 145, 148, 150
ideology, 2, 7, 70-1, 76, 89-91, 97, 128, 132
inequality, 47-8, 52, 59-60, 74, 119, 138-9, 177
influence, 69-70, 79, 91-2, 96, 104, 113, 141-4, 148, 150, 163
inputs, 25, 30
institution/institutional, 12, 20, 28, 60, 80, 83, 97, 107, 115, 117-8, 122, 124-5, 127, 133-6, 159, 163, 172-3, 183
institutionalization, 59, 133-4, 194
institutionalism, 1, 18
interest, 1, 4, 7-8, 44-7, 57, 69, 74, 77, 86-7, 89-91, 97, 99, 104-7, 111, 114-5, 128, 135, 139, 141, 145-6, 150, 152, 169, 184-5
Kautilya, 2
Key, 100, 102, 169

Khaldun, 2
Kothari, 57-8, 102, 106, 135-6, 138-9, 155, 163, 166
Lasswell, 5, 20, 50, 70-1, 95, 112, 118, 174-5
Latham, 76, 81-3
leader/leadership, 68-70, 72, 78-9, 86, 90, 92, 94-7, 104-6, 113-4, 117, 125, 150, 155, 159, 163, 168, 173, 178, 185
legitimacy, 7-9, 116, 127, 135-6, 163, 185
Machiavelli, 1-3
management, 1, 4, 51, 111-2, 116
Marx, Fritz, 116-7
Marx, Karl, 2-4, 11-3, 22, 32-5, 41-2, 45, 48, 51-2, 63, 69, 73, 179, 184
Marxism/Marxist, 32, 34-5, 47-8, 51, 73
Merriam, 5, 141
Merton, 110
Michels, 2, 44, 61-2, 67-9, 95-6
Mills, 62, 70, 168
mobility, 96, 122, 126, 134, 154, 187
mobilization, 8, 56, 58-60, 74-5, 81, 97-8, 100, 106, 122, 124-6, 128-9, 132-5, 144-5, 148, 151, 187
Mosca, 2, 48, 61-2, 65-7, 73
Narain, 56-7, 157, 160, 166
Neo Machiavellians, 62, 118
organization/organize, 1, 50-1, 58, 68-70, 74, 81, 84-6, 91, 94-5, 97, 99-100, 104, 106-9, 111-3, 118, 128, 130, 133-4, 144, 147, 149, 152, 154-5, 163, 168-9, 173, 178, 181
output, 30, 132, 172
Pareto, 2, 12, 44, 48, 50, 61-5
Parsons, 72
Plato, 2, 4-5, 12, 41, 173-4
political culture, 86-7, 96-7, 172, 186
political sub-culture, 96-7, 149, 162
power, 2, 4, 7, 43, 48-51, 54-7, 61-71, 74, 77, 79, 81, 83, 86, 90-1, 94-7, 99-100, 103-4, 106, 112-4, 116, 118, 124-5, 127, 145-6, 168, 186
recruitment, 28, 50, 52, 58, 67, 94-5
residues, 63-5
revolution, 65, 69, 71, 92
Riggs, 115-7
Rousseau, 4, 12, 173-4, 179

Sartori, 9, 98-9
Schumpeter, 61, 71, 90
Sirsikar, 58, 155-6, 158, 166
socialism, 73, 104
socialization, 28
Srinivas, 52-4
stability, 2, 96, 100-2, 104, 115, 129, 149, 162-3, 167, 171, 188
state, 5-9, 12, 82, 116, 147, 167
status, 43, 45-6, 48, 53-4, 56, 74, 96, 107-9, 124, 148-50, 157, 188
system, 16, 23, 25-6, 35, 101, 128, 130-1, 136-7, 156, 163
systems approach, 23, 35
system : Indian political, 102-3; modern political, 30, 133; political, 1, 8, 16, 29, 31, 35, 67, 86-7, 112, 114, 118, 127, 133, 136-7, 141, 144-5, 147, 152, 161, 163, 171-3; social, 101-2, 112, 145
trade union, 84-5
Truman, 76, 79-81, 84, 112
value, 61, 70, 74, 81, 96, 100, 115, 122-3, 126-7, 136, 141, 146, 162, 171-2, 174, 176, 188
Weber, Max, 12-3, 22, 43-4, 52, 90, 107-12, 114-5